SIX METAPHYSICAL POET

A Reader's Guide

Donated By

THE SECOND CENTURY FUND

Preserving A Tradition Of
Citizen Philanthropy

Other Reader's Guides to Literature

SIX METAPHYSICAL POETS

A Reader's Guide
George Williamson

 SYRACUSE UNIVERSITY PRESS

First Syracuse University Press Edition 2001

01 02 03 04 05   6 5 4 3 2 1

Originally published in 1967 by the Noonday Press. Reprinted by arrangement with Farrar, Straus & Giroux.

The paper used in this publication meets the minimum requirements of American National Standard for Information Sciences—Permanence of Paper for Printed Library Materials, ANSI Z39.48-1984.∞™

Library of Congress Cataloging-in-Publication Data

Williamson, George, 1898-1968.
    Six metaphysical poets : a reader's guide / George Williamson.—1st Syracuse University Press ed.
        p. cm.
    Includes bibliographical references (p.) and index.
    ISBN 0-8156-0698-2 (pbk. : alk. paper)
    1. English poetry—Early modern, 1500–1700—History and criticism. 2. English poetry—Early modern, 1500–1700—Handbooks, manuals, etc. 3. Metaphysics in litera-ture—Handbooks, manuals, etc. 4. Metaphysics in literature. I. Title.
    PR541.W54 2001
    821'.309384—dc21   00-053172

Manufactured in the United States of America

Foreword

The method of explication used in this book is a variation of Dryden's "metaphrase"—turning a poem word by word, or line by line, into prose with such glosses and connections as understanding requires.

It is the most economical way to explain prose meaning in a poem, to emphasize losses in poetic effect, and to expose relations of meter and syntax, or the musical order of a poem.

To some, if not to all, it may seem only another way of leaving out difficulties, as Donne said,

> *As slily as any Commenter goes by*
> *Hard words, or sense; or in Divinity*
> *As controverters, in vouch'd Texts, leave out*
> *Shrewd words, which might against them clear the doubt.*

To others it will seem an indignity; but without a sense of fact, as T. S. Eliot said, "Instead of insight, you get a fiction."

G.W.

May 1966

Contents

SIX METAPHYSICAL POETS
A Reader's Guide

I

The Name and Nature
of Metaphysical Poetry

Until this century the Metaphysical Poets owed their name and nature to Dr. Johnson. And they survived, if at all, in the shadow of Milton. Today all that has been changed, and changed by the taste that created modern poetry. The influence of T. S. Eliot has altered the textbooks and the anthologies that we inherited, even *The Oxford Book of English Verse*. Indeed, the reaction went so far that white knights again rode forth in the service of Milton and Spenser. In academic circles they sometimes succeeded in once more hoisting the banner of Milton over a period of more various achievement. But in general the Metaphysical Poets today are numbered among the quick rather than the dead, and Milton himself has benefited by their revival, since he could no longer be taken for granted. To some, however, Donne is known only by his words "for whom the bell tolls" or "No man is an Island."

Of course there is some diversity of opinion as to who are Metaphysical Poets and what is the nature of their poetry. Perhaps the safest approach to these questions is the historical. Criticism learned to distinguish genres or kinds of poetry before it learned to distinguish differences within the kinds. The latter usually belong to the accidentals rather than the essentials of kinds. Hence they belong to the variables that characterize individuality or fashion, and thus resist formulation. The general similarity that produces a school must be found among such variables, and is seldom more than a resemblance. Whatever the cause of the resemblance, the effect is bound to be variable. History often discovers the resemblance that constitutes a school, and such was the case of the Metaphysical Poets. If we inquire into this discovery, we shall see why they came to be regarded as a school. And we shall then be able to compare the historical analysis with the modern analysis of these poets; but, most of all, we shall perceive the elements upon which this analysis was originally based.

Explicit reaction to these poets began with Dryden's *Essay of Dramatic Poesy* (1668), where he relates one extreme of poetry to "catachresis or Clevelandism, wresting and torturing a word into another meaning." It is curious that Dryden's editor, W. P. Ker, here refers to a definition of catachresis that was borrowed from Donne's time. Dryden believes that a poet should not be "too bold in his metaphors and coining words," for which Cleveland has been blamed: "to express a thing hard and unnaturally, is his new way of elocution." Here Dryden allows Donne the advantage over Cleveland in satire: "the one gives us deep thoughts in common language, though rough cadence; the other gives us common thoughts in abstruse words." In Donne the thought is abstruse, in Cleveland the language. Later Dryden becomes less charitable to Donne.

William Walsh first impeached the amorous verse of the Moderns. In his Preface to *Letters and Poems, Amorous and Gallant* (1692) he objected: "The Moderns, on the other hand, have sought out for Occasions that none meet with but themselves, and fill their Verses with Thoughts that are surprising and glittering, but not tender, passionate, or natural to a Man in Love." Then he particularizes this deficiency: "Never was there a more copious Fancy or greater reach of wit than what appears in Dr. Donne; nothing can be more gallant or gentle than the Poems of Mr. Waller; nothing more gay or sprightly than those of Sir John Suckling; and nothing fuller of Variety and Learning than Mr. Cowley's. However, it may be observed, that among all these, that Softness, Tenderness, and Violence of Passion, which the Ancients thought most proper for Love verses, is wanting." If wit and learning get in the way of gallantry, their love poems have a common defect, want of the feeling appropriate to love. Indeed, their violence lies more in metaphor than in passion. This indictment was to have a long life.

Whether or not he was prompted by Walsh, Dryden returned to Donne a year later in *A Discourse concerning Satire* (1693) and enlarged his context: "He affects the metaphysics, not only in his satires, but in his amorous verses, where nature only should reign; and perplexes the minds of the fair sex with nice speculations of philosophy, when he should engage their hearts, and entertain them with the softnesses of love. In this (if I may be pardoned for so bold a truth) Mr. Cowley has copied him to a fault." Thus Dryden suggests the name of the Metaphysical Poets, and agrees with the indictment of Walsh, posing more sharply "nice speculations" against "the softnesses of love," and emphasizing Cowley's imitation of Donne.

Dryden did not employ the term "strong lines" that Izaak Walton still used in his *Compleat Angler* (1661) as a contrast to Marlowe's "smooth song," which he thought "much better than the strong lines that are now in fashion in this critical age." Later he quotes Donne's version of Marlowe's song "to show the world that he could make soft and smooth verses, when he thought smoothness worth his labour." Walton certainly knew, if only from Donne's elegists, that some had "Call'd him a strong lin'd man," and that others had called his "Anniverse,"

> *Indeed so farre above its Reader, good,*
> *That wee are thought wits, when 'tis understood.*

But it is this reputation that Walton wants to counter. Dryden refused the term "strong lines" but kept the traits for which it stood: "rough cadence" and "deep thoughts," now demoted to metaphysical puzzles. They could still make wits, but not poets.

Walsh, however, did not go unchallenged. Charles Gildon, in *Miscellaneous Letters and Essays* (1694), answered Walsh by shifting the ground of propriety to the poet: "A Man that is used to a good Habit of thinking, cannot be without extraordinary Thoughts, on what concerns him so near as the Heart of his Mistress." This plea might have saved the Metaphysical Poets in a less rhetorical age, but Addison (*Spectator* 89) found arguments in Marvell's *Coy Mistress* against coy reluctance to marry, and the future belonged to Pamela.

When Pope made his *Sketch for a History of the Rise and Progress of English Poetry,* his last major school was a "School of Donne." Primarily this included Cowley, Davenant, Drayton, Overbury, Randolph, Sir John Davies, Sir John Beaumont, Cartwright, Cleveland, Crashaw, Corbet, and Lord Falkland. But Pope's views as reported in Spence's *Anecdotes* show more discrimination. There Drayton becomes an imitator of Spenser; Carew remains in the school of Waller; "Crashaw is a worse sort of Cowley"; "Herbert is lower than Crashaw"; "Donne had no imagination, but as much wit, I think, as any writer can possibly have." The last remark is an echo but not the point of Dryden's preface to *Eleonora:* "Doctor Donne, the greatest wit, though not the best poet of our nation . . ." However, Spence's comment explains Pope's remark by example: "He commended Donne's Epistles, Metempsychosis, and Satires, as his best things." Thus wit and imagination are set apart.

On two members of the school of Donne, the remarks of Pope are more enlightening. Of Davenant as the author of *Gondibert* he says: "He is a scholar of Donne's, and took his sententiousness and metaphysics from him." He makes the same point again about Cowley: "Cowley is a fine poet, in spite of all his faults. He, as well as Davenant, borrowed his metaphysical style from Donne." It is probable that Pope was repeating the remarks of Walsh and Dryden, but he was also extending them into a school whose members are insufficiently discriminated. Yet the witty character of its founder has been named more specifically and his influence extended over a considerable span of poetry. Indeed, Edmund Gosse concluded *The Life and Letters of Donne* (1899) by finding his kind of writing in the close of *The Dunciad:* "From him the descent of it is unbroken."

Dr. Johnson christened the Metaphysical Poets and analyzed their school of poetry in his *Life of Cowley*, but in neither instance was he quite new or just. When he begins, "The metaphysical poets were men of learning, and to show their learning was their whole endeavour," we are reminded of Walsh and Dryden, but without his exaggeration. If poetry is an imitative art, says Johnson, they are not poets: "they neither copied nature nor life; neither painted the forms of matter, nor represented the operations of intellect." They may, however, be wits, "for they endeavoured to be singular in their thoughts." Hence Dr. Johnson's definition of wit "as a kind of *discordia concors;* a combination of dissimilar images, or discovery of occult resemblances in things apparently unlike." This ambition explains their need and use for various or diverse learning.

In this search for the unexpected and surprising they forfeited power over the emotions. Johnson again echoes Walsh and Dryden: "Their courtship was void of fondness, and their lamentation of sorrow." Their search for novelty could achieve subtlety, but not sublimity; this deficiency they attempted to supply by figurative violence. At best they could produce both the new and true; at worst they avoided the old.

As English models at this time, Johnson names Donne primarily for cast of sentiments and Jonson primarily for ruggedness of lines. Their successors were Suckling, Waller, Denham, Cowley, Cleveland, and Milton; but imitators of the "metaphysick style" are reduced to Cowley and Cleveland. Thus Johnson actually names and illustrates only Donne, Cleveland, and Cowley as members of the Metaphysical school. Altogether, Johnson's analysis is closer, but his charges are much the same as those of his predecessors, and his bias descended to our time.

This bias was particular with respect to the Metaphysical Poets, but general with respect to the theory of poetry, and it really began with Addison. In his last *Spectator* paper on Wit, Addison formulates the basic doctrine. He realizes that "In order therefore that the Resemblance in the Ideas be Wit, it is necessary that the Ideas should not lie too near one another in the Nature of things; for where the Likeness is obvious, it gives no Surprise." But this requirement of wit seems to him at odds with the requirements of Heroic poetry, and so he divides the old realm of poetic wit to which Donne's monarchy belonged: "For this Reason, the Similitudes in Heroick Poets, who endeavour rather to fill the Mind with great Conceptions, than to divert it with such as are new and surprizing, have seldom any thing in them that can be called Wit." Serious poetry cannot be both sublime and diverting, both moving and witty. Dr. Johnson applied this criticism to the Metaphysical Poets: they are wits rather than poets; their wit denies them emotional power and sublimity.

Matthew Arnold, in his essay on *Thomas Gray*, widened this gulf enough to drown the school of Dr. Johnson: "The difference between genuine poetry and the poetry of Dryden, Pope and all their school, is briefly this: their poetry is conceived and composed in their wits, genuine poetry is conceived and composed in the soul. The difference between the two kinds of poetry is immense." This difference was established in his *Study of Poetry* by the doctrine of "high seriousness," which separated emotional power and sublimity from the less serious products of the wits or a less intense criticism of life. It is ironical that the division of poetry which Addison initiated should engulf Johnson himself by the time of Arnold. Indeed, it split poetry into a kind of Ramist dichotomy of serious poetry and society verse; and the Metaphysical Poets were left, by the friendlier critics, to a kingdom of fancy.

It is not surprising that T. S. Eliot should attack the division of poetry which threatened both his talent and his taste. Or that he should find Arnold a major threat to poetry in his time, insisting that a poet had to take the high road, and not the low road, if he wanted to reach the castle of high seriousness, or to persuade others that he had a soul. In New England the figure of Arnold seemed to Eliot more Hebraic than Hellenic:

> *Upon the glazen shelves kept watch*
> *Matthew and Waldo, guardians of the faith,*
> *The army of unalterable law.*

In *The Use of Poetry and the Use of Criticism* Eliot is severe on the theories of Arnold that produce this division, and on their results in Arnold himself. He turns the tables on Arnold by finding his vision of life not serious enough, and his taste sounder in operation than in principle, his poetry more honest than assured. But it is in Eliot's essay on *Andrew Marvell*, his most serious treatment of wit in poetry, that he puts his finger on the dichotomy in our time: "or we find serious poets who seem afraid of acquiring wit, lest they lose intensity." In modern times Arnold did most to create that fear, and Eliot most to remove it. He concluded that wit "is something precious and needed and apparently extinct; it is what should preserve the reputation of Marvell." At least, it no longer bars the Metaphysical Poets from the sacred precincts of poetry.

II

The Context of Metaphysical Wit

The short view of history which led us to the definition of a Metaphysical school of poetry in the seventeenth century left us with a complex of wit and learning. And this complex was related to metaphysics. If Donne did not debate how many angels could stand on the point of a needle, he did use other potentialities of angels in nice speculations that turned upon wit or required acuteness for their comprehension, as in *Air and Angels* or *The Dream*. Metaphysics was not only an exercise for sharp wits but also a means to the interpretation of life, but with the decline of Aristotelianism such means finally became as idle as the speculations of the Schoolmen. Richard Baxter, who was both a dissenter and a wit, felt the need to sharpen his wits by reading the Schoolmen even when it pleased God to keep him from "tippling and excess."

In criticizing Cleveland for an excessive use of catachresis,

Dryden pointed to the rhetorical forms of wit. Here Dryden was speaking in the rhetorical tradition of his time, and this carries us back to a poet who was associated with Donne and who wrote a popular rhetoric, no doubt because he was a noted wit. It lasted into the fourth quarter of the century through such borrowers as Ben Jonson, Thomas Blount, and John Smith. Moreover, John Hoskins's *Directions for Speech and Style*, which was written about 1599, has special value for its indications of the fashions of his time. Thus it provides a useful approach to the school of Metaphysical wit, which is the essence of "affecting the metaphysics" by figurative employment.

Hoskins's definition of metaphor involves two rules: "A Metaphor, or Translation, is the friendly and neighborly borrowing of one word to express a thing with more light and better note, though not so directly and properly as the natural name of the thing meant would signify." Since a metaphor should avoid extremes, "The rule of a metaphor is that it be not too bold nor too far-fetched." This is the rule that Cleveland violated. The other rule is that a metaphor must not be too base: "But ever (unless your purpose be to disgrace) let the word be taken from a thing of equal or greater dignity," especially if metaphor is to give a "better note." The reason for "more light" is this: "Besides, a metaphor is pleasant because it enricheth our knowledge with two things at once, with the truth and with similitude."

Both "more light and better note" lead to learning in metaphor, and the rule that metaphor be not too base, except by intention, is followed by this observation: "Therefore, to delight generally, take those terms from ingenious and several professions; from ingenious arts to please the learned of all sorts; as from the meteors, planets, and beasts in natural philosophy, from the stars, spheres, and their motions in astronomy, from the better part of husbandry, from the politic government of cities, from navigation, from military profession, from physic; but not out of the depth of these mysteries." This is almost a recipe for Donne; and he erred, if at all, in the last respect, going too deep into these mysteries. An opposite warning, however, is not to go too low in husbandry. In these sources of metaphor we may notice the absence of conventional mythology, the emphasis on the ingenious or variety, and the desire to please the learned.

Now let us see what forms of wit, or various senses of the ingenious, Hoskins finds current or fashionable. First of all there is the bold metaphor that Dryden condemned in Cleveland: "Catachresis (in English, Abuse) is now grown in fashion—as most abuses are. It is somewhat more desperate than a metaphor. It is the expressing of one matter by the name of another which is incompatible with it, and sometimes clean contrary." It abuses metaphor chiefly in the requirement of compatibility, but incompatibility is the basis of its appeal to wit or ingenuity. "This is a usual figure," says Hoskins, "with the fine conversants of our time, when they strain for an extraordinary phrase." In the element of contrariety he relates it to the figure *ironia*.

Amplification in rhetoric has for Hoskins the function of making something appear extraordinary and thus provoke admiration. Comparison is one of the basic ways: "Comparison is either of things contrary, equal, or things different." In things equal "there are to be searched out all the several points of a consorted equality," as in Donne's "conceit." But this is not so forcible an amplification "as when things seeming unequal are compared, and that in similitudes as well as examples; as in my speech of a widow compared to a ship, *both ask much tackling and sometimes rigging*. And you shall most of all profit by inventing matter of agreement in things most unlike, as London and a tennis court: *for in both all the gain goes to the hazard*." As in catachresis, the challenge to ingenuity increases with the incompatibility, and the appeal to admiration with the difficulty of detecting similarity.

"Comparison of contraries," says Hoskins, "is the third and most flourishing way of comparison." This includes the various forms of antithesis, of terms compared by opposition. Thus from an emphasis on contrariety in similitude we pass to the comparison of contraries. But other ways of using contraries engage the attention of Hoskins. *Ironia*, for example, leads to amplification, "but in dissembling sort," because it "expresseth a thing by contrary, by show of exhortation when indeed it dehorteth," or by putting one opposite for another. The appeal to ingenuity is again patent.

There is also "a composition of contraries, and by both words intimateth the meaning of neither precisely but a moderation and mediocrity of both; as, *bravery* and *rags* are contrary, yet somewhat better than both is *brave raggedness*." This figure of amplification he calls Synoeciosis, and it includes oxymoron and other forms of paradox. Observing that "This is an easy figure now in fashion," he remarks: "This is a fine course to stir admiration in the hearer and make them think it a strange harmony which must be expressed in such discords." Here is a supreme achievement in the *discordia concors* of Dr. Johnson or the kind of writing that he connected with Marino.

This figure involves another way of amplification: "Intimation, that leaves the collection of greatness to our understanding, by expressing some mark of it." It requires inference because, like irony, it intimates more than it says. It demands an effort of mind, and so appeals to ingenuity or wit. Except in catachresis, Hoskins seems to be partial to the figures that involve a composition or comparison of contraries or incompatibles. Donne is also partial to these figures of wit.

But Hoskins's attitude is best summed up by his comment on another figure. In prose it relates to Seneca and Bacon, but we must remember that the figures were common to prose and poetry, and occupied a whole book in Puttenham's *Arte of English Poesie*. Here is Hoskins: "Sententia, if it be well used, is a figure—if ill and too much, it is a style; whereof none that writes humorously or factiously nowadays can be clear. For now there are such schisms of eloquence that it is enough for any ten years that all the bravest wits do imitate some one figure which a critic hath taught some great personage." This explains the origin of a style; and, although the allusion may be to Queen Elizabeth, it could also account for the Baconian essayists or the Metaphysical Poets.

Indeed, Hoskins proceeds to consider such fashions in the form and matter of writing: "So it may be within this two hundred years we shall go through the whole body of rhetoric. It is true that we study according to the predominancy of courtly inclinations: whilst mathematics were in request, all our similitudes came from lines, circles, and angles; whilst moral philosophy is now a while spoken of, it is rudeness not to be sententious. And for my part, I'll make one. I have used and outworn six several styles since I was first Fellow of New College, and am yet able to bear the fashion of writing company. Let our age, therefore, only speak morally, and let the next age live morally." Here the wit appears to validate his credentials. Geometrical figures are prominent in Donne.

After Hoskins finds *ironia* related to catachresis and intimation, he treats it as a dissembling sort of amplification. In Fulke Greville's *Life of Sidney* we find a vivid instance of the dissembling character of irony. The hazards of the subject in his own *Treatise of Monarchy*, Greville tells us, delayed its publication. In the attempt to revise it, he began to give it a richer dress: "But while these clothes were in making, I perceived that cost would but draw more curious eyes to observe deformities. So that from these checks a new counsell rose up in me, to take away all opinion of seriousnesse from these perplexed pedigrees; and to this end carelessly cast them into that hypocriticall figure *Ironia*, wherein men commonly (to keep above their workes) seeme to make toies of the utmost they can doe." Although a fancy dress might take away some opinion of seriousness, irony would complete the job by assuming a mask of flippant superiority. This dissembling figure would mock any idea of serious commitment to the views expressed.

But the result seemed to violate his subject: "And yet againe, in that confusing mist, when I beheld this grave subject (which should draw reverence and attention) to bee overspangled with lightnesse, I forced in examples of the Roman gravity, and greatnesse, the harsh severity of the *Lacedemonian* Governement; the riches of the *Athenian* learning, wit, and industry; and like a man that plaies divers parts upon severall hints, left all the indigested crudities, equally applied to Kings, or Tyrants." The result was that his distinctions were blurred, and the right line of descent would not reveal the crooked because it could not be believed. Not only was dissembling irony defeated, but all intimation was utterly frustrated. The mixture of ornament, ironic levity, and sententiousness left him to play the fool in motley. Finally, his revision became a lesson in the conflict of rhetorical means and ends. Nevertheless, gravity "over-spangled with lightness" may stand, as Burton said, like Janus in the field of Jacobean paradox, and Greville may put us on guard.

The poet who did most for Donne's reputation was Thomas Carew, in his *Elegy upon the Author* in the first edition of Donne's *Poems* (1633). For him Donne ruled "the universall Monarchy of wit" first as the priest of Apollo and then of the true God. His divine flame made apparent what could not be imagined:

> *And the deepe knowledge of darke truths so teach,*
> *As sense might judge, what phansie could not reach.*

Later, as we know, Donne was chided for being metaphysical. For Carew his secular fire purged "the Muses garden" of "Pedantique weedes" and "servile imitation." He repaid "the debts of our penurious bankrupt age," our licentious thefts of inspiration, our sly exchanges with the Greek or Latin tongue. Indeed, he has redeemed invention,

> *and open'd Us a Mine*
> *Of rich and pregnant phansie, drawn a line*
> *Of masculine expression,*

ways in which he made poetry new. His "imperious wit" or "Giant phansie" has molded the language to new achievement and exiled classical mythology. But his strict laws will prove too hard,

> *Till Verse refin'd by thee, in this last Age*
> *Turne ballad rime, Or those old Idolls bee*
> *Ador'd againe, with new apostasie.*

Though Donne was a "rebell and atheist" in the old faith, Carew fears for his reformation of poetry. And despairing of measuring up to the demands of the occasion, although he pays the tribute of imitation, Carew concludes with the Epitaph that formulated Donne's title of honor.

About the same time Drummond of Hawthornden was asserting the "new apostasie" in poetry. Whether against Donne or not, he was certainly indicting his strict laws in a letter to Dr. Arthur Johnston: "In vain have some Men of late (Transformers of every Thing) consulted upon her Reformation, and endeavoured to abstract her to Metaphysical Idea's, and Scholastical Quiddities, denuding her of her own Habits, and those Ornaments with which she hath amused the World some Thousand Years . . . What is not like the Ancients and conform to those Rules which hath been agreed unto by all Times, may (indeed) be something like unto Poesy, but it is no more Poesy than a Monster is a Man." Obviously Drummond objects to making poetry new and wants it returned to the garb furnished by the storehouse of classical myth and nature. To him the new poet looks like Samuel Butler's "Metaphysical Sectarian":

He could reduce all things to Acts
And knew their Natures by Abstracts,
Where Entity and Quiddity
The Ghosts of defunct Bodies flie;
Where Truth in Person does appear,
Like words congeal'd in Northern Air.
He knew what's what, *and that's as high*
As Metaphysick wit can fly.

In metaphysical wit abstractions appear at best like words thickened by personification, or like the ghosts of defunct bodies. To denude poetry of her mythology and to analyze experience by abstract ideas is the innovation that Drummond rejected.

Quarles the emblem poet had scorned metaphysical wit in his preface to *Argalus and Parthenia* (1629): "In this Discourse, I have not affected to set thy understanding on the Rack, by the tyranny of *strong lines,* which (as they fabulously report of *China* dishes) are made for the third *Generation* to make use of, and are the meere itch of wit; under the colour of which, many have ventured (trusting to the Oedipean conceit of their ingenious Reader) to write *non-sense,* and feloniously father the created expositions of other men." Not only the difficulty but the prestige of this wit seemed to Quarles such as to tempt some to write nonsense and then to adopt the meaning created by their ingenious readers, those who were good at riddles. It would appear that the "strong lines" of Metaphysical wit had a snob appeal for both writers and readers. In fact, the printer of Donne's *Poems* in 1633 disdained readers and addressed himself "To the Understanders": "For this time I must speake only to you, at another, *Readers* may perchance serve my turne."

In general Carew, Drummond, and Quarles outline the pattern of convention and revolt that obtained about the time of Donne's death. Although Drummond and Quarles do not mention Donne, they describe the poetry of revolt against the conventions which they espouse but Carew deplores. Times will change but this conflict will continue until a new set of conventions is established.

Later, Davenant also related wit to new ways. In the Preface to *Gondibert* (1650) he states this ambition: "nor will I presume to call the matter of which the Ornaments or Substantial parts of this Poem are compos'd, *Wit;* but onely tell you my endeavour was, in bringing Truth, too often absent, home to mens bosoms, to lead her through unfrequented and new ways, and from the most remote Shades, by representing Nature, though not in an affected, yet in an unusual dress." This goes counter to the position of Drummond, and exceeds Hoskins in comparisons drawn "from the most remote Shades."

Hobbes provided the basic psychology for analyzing literary powers at this time. In *Human Nature* (Chap. X) he speaks of the quickness "which is joyned with *Curiosity* of comparing the Things that come into the Mind, one with another: in which Comparison, a Man delighteth himself either with finding unexpected *Similitude* of Things, otherwise much unlike, in which Men place the Excellency of *Fancy*, and from whence proceed those grateful Similes, Metaphors, and other Tropes, by which both *Poets* and *Orators* have it in their Power to make Things please or displease, and show well or ill to others, as they like themselves; or else in discerning suddenly *Dissimilitude* in Things that otherwise appear the same. And this Vertue of the Mind is that by which Men attain to exact and perfect *Knowledge;* and the Pleasure thereof consisteth in continual Instruction, and in Distinction of Places, Persons, and Seasons, and is commonly termed by the Name of Judgement, for, to judge is nothing else, but to distinguish or discern." In repeating these definitions of Fancy and Judgment in the *Leviathan* (1651) he emphasizes the difficulty in each kind of perception as its claim to excellence as an Intellectual Vertue. In literary matters judgment is the faculty of propriety and is related to "exact and perfect Knowledge."

Of course "dissimilitude" was also the basis of various rhetorical figures, and Obadiah Walker classified them in *Some Instructions concerning the Art of Oratory* (1659) as "Dissimilitudes, or Comparisons with, and Illustrations by Contraries." These dissimilitudes were expressed by "Disjunction" in antithesis, or by "Commutation and Inversion" in antimetabole, or by "denominating one of another" in oxymoron. On their paradoxical form Walker sounds like Hoskins: "Which because commonly not done without strength of fancy in the Orator, is the more remarked and admired by the Auditor, much taken to see opposites agree and contradictions true." When Addison finished his *Spectator* papers on wit, he became aware that he had omitted this kind of wit, but he never repaired the omission.

In Hobbes's *Answer to Davenant's Preface* his doctrine took its most persuasive literary form and related fancy and judgment more precisely to knowledge. Here is the work of judgment and fancy respectively: "That which giveth a Poem the true and natural Colour consisteth in two things, which are, *To know well*, that is, to have images of nature in the memory distinct and clear, and *To know much*. A signe of the first is perspicuity, property, and decency, which delight all sorts of men, either by instructing the ignorant or soothing the learned in their knowledge. A signe of the latter is novelty of expression, and pleaseth by excitation of the minde; for novelty causeth admiration, and admiration curiosity, which is a delightful appetite of knowledge." Thus fancy could sanction the Metaphysical Poets. But perspicuity is threatened by scholastic terms and the kind of wit that Quarles rejected: "To this palpable darkness I may also add the ambitious obscurity of expressing more than is perfectly conceived, or perfect conception in fewer words than it requires. Which Expressions, though they have had the honor to be called strong lines, are indeed no better than Riddles, and, not onely to the Reader but also after a little time to the Writer himself, dark and troublesome." Hobbes sees both of the aspects of strong lines that Quarles observed, and rejects them both as related to knowledge and as related to expression. Of course both scholastic terms and strong lines were cultivated by Metaphysical poetry.

After discussing various kinds of propriety or decorum as the business of judgment, Hobbes turns to the product of fancy as related to knowledge: "From *Knowing much,* proceedeth the admirable variety and novelty of Metaphors and Similitudes, which are not possible to be lighted on in the compass of a narrow knowledge. And the want whereof compelleth a Writer to expressions that are either defac'd by time or sullied with vulgar and long use." This want explains and justifies the use of knowledge by the Metaphysical Poets. But Hobbes also includes the effect upon the Reader: "For the Phrases of Poesy, as the airs of musick, with often hearing become insipide, the Reader having no more sense of their force than our Flesh is sensible of the bones that sustain it. As the sense we have of bodies consisteth in change and variety of impression, so also does the sense of language in the variety and changeable use of words." Hobbes's quarrel is not with knowledge, but with the kind that became associated with the Metaphysical Poets, or with such contradictions as "incorporeal substance." But wit had not yet come under the tyranny of decorum which finally outlaws Metaphysical wit for Walsh and Dryden.

Also prefixed to *Gondibert* were two eulogistic poems that are equally conscious of Davenant's claim to new ways of wit. In their way they express the opposition found in Carew's *Elegy on Donne.* Waller praises the new ways in a style entangled in the old ways:

Wherein those few that can with Judgement look,
May find old Love in pure fresh Language told,
Like new stampt Coyn made out of Angel gold.
Such truth in Love as th'antique World did know,
In such a style as Courts may boast of now.
Which no bold tales of Gods or Monsters swell,
But humane Passions, such as with us dwell.
Man is thy theam, his Virtue or his Rage
Drawn to the life in each elaborate Page.
Mars nor Bellona are not named here;
But such a Gondibert as both might fear.
Venus had here, and Hebe been out-shin'd
By thy bright Birtha, and thy Rhodalind.
Such is thy happy skill, and such the odds
Betwixt thy Worthies and the Grecian Gods.

Though the contrast between old and new sources of wit is appropriate, the odds put Waller among those foretold by Carew:

They will repeale the goodly exil'd traine
Of gods and goddesses, which in thy just raigne
Were banish'd nobler Poems, now, with these
The silenc'd tales o'th'Metamorphoses
Shall stuffe their lines, and swell the windy Page.

Waller must have disappointed those who took Hobbes as a guide to Davenant's poem, but Cowley repeated the gospel of Carew in words more acceptable to Hobbes:

Some Men their Fancies like their Faiths derive,
And count all ill but that which Rome does give;
The marks of Old and Catholick would find,
To the same Chair would Truth and Fiction bind.
Thou in these beaten paths disdain'st to tread,
And scorn'st to live by robbing of the Dead.
Since Time does all things change, thou think'st not fit
This latter Age should see all new, but Wit.
Thy Fancie, like a Flame, her way does make,
And leaves bright tracks for following Pens to take.

Sure 'twas this noble boldness of the Muse
Did thy desire, to seek new Worlds, infuse.

In refusing to bind truth and fiction to the same doctrine, Cowley might worry Hobbes a little; but he is definitely a protestant in wit, opposed to Drummond, and oriented toward Donne.

The importance of this prefatory matter is attested in an appropriate way. It first appeared without the poem, which made it a butt of the wits:

A Preface to no Book, a Porch to no house:
Here is the Mountain, but where is the Mouse?

History fixed this order of importance, and in its own way made

Room for the best of Poets heroick,
If you'l believe two Wits and a Stoick;

but more for their reasons than for their alleged conclusion.

The culmination of this concern about the sources of wit is found in Thomas Sprat's *History of the Royal Society* (1667), which was also introduced by a eulogy from Cowley. A year before Dryden's *Essay of Dramatic Poesy*, Sprat is at pains to point out (Part III, Sect. 35) how "Experiments will be beneficial to our wits and Writers." He was in fact promoting natural philosophy as a source of wit. To this end he undertakes a Baconian inventory of the sources of wit: "The several subjects from which it has been raised in all Times, are the Fables, and Religions of the Antients, the Civil Histories of all Countries, the Customs of Nations, the *Bible*, the Sciences, and Manners of Men, the several Arts of their hands, and the works of Nature. In all these, where there may be a resemblance of one thing to another, as there may be in all, there is a sufficient Foundation for Wit." Naturally this list is more extensive than that of Hoskins, but Sprat also imposes new limitations: "To this purpose I must premise, that it is required in the best, and most delightful Wit; that it be founded on such images which are generally known, and are able to bring a strong, and a sensible impression on the mind."

Thus his requirements for the best wit favor both common knowledge and the arts of men's hands and the works of nature. Moreover, they disqualify metaphysics: "The Sciences of mens Brains are none of the best Materials for this kind of Wit. Very few have happily succeeded in Logical, Metaphysical, Grammatical, nay even scarce in Mathematical Comparisons; and the reason is, because they are most of them conversant about things removed from the Senses, and so cannot surprise the *fancy* with very obvious, or quick, or sensible delights." Abstractions do not strike the fancy through the senses, and thus Sprat anticipates Dryden and Walsh by rejecting imagery drawn from abstract learning.

For Sprat, not only is mythology exhausted as a source of wit, but it forces him to join those men who "their Fancies like their Faiths derive," and "To the same Chair would Truth and Fiction bind." For the fables and religions of the ancient world "have this peculiar imperfection, that they were only Fictions at first: whereas Truth is never so well expressed or amplifyed, as by those Ornaments which are True and Real in themselves." So the best wit has to be true as well as real, and this distinguishes the Bible from mythology. Moreover, the natural knowledge of the ancients has also been exhausted as a source of wit, but experiments will soon provide a new storehouse of the best wit. Later it was thought that the old philosophy of "Materia Prima and Occult Qualities" had only given way to "the Reign of Atoms." But Sprat felt that he had established new standards for wit based on the visible world, except for the wit of the Bible, to which some took exception.

This program, however, would restrict their wits and

scholars to terms much more limited than those supplied by the ingenious arts and professions of Hoskins. If they were denied metaphysical terms of art, they were encouraged to use those related to the arts of men's hands. Davenant allowed mechanical as well as liberal terms in the epic, but Hobbes did not. Dryden was tempted by the special terms of naval warfare in his *Annus Mirabilis*. By the time of his translation of Virgil, however, he had changed his mind about such "proprieties" and wrote in general terms for an audience "better bred than to be too nicely knowing in the terms." Or to "parley" metaphysics to a lady.

III

The Two Worlds of Donne

In *The History of the Royal Society* Sprat directed the poet's attention to the visible world rather than the invisible world explored by "the Sciences of men's Brains." Bacon in *The Advancement of Learning* had attacked the "vain matter" of the Schoolmen for this reason: "For the wit and mind of man, if it work upon matter, which is the contemplation of the creatures of God, worketh according to the stuff, and is limited thereby; but if it work upon itself, as the spider worketh his web, then it is endless, and brings forth indeed cobwebs of learning, admirable for the fineness of thread and work, but of no substance or profit." Sprat applied this criticism to the work of wits and writers.

But Cowley prepared the way when his eulogy of *Gondibert* praised Davenant's banishment of the supernatural in favor of the natural in the epic, and when his Preface to *A*

Proposition for the Advancement of Experimental Philosophy (1661) allowed Bacon's principle to apply to both fancy and reason: "Our Reasoning Faculty as well as Fancy, does but Dream, when it is not guided by sensible Objects. We shall compound where Nature has divided, and divide where Nature has compounded, and create nothing but either Deformed Monsters, or at best pretty but impossible Mermaids. 'Tis like Painting by Memory and Imagination which can never produce a Picture to the Life." This is why the Schoolmen did not "so much as touch Nature, because they catcht only at the shadow of her in their own Brains."

Yet in his *Pindarique Odes,* in a note on "The Muse," Cowley allowed fancy greater license: "The meaning is, that Poetry treats not only of all things that are, or can be, but makes Creatures of her own, as Centaurs, Satyrs, Fairies, &c., makes persons and actions of her own, as in Fables and Romances, makes Beasts, Trees, Waters, and other irrational and insensible things to act above the possibility of their natures, as to understand and speak, nay makes what Gods it pleases too without Idolatry, and varies all these into innumerable Systemes, or Worlds of Invention." This license goes beyond Hobbes's limitation of imagination, "the conceived possibility of nature," but not beyond the poetic liberty that Cowley thought proper to the Pindaric muse or the supernatural.

In general Cowley and Sprat would turn the mind from notional philosophy to empirical philosophy even in works of the imagination. But in following Donne, the earlier work of Cowley did not achieve the new orientation, but opened him to the same censure as Donne. Dr. Johnson, however, could relent upon occasion: "where scholastick speculation can be properly admitted, their copiousness and acuteness may justly be admired. What Cowley has written upon Hope shows an unequalled fertility of invention." As with Dryden, the basic issue is propriety, and the intruder is scholastic speculation or notional philosophy; but in Dryden the intrusion is upon formal human nature. These consequences of affecting the metaphysics ought to be kept clearly in mind.

Instead of calling the framework for Donne's speculation "The Elizabethan World Picture," I might call it the metaphysical cosmology to emphasize cosmology as a branch of metaphysics and this cosmos as an orderly system dependent upon the principle of the chain of being. But a definition of metaphysics in Dryden's time is perhaps more to the point. Thomas Blount, in his *Glossographia*, defines "Metaphysicks" as "a Science, which lifting it self above the changeable nature of things, considers of such as subsist in their own essence, not subject to any alteration, dealing onely with Universals, abstracting from Individuals; School Divinity is the highest part of it, consisting chiefly in contemplative knowledge of God, Angels, Souls of Men, &c."

This distinguishes Donne's two worlds: the world of change or alteration, of the body of man; and the world of the unchanging or constant, of the soul of man. In the astronomy of Aristotle and Ptolemy they were divided by the sphere of the moon: all below was the sublunary realm; all above was the superlunary realm. Theologically they reflected the order of nature and the order of grace. In language one is a world of bodies and Individuals, the other a world of abstractions and Universals. Together they provide Donne with the means of analyzing the experience of man. We shall particularize them only so far as to uncover their basic applications to his poetry.

The relevance of Blount's definition to our purpose is supported by his citation from *The Advancement of Learning*: "Physick (says my Lord Bacon) is that which enquires of the efficient cause, and of the matter; Metaphysick, that which enquires of the form and end." These four causes are explained by Sir Thomas Browne in *Religio Medici* (Sect. xiv): "There is but one first cause, and four second causes of all things. Some are without efficient, as God; others without matter, as Angels; some without form, as the first matter: but every Essence, created or uncreated, hath its final cause, and some positive end both of its Essence and Operation." For Bacon to make use of the latter causes was to affect the metaphysics, with or without propriety, and to leave the experimental for the speculative world.

Donne lived in the same divided and distinguished worlds as Sir Thomas Browne, the cosmos defined by the ladder or chain of being and divided by man and the moon. Browne describes these worlds in his *Religio Medici* (Sect. xxxiii), beginning with their basic principle: "for there is in this Universe a Stair, or manifest Scale of creatures, rising not disorderly, or in confusion, but with a comely method and proportion. Between creatures of meer existence, and things of life, there is a large disproportion of nature; between plants, and animals or creatures of sense, a wider difference; between them and Man, a far greater: and if the proportion hold on, between Man and Angels there should be yet a greater." This scale runs from stones to angels, from existence to understanding. Browne speculates on the difference between man and angels: before the Fall, man also was immortal; but the chief difference is that angels know immediately, by intuitive reason; man only mediately, by discursive reason.

Then Browne describes man's place in the cosmos: "We are onely that amphibious piece between a corporal and spiritual Essence, that middle form that links those two together, and makes good the Method of God and Nature, that jumps not from extreams, but unites the incompatible distances by some middle and participating natures. That we are the breath and similitude of God, it is indisputable, and upon record of Holy Scripture; but to call ourselves a Microcosm, or little World, I thought it only a pleasant trope of Rhetorick, till my neer judgement and second thoughts told me there was a real truth therein." This is the basis for cosmological figures. The amphibious nature of man explains Donne's concern with his dual parts of body and soul, as in *Holy Sonnet V:*

> *I am a little world made cunningly*
> *Of Elements and an Angelic sprite.*

In his *Letters* (1651, p. 121) he joins them in his "Philosophy of love; which though it be directed upon the minde, doth inhere in the body, and find piety entertainment there."

Now Browne makes man himself run the entire scale of being: "For first we are a rude mass, and in the rank of creatures which onely are, and have a dull kind of being, not yet privileged with life, or preferred to sense or reason; next we live the life of Plants, the life of Animals, the life of Men, and at last the life of Spirits, running on in one mysterious nature those five kinds of existences, which comprehend the creatures, not onely of the World, but of the Universe." These five levels are defined by mere being, mere life, sense, reason, Spirit; and explain how Donne can figuratively sink or rise in the scale of being, as in *Twickenham Garden* or *A Nocturnal upon St. Lucy's Day.*

Browne concludes: "Thus is Man that great and True *Amphibium,* whose nature is disposed to live, not onely like other creatures in diverse elements, but in divided and distinguished worlds: for though there be but one to sense, there are two to reason, the one visible, the other invisible." In a *Verse Letter to the Countess of Huntington,* Donne puts it this way:

> *The soul with body, is a heaven combin'd*
> *With earth, and for man's ease, but nearer join'd;*
> *Where thoughts the stars of soul we understand,*
> *We guess not their large natures, but command.*

In his *Letters* (p. 46) he says: "Our nature is Meteorique, we respect (because we partake so) both earth and heaven; for as our bodies glorified shall be capable of spirituall joy, so our souls demerged into those bodies, are allowed to partake earthly pleasure." Donne is concerned with these two worlds not only in their material and spiritual aspects, but in the sublunary and superlunary aspects that divide them or distinguish their natures. Thus *A Valediction: Forbidding Mourning* opposes movements of the earth and the spheres to distinguish "dull sublunary lovers" from those "interassured of the mind." Or *A Valediction: Of my Name in the Window* finds hope in a metaphysical compliment:

> *Then, as all my souls be*
> *Emparadis'd in you, (in whom alone*
> *I understand, and grow and see,)* . . .

This is the scale and these are the realms by which Donne's "nice speculations" or scholastic tropes bring meaning to human experience. As his poetry shows, this meaning had little to do with the physical charms or "oldest clothes" of women, and could never be interpreted only by the world of sense, except as lust. Because he had to explore experience or extend its meaning by speculation, Donne laid himself open to the charges of Dryden.

Donne's sublunary world was described in these words by Thomas Digges in 1576: "The Globe of Elements enclosed in the Orbe of the Moone I call the Globe of Mortalitie because it is the peculiar Empire of death. For above the Moone they feare not his force but as the Christian Poet sayth . . . In the midst of this Globe of Mortalitie hangeth this darcke starre or ball of earth and water." The other elements are, of course, air and fire, Cleopatra's final elements according to Shakespeare. Form was mutable, but matter constant. The earth as opposed to the heavens, even for this Copernican, was still confined to the realm of mutability and death, subject to the vicissitude of the four elements. These were composed of the four contraries, cold, hot, moist, and dry, and were the basis of mutability and decay. In *The Dissolution* we find them as elements of love:

> *My fire of Passion, sighs of air,*
> *Water of tears, and earthy sad despair . . .*

In *Elegy XII*, "his parting from her" translates them:

> *I will not look upon the quickening Sun,*
> *But straight her beauty to my sense shall run;*
> *The air shall note her soft, the fire most pure;*
> *Water suggest her clear, and the earth sure.*

The elements corresponded to the humours in man. Cold and dry united in Earth and Melancholy; cold and moist united in Water and Phlegm; hot and moist united in Air and Blood; hot and dry united in Fire and Choler. Virtue is related to the humours in a *Verse Letter to the Lady Carey*. Balance made stability or health among the elements; dominance made complexion among the humours.

Above the moon, according to Plato, the elements were mixed equally; according to Aristotle, all was composed of ether, a fifth element. In *The Good-Morrow* "What ever dies, was not mixt equally"; in *Love's Growth* mixtures and a fifth element are opposed in the analysis of love: if love

> *not only be no quintessence,*
> *But mixt of all stuffs, paining soul, or sense,*

then it belongs to the world of elements, and

> *Love's not so pure, and abstract, as they use*
> *To say, which have no Mistress but their Muse.*

Above the moon, Intelligences, or angels, moved the spheres. The heavens were deemed eternal until they appeared to be invaded by change; as when Donne said in a *Verse Letter to the Countess of Bedford*:

We've added to the world Virginia, and sent
Two new stars lately to the firmament.

For Donne cartography or the mapping of the earth was also an important source of imagery; his *Devotions upon Emergent Occasions* provides the best map of his characteristic imagery. But he also included the regions defined by Hobbes: "As Philosophers have divided the Universe, their subject, into three Regions, *Celestiall*, *Aëriall*, and *Terrestriall*, so the Poets," said Hobbes, "have lodg'd themselves in the three Regions of mankinde, *Court*, *City*, and *Country*, correspondent in some proportion to those three Regions of the World."

Donne analyzes experience in terms of body and soul, their elements or faculties; or in terms of the three souls and the four contraries. The three souls corresponded to the vegetable, animal, and human level on the scale of being: the special powers of the vegetable soul were growth and reproduction; of the animal soul, sense and movement; of the human, reason; but each soul subsumed the powers of the soul below it. This is Robert Burton's threefold division of the Body: "As first of the head, in which the animal organs are contained, and brain itself, which by his nerves gives sense and motion to the rest, and is, as it were, a privy counsellor and chancellor to the heart. The second region is the chest, or middle belly, in which the heart as king keeps his court, and by his arteries communicates life to the whole body. The third region is the lower belly, in which the liver resides as a legate *a latere*, with the rest of those natural organs, serving for concoction, nourishment, expelling of excrements." Here "animal" refers to *anima* or the highest soul. The liver was the seat of physical life, the heart of emotional life, and the brain of rational life, or the immortal soul.

In a *Verse Letter to the Countess of Salisbury*, Donne is more specific about the three souls:

> *We first have souls of growth, and sense, and those,*
> *When our last soul, our soul immortal came,*
> *Were swallowed into it, and have no name.*

Nevertheless he feels indebted to them:

> *I owe my first souls thanks, that they*
> *For my last soul did fit and mould my clay.*

In his *Devotions* (XVIII) Donne emphasizes the last soul. "Man, before hee hath his *immortall soule*, hath a *soule* of *sense*, and a *soule* of *vegitation* before that: This *immortall soule* did not forbid other *soules*, to be in us before, but when this *soule* departs, it carries all with it; no more *vegetation*, no more *sense*." The "spirits," which were expressed from the blood, were the instrument of the soul, or the medium between body and soul. They performed the functions of the liver, heart, and brain, and each kind was made out of the spirits below it. At the rational level they were diffused by the nerves or sinews to the subordinate members. Donne uses them in *The Extasie:*

> *As our blood labours to beget*
> *Spirits, as like souls as it can,*
> *Because such fingers need to knit*
> *That subtle knot, which makes us man.*

They make a knot of man, as man makes a knot of matter and Spirit in the scale of being.

There was also a threefold division of the faculties of the soul: lowest, the five outward senses; middle, the three inner senses—common sense or judgment, fancy, and memory; highest, reason, or understanding and will. Only the highest powers define the rational soul or mind; the other powers belong to the sensitive soul, plus another, movement, or inward appetite and outward motion. Vegetables are not preferred either to sense or to reason. Sometimes the body and soul opposition in Donne is used in this form: " 'Tis not the bodies marry, but the minds"; sometimes the opposition is reduced to sense and mind, or to sense and heart, or to faculties alone:

> *For sense, and understanding may*
> *Know, what gives fuel to their fire.*

In his *Letters* (p. 70) mind also becomes a middle term incapable of this certainty: "for we consist of three parts, a Soul, and Body, and Minde: which I call those thoughts and affections and passions, which neither soul nor body hath alone, but have been begotten by their communication." The passions and diseases of the mind are not easily known and judged by the mind itself, but attempts to follow them may be observed in his poetry. When in doubt, Donne's anatomy of the body and soul may be verified in Robert Burton's *Anatomy of Melancholy* (I. ii. 2).

Donne's poetry was also affected by the invasion of this cosmology by the new philosophy, which brought disorder into the old cosmos:

> *And new Philosophy calls all in doubt,*
> *The Element of fire is quite put out.*

This disorder is the real subject of *An Anatomie of the World*, but not its occasion—"wherein, by occasion of the untimely death of Mistress Elizabeth Drury, the frailty and the decay of this whole world is represented." His *Biathanatos, Ignatius his Conclave*, and the *Anniversaries* all show the impact of the new astronomy on his mind. In this *Anatomie* Donne combines classical and Christian myth and philosophy, so that the Fall of man is also the end of the golden age, the departure of the world-soul or Astraea, the death of virtue and her latest personification. As he said in a *Verse Letter to Mr. R. W.*: in man as a microcosm, "Virtue, our form's form and our soul's soul, is." Both man and his world are decayed.

First, Donne anatomizes the decay of man by all the signs that were used as evidence for this theory. The remedy for man is "The supernaturall food, Religion," and the moral of his condition is summarized thus:

> *Thy better Growth growes withered, and scant;*
> *Be more than man, or thou'rt lesse than an Ant.*

Actually, decay had descended the scale of being to reach the world, and this brings Donne to his second thesis:

> *Then, as mankinde, so is the worlds whole frame*
> *Quite out of joynt, almost created lame:*
> *For, before God had made up all the rest,*
> *Corruption entred, and deprav'd the best:*
> *It seis'd the Angels, and then first of all*
> *The world did in her cradle take a fall,*
> *And turn'd her braines, and tooke a generall maime,*
> *Wronging each joynt of th'universall frame.*
> *The noblest part, man, felt it first; and then*
> *Both beasts and plants, curst in the curse of man.*
> *So did the world from the first houre decay,*
> *That evening was beginning of the day.*

Wronging each joint of the scale or ladder of being, corruption brought decay and death into the world. Disorder came into the cosmos, even change into the superlunary world, largely by astronomical evidence, and weakened the correspondence of heaven and earth. The microcosm and macrocosm, or man and world, provide or involve dual reference for the metaphor of this anatomy, so that the reader feels that both a body and a world are being anatomized. The correspondences are such that a spiritual cause produces physical effects and runs through the scale of being. This conception comes close to involving the first cause in the decay of the world, "almost created lame."

Dryden admired this poem instead of citing it as evidence

of Donne's impropriety in sacrificing ladies to philosophy, although the charge is usually reversed in this case. As if admitting the indictment, Donne begins his final salute with these words:

> *Here therefore be the end: And, blessed maid,*
> *Of whom is meant what ever hath been said . . .*

On the other hand, it would be even more improper to suggest that he meant it lightly. As he said elsewhere, in a *Verse Letter to Mr. S. B.*, "I sing not, Siren-like, to tempt"; his appeal was more intellectual. In a *Verse Letter to Mr. T. W.*, written "where in every street / Infections follow," he begins:

> *Haste thee harsh verse, as fast as thy lame measure*
> *Will give thee leave, to him, my pain and pleasure.*
> *I have given thee, and yet thou art too weak,*
> *Feet, and a reasoning soul and tongue to speak.*

The consequences of such verse have been defined by Thomas Carew, but Donne was more concerned with "a reasoning soul" to inform his verse and speak his "pain and pleasure." The "reasoning soul" was later described as affecting the metaphysics or nice speculation rather than informing his experience.

It is at work in his *Paradoxes*, where it explores questions involved in his verse; for example, the relations of mind and body. In the paradox *That Nature is our worst Guide* he draws this conclusion: "therefore our *Complexions* and whole *Bodies*, we inherit from *Parents;* our *inclinations* and minds follow that: For our *mind* is heavy in our *bodies afflictions*, and rejoyceth in our *bodies pleasure:* how then shall this *nature* [rational nature] governe us, that is governed by the worst part of us?" Again in the paradox *That the Gifts of the Body are better than those of the Minde:* "I say again, that the *body* makes the *minde*, not that it created it a *minde*, but *forms* it a *good* or a *bad minde;* and this *minde* may be confounded with *soul* without any violence or injustice to *Reason* or *Philosophy:* then the *soul* it seems is enabled by our *Body*, not this by it. My *Body* licenseth my *soul* to *see* the worlds *beauties* through mine *eyes:* to *hear* pleasant things through mine *ears;* and affords it apt *Organs* for the conveiance of all perceivable *delight.* But alas! my *soul* cannot make any *part*, that is not of it self disposed to *see* or *hear*, though without doubt she be as able and as willing to see *behinde as before.* Now if my *soul* would say, that she enables any part to taste these *pleasures*, but is her selfe only delighted with those rich *sweetnesses* which her *inward eyes* and *senses* apprehend, shee should dissemble; for I see her often solaced with *beauties*, which she sees through mine *eyes*, and with *musicke* which through mine *eares* she heares. This *perfection* then my *body* hath, that it can impart to my *minde* all his *pleasures;* and my *mind* hath still many, that she can neither teach my *indisposed* part her *faculties*, nor to the best *espoused* parts show it *beauty* of *Angels*, of *Musicke*, of *Spheres*, whereof she boasts the *contemplation.*" However, we must be careful here to distinguish the organs of the body from the faculties of the mind that depend upon them. Elsewhere Donne analyzes the powers of man by means of the three souls, which would be represented here by the sensitive and the rational soul.

For Donne experience had to be fathomed as well as felt. He always sought to know; it was his immoderate hydroptic thirst. When he contemplated the futility of earthly knowledge in *The Second Anniversary*, "Poor soule, in this thy flesh what dost thou know?" he carefully spelled out the limitations of the body.

> *When wilt thou shake off this Pedantery,*
> *Of being taught by sense, and Fantasie?*

> *Thou look'st through spectacles; small things seeme great*
> *Below; But up unto the watch-towre get,*
> *And see all things despoyl'd of fallacies:*
> *Thou shalt not peepe through lattices of eyes,*
> *Nor heare through Labyrinths of eares, nor learne*
> *By circuit, or collections to discerne.*
> *In heaven thou straight know'st all, concerning it,*
> *And what concernes it not, shall straight forget.*

But on earth the rational soul is dependent on the soul of sense, or else can do nothing, as he often says. Here it uses the faculties of that soul to arrive by discursive reason at what angels know immediately in heaven. The Schoolmen divided on this question, and Donne sometimes followed the Scotists, who believed that angels knew intuitively, and sometimes the Thomists, who did not.

Donne never forgot this dependence of man upon the soul of sense, just as he always tried to construct something out of it by reason. In this life the rational soul is less sufficient than in the next:

> *Thinke that it argued some infirmitie,*
> *That those two soules, which then thou foundst in me,*
> *Thou fedst upon, and drewst into thee, both*
> *My second soule of sense, and first of growth.*

Donne never ceased to explore the relations between the higher souls of sense and reason, and never forgot that the three souls made man the most complex creature in the scale of being, with manifold relations to his world. More than anything else, this awareness explains his mode of analysis. Donne defines his feeling by his images and interprets it by their relations; their diversity comes from the various correspondences of his world, their cogency from their connection. Their propriety derives from their force: even "The Holy Ghost is figurative" (*LXXX Sermons*, p. 658); and "No metaphor, no comparison is too high, none too low, too triviall, to imprint in you a sense of Gods everlasting goodnesse towards you" (*Fifty Sermons*, p. 228). Expressiveness must never be sacrificed to decorum.

In general, the Aristotelian and Ptolemaic astronomy divided his cosmos into the sublunary and superlunary realms, extending from the mutable elements to the eternal heavens. This was crossed by the great chain of being extending from stones to God. The animating principles correspondent to the natural orders on this scale were the vegetative, sensitive, and rational souls or faculties; correspondent to the elements were the humours of man. This world of ordered correspondences supported the great analogy of microcosm and macrocosm, or man and world, and this in turn supplied Donne's divergent fields of metaphor, or areas of correspondence. In the analysis of his experience he could pass from the physical to the metaphysical; in exploring the psychological realm he went from anatomy, cosmography, or alchemy, to scholastic philosophy; he could also make Elizabeth Drury superior to the new philosophy on her way to heaven. The same view of the world distinguishes his sermon *At the Funerals of Sir William Cokayne*, December 12, 1626, and explains its remarkable use of learning.

However, Donne was also suspended between two worlds, the old world of Decay and the new world of Progress. The old world is represented in Donne's *Anatomie of the World*, the new world in Bacon's *Advancement of Learning*. The old view was opposed by George Hakewill's *Apologie or Declaration of the Power and Providence of God in the Government of the World, Consisting in an Examination and Censure of the Common Errour Touching Nature's Perpetual and Universal Decay* (1627). This received opinion he refuted by the old idea of constancy in mutability or circular change; his nearest approach to the idea of progress was "a kinde of circular progresse." For Bacon the excessive admiration of Antiquity was an error of learning which produced "a distrust that anything should be discovered in later times that was not hit upon before . . . For thus we seem apprehensive that time is worn out, and become unfit for generation." In a world of change the rule at best was constancy, not progress; the mood that of George Herbert's *Decay*.

But the new astronomers were "exploding" the old doctrine of the heavens set forth by Aristotle and Ptolemy, as Burton tells us in a "Digression of Air" in his *Anatomy of Melancholy*. This controversy aggravated the feeling about the decay of the world, but it also made Burton satiric: "The World is tossed in a blanket amongst them, they hoise the Earth up and down like a ball, make it stand and go at their pleasures." Earlier, in discussing the Center (of earth or universe), he alluded to Donne's satire by calling Hell "Ignatius' Parlour." As late as 1658 Sir Thomas Browne repeated, in *Urne Buriall*, the change in cosmology: "While we look for incorruption in the heavens, we finde they are but like the Earth; Durable in their main bodies, alterable in their parts: whereof beside Comets and new Stars, perspectives begin to tell tales." Although he did not accept the theory of decay, he concluded: " 'Tis too late to be ambitious. The great mutations of the world are acted, or time may be too short for our designes." Mutability had done its work, and allotted time was short. Dr. Johnson found in Milton a hint of belief in "the decrepitude of Nature." Although Milton had argued against decay while a student, he seems to have become less confident of time and place in *Paradise Lost*, "unless an age too late, or cold / Climat, or Years damp my intended wing."

In Donne's world the emotions and imaginations of men were still involved in the Ptolemaic order, in which the new astronomy had destroyed the distinction between the Globe of Mortality and the immutable Heavens, thereby accelerating the decay of the world. By Dryden's time the conflict between the old world of Decay and the new world of Progress had developed into parties of the Ancients and the Moderns. Cowley's prophets of progress were Bacon, Hobbes, and the Royal Society. No doubt Cowley's example encouraged Dryden to apply the idea of progress to literature.

IV

John Donne
1572-1631

"John Donne, Anne Donne, Un-done," thus Donne turned his wit upon himself. It was in the cards that the rebel and atheist of love should find marriage the momentous event of his life. It changed everything. After Anne More's death, he never remarried; Milton, bereaved similarly, remarried twice. In the dark days of Mitcham, when his fortunes were lowest, Donne wrote a strange *Litanie*, more to liberate himself than others: as he

> *Halfe wasted with youths fires, of pride and lust,*
> *Must with new stormes be weatherbeat.*

In his *Letters* (p. 27) he wrote from Mitcham: "I have ever seen in London and our Court, as colours, and habits, and continuances, and motions, and phrases, and accents, and songs, so friends in fashion and in season"—and as suddenly abandoned. Conscious of his "excesse / In seeking secrets, or Poëtiquenesse," he included in his *Litanie* sins unknown to the simple man as well as more personal temptations:

> *From being anxious, or secure,*
> *Dead clods of sadnesse, or light squibs of mirth,*
> *From thinking, that great courts immure*
> *All, or no happinesse, or that this earth*
>   *Is only for our prison fram'd,*
>   *Or that thou art covetous*
> *To them thou lovest, or that they are maim'd*
> *From reaching this worlds sweet, who seek thee thus,*
> *With all their might, Good Lord deliver us.*

But in all his contrarieties of mind he still wanted to make the most of both worlds. Yet he did not want the Prophets, who had harmonized nature and grace, to excuse his "excess in seeking secrets," which was the sin of his inquiring mind.

It is also the key to our understanding of Donne. Even in his early work, in *Loves Deitie* and *Satyre III*, he began to question both love and religion. But how did he regard his adventures "in seeking secrets, or poeticness"? In a letter probably written to Sir Henry Wotton, around 1600, Donne exhibits the questioning for which he asks forgiveness in *The Litanie*, with similar contrariety: "Only in obedience I send you some of my paradoxes: I love you and myself and them too well to send them willingly, for they carry with them a confession of their lightnes, and your trouble and my shame. But indeed they were made rather to deceave tyme than her daughter truth: although they have beene written in an age when any thing is strong enough to overthrow her. If they make you to find better reasons against them they do their office: for they are but swaggerers: quiet enough if you resist them." Thus, despite his diffidence, his paradoxes have an office: they follow the Scriptural injunction, "try all things," as defined by the dictionary, "to test or make trial of, put to proof." Their lightness and swagger express his contempt for the frailty of truth in his time. They may also have some literary merit: "If perchaunce they be pretyly guilt, that is their best, for they are not hatcht: they are rather alarums to truth to arme her than enemies: and they have only this advantadge to scape from being caled ill things that they are nothings." Although they are not fully developed, they may serve to warn truth against some weakness, or to provoke thought about something.

Without a promise "that no coppy shall bee taken," he says, "I shall sinn against my conscience if I send you any more. I speake that in playnes which becomes (methinkes) our honestyes; and therefore call not this a distrustfull but a free spirit: I meane to aquaint you with all mine: and to my satyres there belongs some feare and to some elegies and these perhaps, shame." His satires might entangle him with the law, and his elegies or paradoxes with the moral code. He seems a little ashamed of his timidity: "Against both which affections although I be tough enough, yet I have a ridling disposition to bee ashamed of feare and afrayd of shame. Therefore I am desirous to hyde them with out any over reconing of them or their maker." This riddling disposition was still troubling him in *Holy Sonnet XIX*, but even when he made things "rather to deceive time than her daughter truth," the daughter could prove frail and her seducer vulnerable. Again and again he asked his friends to "let go no copy" of works that only ordination might halt.

In a letter to Sir Henry Goodyer about 1608 he mentions the composition of his *Litanie*, tells why he cannot provide a copy of his *Biathanatos*, and then seems to express, after a lacuna in the text, his view of his secular verse: ". . . opinion of the song, not that I make such trifles for praise, but because as long as you speak comparatively of it with mine own, and not absolutely, so long I am of your opinion even at this time; when I humbly thank God, I ask and have, his comfort of sadder meditations; I doe not condemn in my self, that I have given my wit such evaporations, as those, if they be free from prophaneness, or obscene provocations." Although, even at this serious time, he does not condemn such verses, he does require them to be "free from profaneness or obscene provocations." Presumably, however, the verse in question was open to other objections, but still he does not condemn what seems to have provided another kind of comfort. Indeed, he suggests his need for such "evaporations."

In a *Verse Letter to Mr. Rowland Woodward* he had already expressed a sense of conflict between his poetry and religion:

> *Like one who'in her third widdowhood doth professe*
> *Her selfe a Nunne, tyed to retirednesse,*
> *So'affects my muse now, a chast fallownesse;*
>
> *Since shee to few, yet to too many'hath showne*
> *How love-song weeds, and Satyrique thornes are growne*
> *Where seeds of better Arts, were early sown.*
>
> *Though to use, and love Poëtrie, to mee,*
> *Betroth'd to no'one Art, be no'adulterie;*
> *Omissions of good, ill, as ill deeds bee.*
>
> *For though to us it seeme, 'and be light and thinne,*
> *Yet in those faithfull scales, where God throwes in*
> *Mens workes, vanity weighs as much as sinne.*

But in his *Litanie* the works of levity can become even more paradoxical, "When wee are mov'd to seeme religious / Only to vent wit."

He came to regret the publication of verse of a very different kind. In a letter to George Gerrard, 14 April 1612, he writes: "Of my Anniversaries, the fault that I acknowledge in my self, is to have descended to print any thing in verse, which though it have excuse even in our times, by men who professe, and practise much gravitie; yet I confesse I wonder how I declined to it, and do not pardon my self: But for the other part of the imputation of having said too much, my defence is, that my purpose was to say as well as I could," and of "such a person, as might be capable of all that I could say." Thus when he was beginning to practice more gravity, he came to grief for overpraising virtue. But he was really more concerned with criticizing life than with praising Elizabeth Drury, who gave him an excuse for hyperbolic contrast.

His other poems brought him the greatest embarrassment just before ordination. Again he writes to Sir Henry Goodyer, on Vigilia St. Tho (Dec. 20) 1614 : "One thing more I must tell you; but so softly, that if that good Lady were in the room, with you and this Letter, she might not hear. It is, that I am brought to a necessity of printing my Poems, and addressing them to my L(ord) Chamberlain. This I mean to do forthwith; not for much publique view, but at mine own cost, a few Copies. I apprehend some incongruities in the resolution; and I know what I shall suffer from many interpretations: but I am at an end, of much considering that; and, if I were as startling in that kinde, as ever I was, yet in this particular, I am under an unescapable necessity, as I shall let you perceive, when I see you." In short, he feels himself under great pressure, and is reconciled to suffer from interpretation, but implies a change in his verse, "if I were as startling in that kinde, as ever I was." Another mitigation is that it will be a semiprivate distribution at most. Let us note, however, that he thinks his earlier verse more "startling" than his later verse.

And this is the cause of his concern: "By this occasion I am made a Rhapsoder of mine own rags, and that cost me more diligence, to seek them, than it did to make them. This made me aske to borrow that old book of you, which it will be too late to see, for that use, when I see you: for I must do this, as a valediction to the world, before I take Orders." This is the nearest we come to Donne's own collection of his poems. No doubt, among his valedictions, his *Farewell to Love* worried him most as he prepared to turn all of his poems into a valediction to the world. The metaphor "rags" was almost a trademark of Donne, as a correspondent in the Tobie Mathews Collection suggests when he becomes solicitous to a Lady: "and that all the raggs of time, as *Dunne* calls them, may prove no worse than fair Embroideries to you."

Then Donne gives the reason for speaking softly at the beginning: "But this is it, I am to aske you; whether you ever made any such use of the letter in verse, *A nostre Countesse chez vous*, as that I may not put it in, amongst the rest to persons of that rank; for I desire very very much, that something should bear her name in the book, and I would be just to my written words to my L. *Harrington*, to write nothing after that." It appears that Donne intended to group his verse letters according to titles of honor, and that he wanted to honor his conclusion to *Obsequies to the Lord Harrington* (1614), brother to the Countess of Bedford:

> *Do not, faire soule, this sacrifice refuse,*
> *That in thy grave I doe interre my Muse,*
> *Who, in my griefe, great as thy worth, being cast*
> *Behind hand, yet hath spoke, and spoke her last.*

His concern how to honor both brother and sister bears witness to the seriousness of this pledge, and we may believe at least that it was not lightly broken. Thus he had two reasons to sacrifice his Muse, but the necessity of printing his poems seems to have passed without further embarrassment.

The explanation may be found in the change that overtook the Lord Chamberlain and inspired this poem by Sir Henry Wotton, *Upon the sudden Restraint of the Earl of Somerset, then falling from favour:*

> *Dazled thus with height of place,*
> *Whilst our Hopes our wits Beguile,*
> *No man marks the narrow space*
> *'Twixt a Prison and a Smile.*

Then since Fortunes favours fade,
You that in her arms do sleep,
Learn to swim and not to wade;
For the Hearts of Kings are deep.

But if Greatness be so blind,
As to trust in Towers of Air,
Let it be with Goodness lin'd,
That at least the Fall be fair.

Then though darkned you shall say,
When Friends fail and Princes frown,
Vertue *is the roughest way,*
But proves at night a Bed of Down.

If Donne exchanged one kind of pressure for another in the life of favor, he must also have been moved to the bitter wisdom that sought comfort in virtue. At least, the tangled events before his ordination may have brought to mind the words he once wrote to Wotton:

Beleeve mee, Sir, in my youths giddiest dayes,
When to be like the Court, was a playes praise,
Playes were not so like Courts, as Courts'are like
   playes.

The most complex example of Donne's attitude toward his own work is provided by *Biathanatos*. In 1608 he told Sir Henry Goodyer, "nor ever purposed to print it," and in 1619 he wrote Sir Robert Carre (Ker): "I have always gone so near suppressing it, as that it is onely not burnt." He added that no one had copied it, few read it, and "some particular friends in both Universities" had said, "That certainly, there was a false thread in it, but not easily found." If Ker should let any see it, he must give its date: "that it is a Book written by Jack Donne, and not by D. Donne." But Dr. Donne had not lost the riddling disposition of Jack Donne, for he concluded: "I only forbid it the Presse, and the Fire." Indeed, not long before ordination, he had written to Ker (*Letters*, p. 299): "I begin to be past hope of dying: And I feel that a little rag of *Monte Mayor*, which I read last time I was in your Chamber, hath wrought prophetically upon me, which is, that Death came so fast towards me, that the over-joy of that recovered me."

Donne wrote prefaces for only two major works that were unpublished at his death, *The Progresse of the Soule* and *Biathanatos*. This fact implies an intention to publish, since private circulation would justify neither the preface nor the scale of each work. He did not finish *The Progresse of the Soule*, except in *Ignatius his Conclave*, and for *Biathanatos* he left the prohibition: "publish it not, but yet burn it not." In short, cause and effect were still at odds in this work. Although he had reason to fear the effect of both works, it had not been enough to prevent their creation.

Yet his great paradox on suicide, *Biathanatos*, was originally intended for publication, because the Preface is obviously addressed to readers and possible objections to his book. A reference to publication in a letter to Sir Henry Goodyer, about the end of 1611, may be to this book. Donne informs Goodyer of "two millions confiscated to the Crown of England," and then makes this request: "After you have served yourself with a proportion, I pray make a petition in my name for as much as you think may be given me for my book out of this; for, but out of this, I have no imagination." If this letter is jocose, it issued out of illness, and says at least that Donne cannot think of any other way to publish his book, which could have been *Biathanatos*.

The same attitude, the same explanation, as for his other paradoxes may be found in the Preface to *Biathanatos*: "And though I know, that the malitious prejudged man, and the lazy affectors of ignorance, will use the same calumnies and obtrectations toward me, (for the voyce and sound of the Snake and Goose is all one) yet because I thought, that as in the poole of *Bethsaida*, there was no health till the water was troubled, so the best way to finde the truth in this matter, was to debate and vexe it, (for [We must as well dispute de veritate, *as* pro veritate,]) I abstained not for feare of mis-interpretation from this undertaking." This covers a defense of suicide as well as A *Defence of Womens Inconstancy:* both dispute of truth rather than for truth. The lighter paradox, like his lighter poem, also asks this question: "Are not your wits pleased with those jests, which cozen your expectation?" But in the process, his speculative wit dances through his whole cosmology as it relates women to the delightful variety of the world.

Donne was closer to the Schoolmen than to Bacon, for this Preface observes: "Contemplative and bookish men, must of necessitie be more quarrelsome than others, because they contend not about matter of fact . . . But as long as they goe towards peace, that is Truth, it is no matter which way." This is the spirit and the way not only of *Satire III* but of his more paradoxical inquiry, even when he seems to vex rather than debate the subject. And this attitude explains the kind of readers he wants: "If therefore, of Readers, which *Gorionides* observes to be of foure sorts, [Spunges which attract all without distinguishing; Howre-glasses, which receive and powre out as fast; Bagges which retaine onely the dregges of the Spices, and let the Wine escape; And Sives, which retaine the best onely], I finde some of the last sort, I doubt not they may bee hereby enlightened." Though he sometimes troubled the waters to little effect, he usually discouraged complacency either of wit or opinion, and often discovered new depths of perception. At least, his anxiety about his work was not because it was trivial, but because it often challenged custom or opinion or even law, sometimes merely by flippancy.

In his poetry the most obvious example of this kind of inquiry or challenge is the search for true religion in *Satire III*, especially because it requires valor to serve "our Mistresse

faire Religion" or to fear damnation: "This feare great cour-
age, and high valour is." Then he enumerates the acts that are
mistaken for those of courage, such as his own in *The Storme*
and *The Calme,* and that culminate in bravado:

> *and must every hee*
> *Which cryes not, Goddesse, to thy Mistresse, draw,*
> *Or eate thy poysonous words? courage of straw!*

Thus the desperate coward leaves the appointed field of moral
warfare with the devil, the world, now "in her decrepit
wayne," and the flesh. He yields to the joys of the flesh and
hates the soul "which doth / Give this flesh power to taste
joy," and whose true mistress he ought to seek. But where is
she to be found? At Rome, Geneva, or London? Phrygius
rejects all mistresses, for fear all are false. Graccus "loves all
as one," and "this blindnesse too much light breeds," for they
cannot all be true, and there is legal compulsion: "Of force
must one, and forc'd but one allow."

When repeated in his *Litanie,* "Let not my minde be
blinder by more light," this paradox relates to faith and rea-
son; here it leads to a gospel of doubt:

> *though truth and falsehood bee*
> *Neare twins, yet truth a little elder is;*
> *Be busie to seeke her, beleeve mee this,*
> *Hee's not of none, nor worst, that seekes the best.*
> *To adore, or scorne an image, or protest,*
> *May all be bad; doubt wisely; in strange way*
> *To stand inquiring right, is not to stray;*
> *To sleepe, or runne wrong, is. On a huge hill,*
> *Cragged, and steep, Truth stands, and hee that will*
> *Reach her, about must, and about must goe;*
> *And what the hills suddennes resists, winne so.*

In a letter from Mitcham raising questions about the soul, he
writes on belief (*Letters,* p. 18): "I am ashamed that we do

not also know it by searching farther: But as sometimes we had rather beleeve a Travellers lie than go to disprove him; so men rather cleave to these ways than seek new: yet because I have meditated therein, I will shortly aquaint you with what I think; for I would not be in danger of that law of *Moses,* That if a man dig a pit, and cover it not, he must recompense those which are damnified by it: which is often interpreted of such as shake old opinions, and do not establish new as certain, but leave consciences in a worst danger than they found them in." In his *Satire* he concludes that the soul must not be tied to laws by which she will not be tried at the last judgment. Although Geneva represents Calvinism, Luther is blamed for such subservience, just as he and not Calvin is named in *The Progresse of the Soule.* And this is why it requires true valor to serve "our Mistresse faire Religion." And thus Donne anticipates the connection of sacred and profane love in his later *Holy Sonnets.* When he wrote *The Litanie* he said (*Letters,* p. 29) that these religious divisions "are all virtuall beams of one Sun."

Valor is given another context in one of Donne's contributions to that witty collection of Characters called Overbury's *Wife* (1622). It is *An Essay of Valour* and is related to love rather than religion, and to a change in love from the romantic to the cynical. What is now passé suggests Sidney or Montemayor's *Diana,* from which Donne took his motto, *Antes muerto que mudado,* for a romantic picture with sword at the age of eighteen. "Whilome before this age of wit, and wearing black broke in upon us," he wrote, "there was no way knowne to win a Lady, but by Tilting, Tournying, and Riding through Forrests, in which time these slender striplings with little legs, were held but of strength enough to marie their widowes." Nowadays "servingmen" prove more valorous with their mistresses than gallants dressed in melancholy black; but not, presumably, than the veteran of *His Picture,* still "rather dead than changed."

Are there any other means to win a lady? Donne makes this concession: "Now as for all things else, which are to procure Love, as a good face, wit, cloathes, or a good body; each of them I confesse may worke somewhat for want of a better, that is, *if valour be not their Ryvall.*" And he uses "*Ovid* who writ the Law of Love," to disparage gifts, whether sent as gratuities or bribes. As for wit, it has as great a disability as heart or mind in *The Blossome*, or as Walsh thought: "Wit getteth rather promise than Love. Wit is not to bee seene: and no woman takes advice of any in her loving; but of her own eies, and her wayting womans: Nay which is worse, wit is not to be felt, and so no good Bed fellow: Wit applied to a woman makes her dissolve her sympering, and discover her teeth with laughter, and this is surely a purge for love; for the beginning of love is a kind of foolish melancholy."

In a *Verse Letter to the Countess of Huntington* Donne calls this, passion or lust rather than love:

> *He much profanes whom violent heats do move*
> *To stile his wandring rage of passion, Love.*

But neither is love Petrarchan:

> *Yet neither will I vexe your eyes to see*
> *A sighing Ode, nor crosse-arm'd Elegie.*
> *I come not to call pitty from your heart,*
> *Like some white-liver'd dotard that would part*
> *Else from his slipperie soule with a faint groane,*
> *And faithfully, (without you smil'd) were gone.*
> *I cannot feele the tempest of a frowne,*
> *I may be rais'd by love, but not throwne down.*

Is Donne practicing valor, or being Petrarchan with a difference? Surely no lady could find Petrarchan homage in such poems as *Twicknam Garden* or *The Primrose?* Else why distinguish, with Grierson, between "the Colonel's Lady and

Judy O'Grady"? But Donne is not through rejecting the guise of the Petrarchan lover:

> *Let others sigh, and grieve; one cunning sleight*
> *Shall freeze my Love to Christall in a night.*
> *I can love first, and (if I winne) love still;*
> *And cannot be remov'd, unlesse she will.*
> *It is her fault if I unsure remaine,*
> *Shee onely can untie, and binde againe.*
> *The honesties of love with ease I doe,*
> *But am no porter for a tedious woo.*

Then he proceeds, as he hinted, to "be rais'd by love," to a truly Platonic level, devoid of Petrarchan trappings and of spiritual backsliding. He seemed to distinguish kinds of love with greater precision than many of his critics, and this verse letter traces its progress.

Donne's concern for "the honesties of love" turned him into a rebel and atheist of love. Valor seemed as necessary to love as to religion; he was tired of love that ended "not with a bang but a whimper." In *Loves Deitie* he protests against the long tyranny of Cupid:

> *I long to talke with some old lovers ghost,*
> *   Who dyed before the god of Love was borne:*
> *I cannot thinke that hee, who then lov'd most,*
> *   Sunke so low, as to love one which did scorne.*
> *But since this god produc'd a destinie,*
> *And that vice-nature, custome, lets it be;*
> *   I must love her, that loves not mee.*

The modern form of this destiny, which custom preserves, is the Petrarchan formula of being "Sunke so low, as to love one which did scorne." Love should be mutual—the idea on which the refrain of each stanza turns. Though a rebel to the law and an atheist to the god of love, Donne's honesty or cynicism foresees a worse fate than unrequited love:

> Rebell and Atheist too, why murmure I,
>   As though I felt the worst that love could doe?
> Love might make me leave loving, or might trie
>   A deeper plague, to make her love mee too,
> Which, since she loves before, I'am loth to see;
> Falshood is worse than hate; and that must bee,
>   If shee whom I love, should love mee.

Apparent cynicism becomes honesty when he feels that it is worse to falsify love than not to return it, or to give up loving for the same reason. This is not the paradox of *The Indifferent*, in which "Heretiques in love" are those "Which thinke to stablish dangerous constancie," or the extreme of *The Calme*, "to disuse mee from the queasie paine / Of being belov'd, and loving." Nor does it preach the gospel of variety found in *Elegie XVII* or *A Defence of Womens Inconstancy*.

Certainly it does not approach *Elegie XVII* in the boldness of its revolt against opinion or custom, or its treatment of love as an appetite. There he is indifferent to constancy, to all but the service of beauty, in which that elegy rises above the witty *Indifferent*:

> The last I saw in all extreames is faire,
> And holds me in the Sun-beames of her haire.

There he dedicates himself to the service of love as it prevailed before the modern god was despoiled by opinion:

> Onely some few strong in themselves and free
> Retain the seeds of antient liberty,
> Following that part of Love although deprest,
> And make a throne for him within their brest,
> In spight of modern censures him avowing
> Their Soveraigne, all service him allowing.
> Amongst which troop although I am the least,
> Yet equall in perfection with the best,
> I glory in subjection of his hand,

> *Nor ever did decline his least command:*
> *For in whatever forme the message came*
> *My heart did open and receive the same.*

Some of these pretty forms he has described, but his subjection must finally come to an end:

> *But time will in his course a point discry*
> *When I this loved service must deny,*
> *For our allegiance temporary is,*
> *With firmer age returnes our liberties.*

Some time must be reserved for wisdom and its preferences:

> *What time in years and judgement we repos'd,*
> *Shall not so easily be to change dispos'd,*
> *Nor to the art of severall eyes obeying;*
> *But beauty with true worth securely weighing,*
> *Which being found assembled in some one,*
> *Wee'l love her ever, and love her alone.*

Thus the service of variety ends in constancy, and this appetite is not mere lust, which is indifferent to beauty; it has some relation to wonder in love, rather than the disillusionment of his *Farewell to Love*. The pursuit of beauty at last ends in worth, its final cause; in life her name was Anne More.

The best of Donne's *Elegies* are marked by unusual rhythmic vitality. The excitement of a voyage of discovery is felt in the physical adventure of *Elegie XIX: Going to Bed*, and the incantation of passion in *Elegie XVI: On his Mistris*. The range of love is from physical lust to the Platonic homage of *Elegie IX: The Autumnall*. In the best, the couplets achieve the excellence of the *Anniversaries;* in the worst, we find as nowhere else "the queasie paine" and disgust of love. However, it is not here that we look for Donne's supreme achievements in profane love poetry, but in the *Songs and Sonets*. George Gascoigne, in *Certayne Notes of Instruction*, prepares us for this group of poems: "some thinke that all Poemes (being short) may be called Sonets." He even anticipates Donne: "Sonets serve as well in matters of love as of discourse"; for Donne combined love and argument.

Another caution is in order. The *Verse Letters* provide ample evidence that Donne knew how to pay compliments to noble ladies without resorting to the passion that Grierson calls Petrarchan in such poems as *Twicknam Garden* and *The Primrose*. Donne was not so inept as to mingle insult and compliment, or to confuse realism with idealism, or to make the Petrarchan convention encroach upon the Ovidian. His dejection in love is never what he calls "white-liver'd":

> *Though I can pittie those sigh twice a day,*
> *I hate that thing whispers it selfe away.*

Moreover, as his *Litanie* suggests, pride made him a poor "porter for a tedious woo." The abject subservience of the Petrarchan is absent; love was not an ideal devotion, but an experience. Donne's attitude transforms his use of Petrarchan material, whether flippant in *The Indifferent* or mocking in the irony of *Twicknam Garden*. His *Nocturnall upon S. Lucies Day* is no Petrarchan complaint of a scorned lover, but a triumphant dirge for lost love. Donne may be a martyr to love, but not to a Petrarchan lady.

Songs and Sonets

The Good-Morrow is not merely the salutation of a new day but the discovery of something more real and strange than anything they have known, an absorbing love. This idea governs the imagery and development of the poem. Hence it begins with ordinary reality, in which love makes all past experience seem childish or an oblivion as deep as that of the seven sleepers, who slept nearly two hundred years. Any former love becomes only a Platonic dream of this new love. / Now that their souls have wakened to a new day, they become absorbed in one another; love, not fear, restricts their attention to each other, and yet makes their room a world. No voyager or map-reader can find a world more wonderful than they find in each other. But their world still manifests duality more than unity. / When each one is reflected in the other, then their world includes them as two hemispheres, but without the usual shortcomings of a cold North or sinking West. Yet how can their love escape change in a mutable world? Though one in love, they are two beings. But in scholastic doctrine neither a simple unity, like the soul, nor a compound without contrariety can be dissolved; and so either simple oneness or equality of love will preserve their love. Dr. Johnson complained of the hyperbole by which Donne extended tears into worlds, but such extension belonged to his mode of imagination and of exploring experience.

The Undertaking begins by arousing curiosity about a deed more admirable or heroic than the deeds of the Nine Worthies, and yet it has a braver consequence, which is to conceal it. / For it would be madness to impart the skill to cut specular stone, so as to make it transparent, when it can no longer be found. In his sermons Donne has "Temples made of *Specular stone*," so as to reveal their interiors. / So, if he should impart his secret, others would still love as before, for lack of such stuff to work upon. / But the lover who has seen loveliness within (women) is not limited, like others, to love their physical dress. / So, if you also can see "vertue attir'd in woman," and dare love that, and admit it, and forget about sex; / And if this love, though placed in virtue, you hide from profane men, who will not believe it, because faith is required for the unseen; or if they do, will laugh in contempt: / Then you have done what I have done, "and a braver thence will spring," because you have to conceal a love of virtue. There is no way of proving the spiritual to those who believe or admit only the physical.

The Sunne Rising, the ruler of time and space, is greeted with impudence and told to mind his own business, the various chores of the day; for love is not limited by time, which is contemptuously reduced to its "rags" or scraps. / Why should the sun think his beams so strong, when the lover could eclipse them with a wink, were he willing to lose sight of his mistress that long. If her eyes have not blinded the sun, let him see whether the Indias of spice and gold are where he left them or lie here with me; and likewise with the Kings he saw yesterday. And he shall learn that love is not limited by space. / In fact, love "makes one little room an everywhere," the lovers all states and princes. They are reality, the rest appearance. This reduction of the world may be the sun's gain by making him half as happy as they and by curtailing his duties. He may perform them by becoming their servant: "This bed thy center is, these walls, thy spheare." So the ruler of time and space is neither for these lovers, but rather their subject; his world shrinks as much as theirs expands.

Loves Usury is a bargain with the God of love, giving twenty-to-one odds for allowing his body or lust to reign, and sparing him any emotional involvement until he is gray. He itemizes all the incidents that are indifferent to lust but not to love. He does not want to love even the sport of lust, or to be carried from country to Court or city by any transport except rumor. / If he is inflamed by Love when he is old, and Love covets his own honor or his victim's shame or pain, he will gain most at that age. Then Love may choose the subject, degree, and fruit of love; but until then spare him from and Love covets his own honor or his victim's shame or pain,

The Canonization is an answer to a dissuasion from love in which the worldly argument against love is rejected for an unworldly progress in love that leads to canonization. The first stanza offers other objects of attack, such as palsy, gout, gray hair, ruined fortune; and rejects the inducements of a career at Court: all for love. The second stanza refutes economic, social, and civil liabilities that might be charged to their love. / The third stanza reaches the stage of transcending their alleged faults or conflicts by means of a series of images rising to the Phoenix, the apotheosis of self-immolation. They add wit to the Phoenix riddle by "two being one"; but this duality does not change its manner of regeneration, because sex is neutralized in them, and so their love proves as mysterious as the Phoenix. / "Wee can dye by it, if not live by love," answers the implied objection of the preceding stanza, but does not make sexual expiration the way to martyrdom. It is the character of their love that makes them eligible for canonization; and by sonnets of love, against the objector of the first stanza, "all shall approve / Us Canoniz'd for Love." / And all will invoke these saints of love to intercede for them. Among their qualifications for being invoked to beg from above a pattern of their love are their appeasement of Love and their understanding: who did contract and drove the world's soul into the glasses of their eyes, thus made such mirrors and spies that they did epitomize all—countries, towns, courts (which Hobbes said were "all" to poets). For the concord of "did contract and drove" compare "doth see And adds" in *Holy Sonnet VIII*.

Lovers Infinitenesse is their desire for all in a finite world that frustrates its realization. It begins on the assumption that love is an exchange between two people and then follows its fortunes in a world of time and change. / The first stanza encounters the limitations of their original contract: if he does not have all her love, he cannot buy more because he has spent all; if she did not give all, then he shall never have her all. / Or if she gave all, it was all she had then. But if new love is created in her by other men, this love was not vowed by her. And yet it was, because she gave her heart, and therefore he should have it all. Change has now become a threat to their bargain. / Yet he would not have all yet, because he that hath all can have no more; and he finds that his love grows, so that she ought to have new rewards in store; but she cannot give her heart every day, or else she never gave it. Love's riddles are that hearts really cannot be exchanged in a bargain. The only way to satisfy lovers' demands is more liberal than an exchange of hearts—that is to unite them, for then two lovers can escape their finiteness and "Be one, and one anothers All."

Nothing is more common in Donne than the idea that parting is like death, whether given sardonic form in *The Legacie* or fervent form in the *Song: Sweetest love*. But it is novel to find death a cause to hate the beloved, as in *A Feaver*, or rather to hate all women so much that he shall not commemorate her when he remembers she was one. Yet her uniqueness, which inspires this music, will refute that possibility, which remains hypothetical. / But he finds comfort in the hyperbole by which he denies her possible death, moving from all women to the whole world, which would go out with her breath. / Or if when she, the world's soul, goes, the world remains, it ill only be her carcass, the fairest woman only her ghost, the worthiest men only corrupt worms. / Why did the quarreling schools of philosophy that search what fire shall burn this world not have sense enough to aspire to the knowledge that this her fever might be it? / And yet she cannot waste by this fever, nor long bear this painful wrong, for she does not have enough (much) corruption to fuel such a fever long. / These burning fits are only meteors, which are sustained by matter in the sublunary realm. Her beauty and all intrinsic parts are unchangeable heaven. The cosmological basis of Donne's woman-world hyperbole now comes into the open, and prepares the supreme compliment. / Yet the fever was of like mind with him in seizing her, though it cannot live long in her, for he had rather be owner of her one hour than of the world forever.

Aire and Angels introduces a phantom love, without face or name, but likened to the apparition of angels in a voice or shapeless flame. Yet his sense of her identity is strong: "Some lovely glorious nothing I did see." It is a love of the soul, and since the soul can do nothing without limbs of flesh, its love must not be more refined than the soul, but take a body too. "And therefore I bid Love ask what and who you were, and now I permit it to assume your body and identify itself with you." The object of his love has been associated with angels, and they with air only in voice or flame, before reaching this embodiment. In his paradox *That the Gifts of the Body are better than those of the Minde* he says: "then the *soul* it seems is enabled by our *Body*, not this by it." / While he thought thus to ballast love so that it would be more stable, he saw that he had overloaded love's light vessel with wares that would sink admiration. Her every hair is much too much for love to act upon; some fitter embodiment must be sought. For neither in the glorious nothing, nor in the scattered brilliance of her body, can love inhere. (Love can only inhere in love, be reciprocal.) Then as an Angel puts on face and wings of (thickened) air, not quite so pure as its essence (in order to appear to man), so her love may become his love's sphere, corporeal enough for his love to inhere in and acquire stability. Just such difference as there is between the spirit and substance of Air and Angels, there will always be between women's love and men's, for man's love always seeks realization. / Air and angels are not distributed in the proportion between woman and man, but define their relation in love. The likeness of woman to angel is made at the beginning, and at the end her accommodation to man is also made by a physical manifestation. Neither love of the soul nor love of the body enabled his love to realize the potentiality sought in the first stanza.

The Anniversarie arrives because everything, all earthly glories, even the Sun, which makes times that pass, is older by a year than it was when they first met. All other things are subject to the decay of the sublunary world, but not their love. This has neither tomorrow nor yesterday; though running it never runs away from them, but remains constant, unchanged from first to last, everlasting. Their love is superior to time. / But as human beings they are not. Two graves must hide their bodies; death will separate them. After all, they are like other Princes, subject to sublunary law, and must leave their bodies in death. But souls where nothing is permanent but love (all other thoughts being transient) then shall manifest this love, or a greater love in heaven, when bodies move to their graves, souls from their bodily graves. / And then they shall be supremely happy, but no more than all the rest. It is here upon earth that they are supreme and without rivals. No one can betray them except each other. So let them restrain true and false fears, love nobly, and live, and add years unto years until they reach their diamond anniversary: this is the second of their reign. Their love, after all, is related to time, and their triumph over time is measured by time.

Twicknam Garden opens with metrical vehemence and exaggerated tokens of love. Coming to seek the spring, he receives such balms as would otherwise cure everything. But unfortunately he betrays himself by bringing the spider love that transubstantiates all, and can convert the sweet to bitter; indeed, he has brought the serpent so that this place may be thought true Paradise. Thus his love discovers an emotional incongruity between his feeling and the garden which suggests betrayal. / But it is a false paradise for him and would be more wholesome if winter "benighted" its glory and frost greeted him instead of happy trees. His problem is how to escape having to endure this disgrace and yet not leave loving. So he asks Love to let him become an unfeeling piece of the garden: to sink below the sensitive soul, become a mandrake, a manlike vegetable which by legend could simulate the expression of pain; or on the lower level of mere existence, a stone fountain giving the illusion of weeping. / Hither let lovers come to get vials of his tears by which to test whether their mistress's tears are true or false. For appearances are deceiving and you cannot judge a woman's thoughts by her tears. Woman is only true out of perversity or malice, because her truth to another kills him. Thus her garden was a false appearance of her real feeling and a mockery of his. If this poem was a Petrarchan compliment, who was finally mocked?

A Valediction: of the Booke makes love something like a liberal education, by which one is freed. He will tell her how to anger destiny, or to defeat his absence, and let posterity know her triumph. While he is removed (esloygne) by fate, she may win glory longer than the Sibyl's, greater than (Corinna's) the rival of Pindar, or Lucan's wife, or a female rival of Homer. / Study our letters and then write our Annals. In them will be found rule and example to all whom love's refining fire invades; there no schismatic will dare to challenge the soundness of any fundamental, who sees how Love affords this grace to us, to make, to keep, to use, to be these records of his, / This Book, as long-lived as the elements, or as the world's form, this engraved tome, written in cypher or artificial lingo; We are documents only for love's clergy, when this book is made thus; Should the ravenous Vandals and Goths again inundate us, Learning would be safe; in this our Universe, schools might learn systems of knowledge, spheres music, angels verse. (Connections with the cosmological background are made at various points. Then three stanzas exemplify the kinds of learning available, first for love's clergy.) / Here Love's Divines, (since all Divinity is love or wonder) may find all they seek, whether they like abstract spiritual love, in which their souls are evaporated by the invisible; or, reluctant so to beguile the weakness of faith, they choose something concrete; For, although mind may be the heaven where love resides, Beauty may be a convenient form to embody it. / Here Lawyers may find more than in their own books: both by what rights mistresses are ours, and how these estates are devoured by privilege, transferred from Cupid himself to womankind, who, although they exact great subsidies from heart and eyes, forsake him who relies on them, and for the reason, give honor or conscience, chimeras as vain as they or their special privilege. / Here Statesmen, (or of them, those who can read) may find the fundamentals of their occupation: it strikes to the heart of both love and politics; If one proceeds to consider what the secret is, in both they excel who are good opportunists, and whose weakness none doth or dares tell. In this your book, such will there something see, as in the Bible some can discover alchemy (a fraud). Presumably the art of deception must be maintained by the pretense of finding something. If the reading is "there nothing," then they will see nothing, as those who claim to find alchemy in the Bible. / Thus express (relieve) your thoughts; abroad I'll study you, as he that measures great heights, moves far off; presence makes the best test of how great love is, but absence tries how long this love will be; thus to take a latitude, sun or stars are best viewed at their brightest, but to conclude of longitudes, we must mark when and where the dark eclipses be. Thus his separation will allow him to measure the length of this love by absence. It may also be measured by the increasing cynicism with which he has described her book.

Loves Growth involves a power of the vegetal soul, or a change that puts it in the sublunary rather than the superlunary realm. Hence he cannot believe his love as pure as he thought, because it undergoes change and season, like the grass; he lied when he swore it was infinite, because the infinite cannot grow. But if this medicine, love, which cures all sorrow with more (the Paracelsian way), not only is no fifth essence of heaven, but a mixture of all stuffs that hurt soul or sense, and borrows its active vigor from the sun, then love is not so pure and separated from matter, as they commonly say, who have no mistress except their Muse; but like all other mixtures of things (here soul and body), love would sometimes meditate, sometimes act, or be both passive and active. / And yet his love is not grown larger by the Spring, but more prominent: as in the heaven, stars are not enlarged, but revealed by the sun. Gentle love deeds, like blossoms on a bough, bud out now from love's awakened root. If love take such additions, as more circles are produced by one stirred in water, those, like so many spheres, make only one heaven, for they are all centered in her. And though each spring adds new heat to love, as princes levy new taxes in times of war, and do not remit them in peace, no winter shall reduce the spring's increase. Thus love is not like grass, but more like heaven; rather, it combines both realms and is constant in change.

Loves Exchange is a quarrel with Cupid that disguises a stubborn love. Any other devil except Cupid gives something in exchange for a soul; at Court his fellows every day give the art of rhyming, hunting, or gambling, for souls already possessed by them; only he, who gave more, has nothing; but is, by being humble, lower still. (Presumably he might have expected to get the art of love.) / He does not ask for release from any former obligation, or sue for any exception or "notwithstanding" on nature's law. These are special privileges, they inhere in Cupid and his own; no one should forswear unless he were Love's creature. / But give me thy weakness, make me blind, as thou and thine, both in eyes and mind; Love, let me never know that this is love, or that love is childish. Let me not know that others know that she knows my pains, lest a tender shame add me to my other woe. / If thou give nothing, yet thou art just, because I would not believe your first impulses; small towns that resist until great shot forces them, by war's law cannot make conditions. In love's warfare such is my case, I may not contract for mercy, having forced Love to show this face (which may remind readers of Marlowe's Helen). / This face, by which he could command and change the idolatry of any land; this face, which wheresoever it comes, can call men from celibacy, raise the dead, warm the poles, populate the deserts, and enrich the earth. / For this obduracy, Love is enraged with me, but kills not. If I must be an example to future Rebels; if the unborn must learn, by my being cut up, and torn: Kill, and dissect me, Love; for this torture is against your own end, carcasses torn on the rack make poor bodies for dissection (autopsies). Although stubborn to the last, he argues for an end to his misery on the grounds that torture will spoil the anatomy lesson that might deter future rebels.

The Dreame endeavors to translate a happy fiction into reality. For nothing less than the object of the dream would he have broken it. She waked him wisely, because it was a theme for reason, much too strong for phantasy (which rules the mind during sleep); yet she did not break his dream, but continued it (as its subject); she is so truth-like that thoughts of her suffice to make dreams real and fables actual: "Enter these arms, for since you thought it best, not to dream all my dream, let's act the rest." Thus her truth or verisimilitude is urged to complete the translation of dream into reality. / As lightning or a candle, her eyes, not noise, waked him; yet he thought her (for she loves the truth) an angel at first sight, but when he saw that she saw his heart, and knew his thoughts, past an angel's skill, when she knew what he dreamt, when she knew excess of joy would wake him, and came then, he must confess, it could only be profane, to think her anything but herself. Here Donne denies the angel intuition, but gives the lady angelic powers and effects. / Coming and staying showed that she was she, but rising makes him think that now she is not herself. That love is weak, where fear is as strong as he; love is not all spirit, pure, and brave, if it have mixture of fear, shame, honor. Perhaps she deals with him as men do with torches, light and put out to make them ready for use, so she came to kindle and goes to return; then he will dream that hope again, but otherwise would die. Here pure substance versus mixtures becomes a sophistic opposition by its application to moral qualities. Thus seduction by angelic parallels finds an ingenious path from lightning and tapers to torches.

A Valediction: of Weeping explores the significance of tears in the separation of lovers. He asks permission to pour forth his tears while he remains, for her face coins, stamps, and gives them value, and thus they become full of her significance to him; they are effects of much sorrow, but images of more; when a tear falls, that image of her which it bore falls, so she and he are nothing (by this Mintage) when on a different shore (when tears become a sea of separation). / On a round ball a workman who has copies ready, can lay an Europe, Africa, and Asia, and quickly make that which was nothing, All; so doth each tear which wears her image, a globe, yea world by that impression grow, until her tears mixt with his do overflow this world, by waters sent from her, his heaven dissolved in tears. Thus her tears may bring a deluge to the world imaged in his tear, the extension that distressed Dr. Johnson. / So he implores her as a moon controlling the tides not to drown him in the world of her image; not to weep him dead in her arms, not to teach the sea what it may do too soon; not to give the wind an excuse to do him more harm than it intends: Since they sigh each other's breath, whoever sighs most is cruellest, and hastens the other's death. Thus tears, though fruits of her creation, may become emblems of his destruction by sea, and ought to be forborne.

Loves Alchymie finds love like alchemy in its search for the elixir of life. Appropriately it begins with a mine, where one might discover the supreme mystery of alchemical gold. Let some who have digged deeper into love than he, tell where love's central happiness lies. He has loved, possessed, and told what he found, but should he do this until he were old, he should not find that hidden mystery; oh, it is all imposture: And just as no alchemist has yet got the Elixir, but glorifies his potent pot, if to him befall by the way some odorous substance or nostrum, so lovers dream of a rich and long delight, but get a rather cold and short night. / Our ease, our thrift, our honor, and our day, shall we pay for this vain bubble's shadow? Does love end in this, that his servant can be as happy as he can, if he can stand the short disdain of a bridegroom's play? That loving wretch that swears, it is not the bodies that marry, but the minds, which he finds angelic in her, would swear as justly that he hears in the wedding day's raucous minstrelsy the music of the spheres. Do not hope for mind (rational soul) in women; at their best they are sweetness and wit (sensitive soul), but only body or mummy when enjoyed (rather like the fraud of the alchemist's pot).

A Nocturnall upon S. Lucies Day begins with the midnight of the shortest day and ends with a vigil of grief in the calendar of love. This midnight belongs to the year, the day, and Lucy, who as light unmasks herself scarcely seven hours; the Sun is exhausted, and now his powder-horns send forth light flashes, no constant rays; the world's vital sap is sunk: The general preservative balm (of alchemy) the thirsty earth has drunk, whither, as to the beds-foot, life is shrunk, dead and buried; yet all of these seem happy, compared with me, who am their memorial. (On balm Donne writes in his *Letters*, p. 97: "The later Physitians say, that when our naturall inborn preservative is corrupted or wasted, and must be restored by a like extracted from other bodies; the chief care is that the Mummy have in it no excelling quality, but an equally digested temper.") / Let them study me then, who shall be lovers at the next world, that is, at the next Spring: For I am every dead thing, in whom love wrought a new kind of alchemy. For his art did extract a fifth essence (latent only in things) even from nothingness, from dull negations, and lean hollowness: "He desolated me, and I am re-begot of absence, darkness, death; things which are not" (privations of presence, light, life). / All others draw all that is good from all things, life, soul, form, spirit, from which they derive their being; I, by virtue of love's still (alembic), am the grave of all that is nothing. Often we two have wept a flood, and so drowned the whole world, us two; often we did grow to be two Chaoses, when we did show concern for anything else (chaos being the privation of form); and often absences withdrew our souls (source of life), and made us carcasses. (These are various forms of love's desolation.) / But I am by her death (which word denies her being) grown the quintessence of the original nothing (before Creation); if I were a man, I would know that I were one by reason; if I were any beast, I should favor by sense some ends, some means; yes plants, yes even stones (loadstones) reject and choose; everything is endowed with some attributes; if I were an ordinary nothing, such as shadow, a light and body must be here to make it. (He has sunk in the scale of being as far as he can go.) / But I am none of these; nor will by Sun renew. You lovers, for whose sake the lesser Sun at this time has run to

Capricorn to fetch new lust, and give it to you, enjoy your summer all: Since my Sun enjoys her long night's festival of darkness, let me prepare in devotion to meet her, and let me call this hour of grief her Vigil and her Eve, since it is the midnight both of the year and the day.

A Valediction: Forbidding Mourning begins with the separation of body and soul in death and proceeds to relate this separation to love. As virtuous men pass away gently and unobtrusively, / So let us dissolve in separation, without making any noise or rousing any tear-floods or sigh-tempests. It would profane our joys to reveal our love to the public. / Movement of the earth (earthquake) brings hurts and fears, men consider what it did and meant, but quaking (trepidation) of the spheres, though far greater, is free from harms and fears (sublunary movement is more alarming than superlunary movement). / The love of dull sublunary lovers (whose soul is that of sense) cannot allow absence, because it removes the physical elements that compound it. / But we who are so much refined by a love, that we ourselves do not know what it is, mutually secured against change by the mind (rational soul), are less concerned to miss eyes, lips, and hands (which element the physical love of sublunary lovers). / Our two souls therefore, which are united in love, although I must go, still do not suffer a break, but an extension, like gold beaten to airy thinness (their triumph over a sublunary element). / If they be two beings, still they are such as stiff twin compasses are two, thy soul as the fixed foot, does not pretend to move, but does if the other moves. / Their relations are reciprocal, but the compass figure enacts her role in separation, leaning and inquiring after the wandering foot, but growing erect as that comes back to her, the fixed foot. / Such you will be to me, who must run declining, like the roving foot: Thy steadfastness makes my circle true, and makes me end where I began. Thus a superlunary love justifies its relation to the death of virtuous men, and triumphs over its own sublunary difficulties.

The Extasie is one of the poems that descend from a Song in Sidney's *Astrophel and Stella*, "In a Grove most rich of shade." Donne uses the ecstasy as a means to raise his dialogue on love above the pastoral setting inherited from Sidney, and then to unite the souls of the lovers in a soul capable of speaking for both in monologue. / Donne has fecund nature at once mingle indoors and outdoors in the pastoral setting. The lovers are joined by hands firmly cemented by their own preservative balm; their eye-beams twisted and threaded their eyes upon one double string; so to intergraft their hands was as yet all the means to make them one, and to produce reflections in their eyes was all their propagation. / As between two equal armies, Fate suspends uncertain victory, their souls, which had gone out to advance their status, hung between her and him. (While amatory union remains undecided, their rational souls come between them.) And while their souls negotiate the outcome, their bodies remain like burial statues, all day in the same posture, silent all day. / If any, so refined by love, that he understood soul's language, and by good love were grown all mind (rational soul), he (though he did not know which soul spake, because both meant and spoke alike) might take a new refinement from them, and part far purer than he came. / This Ecstasy (we said) doth explain and tell us what we love, we see by this, that it was not sex, we see that we saw not what did move us: But as all separate souls contain a mixture of they know not what things, Love doth mix again these mixed souls, and make both into one, each this and that. (Thus unity is achieved on the spiritual level, but now the pastoral setting advances the argument.) Transplant a single violet, and the strength, color, and size (all that was poor and scanty before) redoubles still and multiplies. / When love thus mutually invigorates two souls with one another, that abler soul, which flows from them, controls the wants of loneliness. We then, who are this new soul, know of what we are composed and made, for the Atoms out of which we grow, are souls, whom no change can invade. (Now they know their composition, which makes them superior to the world of mutability, but they have not finished their negotiation.)

Why do they stay away from their bodies so long and so far? They are ours, though they are not we (who have superior status), We are the intelligences (angels), they the spheres we control. We owe them thanks, because they first conveyed us to each other, lent their senses' powers to us, and are not waste to us, but alloy of strength. Heaven's influence acts not thus on man, unless it first imprints the air, so soul may flow into soul, though it first resorts to body (as a medium). / As our blood works to produce spirits resembling souls, because such agents are needed to knit body and soul together: so must the souls of pure lovers descend to affections and faculties, which the senses of the body may reach and grasp, otherwise a great Prince (the soul) is imprisoned. / Let us return then to our bodies, so that weak men may look on love revealed; love's mysteries do grow in souls, but yet the body is his book of revelation. (Weak men cannot understand soul's language.) And if some lover like us, may have heard this dialogue of one, let him still observe us, and he shall see little change, when we have gone to bodies. Presumably a lover like them will not find "this dialogue of one" corrupted by their return to bodies. Thus the place of the body in love (it enables the soul) is justified without loss of status to the soul.

In *The Will* the close of each stanza tells how Love has taught him the principle of the bequests he has just made. By making him serve her who had twenty other lovers, Cupid taught him that he should give to none but such as had too much before.

Argus, for example, already had a hundred eyes. / In the second stanza Love teaches him, by making him love where no love can be received, Only to give to such as are incapable of using his bequests. Here "ingenuity" means ingenuousness, and a Capuchin was vowed to poverty. / In the third stanza Love teaches him, by making him love her who regards his love as beneath her, Only to give to those that think his gifts dishonorable (unworthy of them). / In the fourth stanza Love, by making him adore her who begot his love, Taught him to pretend to give when he did only restore. / In the fifth stanza Love, by making him love one who thinks friendship a proper lot for younger lovers, becomes responsible for making his gifts just as incongruous. / Therefore he will give no more, but undo the world by dying; because love dies too:

> *Then all your beauties will be no more worth*
> *Than gold in Mines, where none doth draw it forth;*
> *And all your graces no more use shall have*
>   *Than a Sun dyall in a grave.*

Thus Love taught him, by making him love her who neglects both him and Love, to invent and practice this one way to annihilate all three. But this is not the school of love kept by Petrarch.

The Funerall prepares for the burial of the most striking symbol in Donne. He asks that whoever comes to put him into his shroud, do not harm or inquire into the artful wreath of hair which crowns (adorns and rules) his arm; the enigma, the sign you must not touch, because it is his external soul, viceroy to that soul, which being gone to heaven then, will leave this soul to control, and keep these limbs, her Provinces, from dissolution. (Clearly he is her subject; but should he begin to question the wreath himself?) / For if the nerves his brain lets fall through every part, can tie those parts together and unify him, these hairs which grew upward, and have strength

and art from a better brain, can do it better; unless she meant
that he should know his pain by this, as prisoners are mana-
cled then, when they are condemned to die. (Thus a subject
becomes a prisoner.) / Whatever she meant by it, bury it
with him, for since he is love's martyr, it might breed idola-
try, if these love relics came into other hands; as it was humil-
ity to give to this sign (of the lady) all that a Soul can do, so
it is some bravery (bravado), That since she would save none
of him, he bury some of her (hair). As love's martyr, he must
prevent idolatry and avenge his servitude.

The Blossome begins by observing the sudden growth of
love, like a blossom on a bough, unmindful of the freeze that
by tomorrow will destroy it. Then the heart, which labors to
settle in "a forbidden or forbidding tree" of love, is warned
that tomorrow before that sun (the lady) wakens, it must
take a journey with this sun and him. / But the thinking
heart, which loves to plague itself with subtleties, replies that
its business is here, and that he goes to pleasures of the senses:
if then your body (senses) go, what need you a heart (emo-
tions)? / Well then, the heart may stay, but it will be to no
avail. A naked thinking heart that gives no sensuous evidence
of itself is to a woman only a kind of ghost. How shall she
know his heart, or indeed recognize a heart? Practice may
make her know some other part, but not a heart. / Let his
heart meet him at London twenty days from now, and it will
find him in better shape than if he had stayed behind to pine
away. If possible, let his heart be unwasted too, because he
would give it to another friend, as glad to have his body as his
mind. Thus, if he proves his case for the body, mind and
body unite in the final solution.

The Primrose begins with a primrose hill, where the prim-
roses can translate the rain of heaven into divine nectar, and
where in form and number they make an earthly galaxy, like

the stars in the sky: there he walks to find a true love, and realizes that she must be exceptional, not merely a woman, but more or less than common—in flower language, not the five-petalled primrose. / Yet he does not know whether he wants the exception to have six or four petals. If she were less than a woman (or four), she would be scarcely anything; but if she were more (or six), she would get above all thought of sex, and think to move his heart to study her, not to love: Both of these would be abnormal (monsters); but since there must be falsehood in woman (remember Eden), he would prefer her to be falsified by art rather than by nature, or above the thought of sex rather than below the capacity. / In the last stanza Donne uses numbers as in his *Essays in Divinity* (ed. Simpson, p. 59): "*Ten* cannot be exceeded, but that to express any further Number you must take part of it again"; (p. 46) "from *Sarai's* Name he took a letter, which expressed the number *ten*, and repos'd one, which made but *five;* so that she contributed that five which man wanted before, to show a mutuall indigence and Supplement"; (p. 10) five is "compos'd of the first even, and first odd" number. / So he salutes the true primrose of love as the one of five petals, and urges woman, whom this flower doth represent, to be content with this mysterious number (which he proceeds to explicate): Ten is the farthest basic or inclusive number (one is not a number); if half ten (five) belong to each woman, then each woman may take half of ten from us men; or if this is not enough for them, since all numbers are odd, or even, and they fall (as two and three) first into this five, women may take us all (thus five can replace ten as the inclusive number). Hence the normal woman is both more mysterious and more able to satisfy her ambition than the exceptional woman.

The Relique begins with the final metaphor of *The Funerall* as it unites, in "A bracelet of bright haire about the bone," two of Sir Thomas Browne's "minor monuments" of identity after death. When burial ground was limited, it was used more than once; so graves have learned the kind of woman-hood that explains the second guest and anticipates the loving couple symbolized by the bracelet of hair about the bone. He asks the grave-digger to let them alone, because they thought by this device to make their souls meet at this grave on judgment day. / If this digging should happen in a time or land, where mis-devotion (Roman Catholicism) rules, then the grave-digger will bring them to the Bishop and the King, to make them relics; then she shall become a Mary Magdalen, and thereby he something other than himself; all women shall adore them thus romanticized, and some men; and since miracles are sought at such times, he would have that age taught by this poem what miracles such innocent lovers wrought. / First, they loved well and faithfully, without knowing what they loved or why, difference of sex they knew no more, than their Guardian Angels do; coming and going, perhaps they used the ceremonial kiss, but not between those customary occasions; their hands never touched the physical seals that later law fastens but nature releases (see *Elegy XVII*). These miracles they did; but now alas (how can he describe the miracle of her being?) he should pass all measure and all language, if he told what a miracle she was (which really made him "something else thereby").

Negative Love is a love that escapes definition by body and soul. To understand his love he must know himself, which is impossible. He never stooped so low as the sublunary lovers of body, seldom to the Platonic lovers of soul, for sense and understanding may know and hence define the nature of their love. (Thus a *tertium quid* escapes a dichotomy supposed to be exhaustive.) His love, though ignorant, is more daring; for may he miss the mark, whenever he craves love, if he knows yet exactly what he wants. / If perfection can only be expressed by Negatives (like God, who cannot be defined positively), his love is such. To All that everybody else loves, he says no. If any that interpret best, can know what we know not, ourselves, let him teach me that unknown (nothing: a privation of knowledge): This as yet is my ease and comfort, though I do not succeed in knowledge, I cannot fail in practice. If he is intuitive in love, his divinity is certainly wonder.

Farewell to Love is a valediction to sublunary love which exposes its mystery. While yet untried, he thought there was some Deity in love, so he did reverence and worship it; as Atheists at their dying hour call, what they cannot name (being atheists), an unknown power, as ignorantly did he crave (as in *Negative Love*): Thus when things as yet unknown are coveted by men, our desires give them shape, and so as desires decrease, their objects shrink, as desires increase, their objects swell. / But a gingerbread prince on a golden throne from a recent fair, is not less cared for by children after three days, than the thing which lovers admire so blindly, and woo with such worship; once possessed, its enjoyment decays: And afterwards, what before pleased all senses, takes only one sense (touch), and that so weakly, that it leaves behind a kind of sorrowing dullness to the mind. / Alas, why cannot we, as well as Cocks and Lions, be jocund after such pleasures? Unless wise Nature decreed it (since the act is said to shorten life), as though she would that man should despise the sport, because that other curse of being short, and only for a minute made to be keen, desires to propagate or multiply itself. (Thus the curse of dullness is necessary to counteract the curse of brevity that promotes overindulgence.) / Since this is so, my mind (not body) shall not desire what no other man can find (satisfaction in love), I will no more be foolish and run after things which would injure me. And when I come where moving beauties are, as men do when the summer sun grows great, though I admire their greatness, shun their heat; each place can provide shadows. If everything else fails, it is only a matter of applying some anaphrodisiac like wormseed.

Divine Poems

If Donne's *Litanie* exposed deep personal temptations, his *Essays in Divinity* revealed a later sense of deliverance from his worst torments: "Thou hast delivered me, O God, from the Egypt of confidence and presumption, by interrupting my fortunes, and intercepting my hopes; And from the Egypt of despair by contemplation of thine abundant treasures, and my portion therein; from the Egypt of lust, by confining my affections; and from the monstrous and unnaturall Egypt of painfull and wearisome idleness, by the necessities of domestick and familiar cares and duties. Yet as an Eagle, though she enjoy her wing and beak, is wholly prisoner, if she be held by but one talon; so are we, though we could be delivered of all habit of sin, in bondage still, if Vanity hold us but by a silken thred" (ed. Simpson, p. 75). If religious conviction brought him this sense of deliverance, the sins are vivid reminders of his biography. And when he adds that God "contenting thy self with being my Medicine, allowest me to be my Physician," he reminds us how providence delivered him from these habits of sin, though he never broke the silken thread of vanity.

In his *Letters* (p. 228) Donne later excuses himself for writing his sermons: "for since I have not utterly delivered my self from this intemperance of scribling (though I thank God my accesses are lesse and lesse vehement), I make account that to spend all my little stock of knowledge upon matter of delight, were the same error, as to spend a fortune upon Masks and Banqueting houses: I chose rather to build in this poor fashion, some Spittles, and Hospitals, where the poor

and impotent sinner may finde some relief, or at least under-
standing of his infirmity."

Sacred and profane love had already met in the analysis of
Satire III, but since then he had gone about and about the hill
of truth before reaching his later service of "our Mistresse
faire religion." The story of that service he told unexpectedly
in the true sonnets of his *Holy Sonnets*. In *Religion and Litera-
ture* T. S. Eliot says there is a kind of religious poet who
seems to be "leaving out what men consider their major pas-
sions, and thereby confessing his ignorance of them." Donne
confessed no such ignorance either in *Satire III* or in his *Di-
vine Poems*, but even the contrary, or that soul gave "flesh
power to taste joy," which he seemed to reverse in the para-
dox *That the Gifts of the Body are better than those of the
Minde*. He has also told us, in his verses *To Mr. Tilman*, what
taking orders meant to his world:

> *Why doth the foolish world scorne that profession,*
> *Whose joyes passe speech? Why do they think unfit*
> *That Gentry should joyne families with it?*
> *As if their day were onely to be spent*
> *In dressing, Mistressing and complement;*
> *Alas poore joyes, but poorer men, whose trust*
> *Seemes richly placed in sublimed dust;*
> *(For, such are cloathes and beauty, which though gay,*
> *Are, at the best, but as sublimed clay.)*

Other worldly values were rejected for love in *The Canoniza-
tion*. But religion finally became much more disturbing to
Donne than the question of moral virtue in *Satire III* or of
vanity in his *Litanie*.

The delight in variety that led Donne to praise inconstancy
in woman and the world included an argument that finally
turned against him: "It is the nature of nice and fastidious
mindes to know things only to be weary of them." In *Satire
III* he said of truth, "Be busie to seeke her," and

>   *doubt wisely; in strange way*
> *To stand inquiring right, is not to stray;*
> *To sleepe, or runne wrong, is.*

By *The First Anniversary* (1611) this search has been complicated by a new source of disorder:

> *The new Philosophy calls all in doubt,*
> *The Element of fire is quite put out;*
> *The Sun is lost, and th'earth, and no mans wit*
> *Can well direct him where to looke for it.*
> *And freely men confesse that this world's spent,*
> *When in the Planets, and the Firmament*
> *They seeke so many new; then see that this*
> *Is crumbled out againe to his Atomies.*
> *'Tis all in peeces, all cohaerence gone;*
> *All just supply, and all Relation.*

In *The Second Anniversary* he has grown weary in the search:

> *Be not concern'd: study not why, nor when;*
> *Doe not so much as not believe a man.*
> *For though to erre, be worst, to try truths forth,*
> *Is far more businesse, than this world is worth.*

And he has learned the opening theme of his *Devotions upon Emergent Occasions,* "Variable, and therefore miserable condition of Man," in terms of his secular devotion:

> *And what essentiall joy can'st thou expect*
> *Here upon earth? what permanent effect*
> *Of transitory causes? Dost thou love*
> *Beauty? (And beauty worthy'st is to move)*
> *Poore cousened cousenor, that she, and that thou,*
> *Which did begin to love, are neither now;*
> *You are both fluid, chang'd since yesterday;*
> *Next day repaires, (but ill) last dayes decay.*
> *Nor are, (although the river keepe the name)*

> *Yesterdaies waters, and to daies the same.*
> *So flowes her face, and thine eyes, neither now*
> *That Saint, nor Pilgrime, which your loving vow*
> *Concern'd, remaines; but whil'st you thinke you bee*
> *Constant, you'are hourely in inconstancie.*

Thus the sublunary world took revenge upon the constancy of his saint and pilgrim through the passage of time, if not of love.

Holy Sonnet I opposes the motion that pulls him downward toward hell to the force that draws him toward God. The first line states the question, "Thou hast made me, And shall thy worke decay?" The next lines develop his sense of approaching death, and his fear, despair, and terror as sin "weighs" his weak flesh down towards hell. Only God is above, and when he is allowed to look towards God, he rises in spirit again; but the devil so tempts him that not one hour can he keep upright. God's grace may support him enough to hinder the devil's craft, and God, like a magnet, may draw his heavy but responsive heart (adamant draws by magnetic attraction). Thus the initial question is answered by the admission of dependence on God's will by one of his willing but weak creatures.

Holy Sonnet III turns on the point that, unlike other sinners, his punishment and sin are the same. Hence he wishes he had back again all the sighs and tears that he has spent, so that in this holy discontent he could mourn with some profit, as he has mourned in vain; in his Idolatry (of women) what showers of tears wasted his eyes! what griefs rent his heart! Now he repents that indulgence in suffering was his sin (instead of something else); because he did indulge he must endure pain. The thirsty drunkard, nocturnal thief, itchy lecher, and self-pleasing proud have (what he has not) the memory of past joys, for relief from coming ills. Only he is allowed no respite (in memory); for long, yet vehement grief hath been both the effect and the cause, both punishment and sin. This is why his state is worse than that of other sinners, and why he repents especially the nature of his sin.

Holy Sonnet V gives cosmological extension to his sinful state in the Biblical terms of 2 Peter iii, 5-7. As a microcosm he is made of the elements (earth, water, air, fire) and an angelic spirit, but black sin has betrayed both parts of his world to endless night, and so both parts must die. You who have found new spheres beyond that heaven which was most high (but is so no longer), and can write of new lands, pour new seas (from that new world) in my eyes, that so I might drown my world, with sincere weeping (as the Deluge drowned a sinful world), or wash it if it must be drowned no more (according to God's covenant). Here we may recall that other world of love in *A Valediction: of Weeping:*

> *Till thy teares mixt with mine doe overflow*
> *This world, by waters sent from thee, my heaven dissolved so.*

But oh (he continues according to Scripture) it must finally be burnt! alas the fire of lust and envy have burnt it heretofore, and made it fouler: Let their flames retire, and burn me O Lord, with a fiery zeal of thee and thy house, which doth in eating heal. Thus divine fire (not elemental) may cleanse him.

Holy Sonnet VII is a vision related to the Resurrection and Judgment in Ezekiel (37) and Revelation (7). Donne modernizes "the four corners of the earth" in Revelation as his Angels blow their trumpets to wake the dead for something like Ezekiel's "resurrection of dry bones." The dead include all those whom the Flood did, and Fire shall overthrow, all those slain by war, dearth, age, agues, tyrannies, despair, law, chance, and even those who shall behold God without dying (Exodus 33, 20, said: no man shall see God's face and live; yet I Cor. 15, 51, said: "We shall not all sleep, but we shall all be changed"). But let them sleep, Lord, and me mourn a space, for if my sins abound above all these, it is too late to ask for abundant grace, when we are before the judgment seat; here on this humble ground, teach me how to repent; for that is as valid as if you had sealed my pardon with your blood (instead of all men's on the same condition). Thus his desire for that time and place is dramatically checked by his sense of unworthiness.

Holy Sonnet VIII considers the evidence of his spiritual state as it relates to angels and men. Scotus held that Angels "have a natural power to understand thoughts"; Aquinas denied this power (to angels as well as men). This conflict gives the alternatives considered here. If the souls of the faithful are glorified like Angels, then his father's soul doth see that he bravely strides over hell's wide mouth, and adds this fact even to complete felicity. But if our minds are made known to these souls by circumstances—not immediately, but mediated by signs apparent in us—how shall his mind's innocence be judged by them? They see outward signs of devotion in idolatrous lovers, blasphemous Conjurers, and Pharisaical dissemblers (his appearance also varies from his inward truth). Then turn, O anxious soul, to God, for he knows best thy true remorse, since he put it in thy breast.

Holy Sonnet IX is a questioning sonnet. Why is man subject to damnation, if poisonous minerals, the tree that brought death to otherwise immortal man, lecherous goats, or envious serpents cannot be damned? Why should will or reason, which are born in man (his distinctive faculties), make sins, which are otherwise equal, more heinous in man? And since mercy is easy, and brings glory to God, why does he threaten

in his stern wrath? But who am I, that dare dispute with thee
O God? Oh! out of thy only worthy blood, and my tears,
make a heavenly river of oblivion (Lethe was in Hades), and
drown in it the black memory of my sin. Some claim as debt,
that thou remember their sins (so as to forgive them), I
think it mercy, if thou wilt forget.

If the question is answered here by contrition, in *Holy Son-
net XII* it is answered by man's relation to nature and God:
Created nature is subjected to us; but its Creator, whom
neither sin nor nature bound, hath died for us, his Creatures,
and his foes.

In *Holy Sonnet X* the only difficulty presented by death is
in the line, "And soonest our best men with thee doe goe,"
where "soonest" means "most readily."

Holy Sonnet XIII is another anticipation of the last Judgment.
What if this were the world's last night? He calls upon his
Soul to look at the picture in his heart, which is that of Christ
crucified, and tell whether that countenance is terrifying;
tears in his eyes put out the astounding light, blood fills his
frowns, which fell from his pierced head (these aspects com-
bine opposites of mercy and justice). And can that tongue
which prayed to forgive the fierce hate of his foes condemn
thee to hell? No, no; but as I said in my idolatry to all my
profane mistresses, beauty is a sign of pity, only ugliness is a
sign of harshness: so I say to thee, frightful shapes are as-
signed to wicked spirits, this beauteous form ensures a pitiful
mind. In his paradox *That the Gifts of the Body are better
than those of the Minde* he says: "And in a faire body, I do
seldom suspect a disproportioned minde, and as seldome hope
for a good, in a deformed."

Holy Sonnet XIV is a sonnet of violence, in which reason has
surrendered to passion and can only be restored to power by
counter-violence. In the opening lines he calls for the kind of

treatment that is used to explain his hardship in the hymn on his illness. Like a usurped town owed to another, he labors to admit God, but to no avail, because reason, which is God's viceroy in him and should defend him, is captivated, and proves weak or untrue. Yet he loves God dearly, and wants to be loved, but is betrothed to his enemy: he calls upon God, to divorce, untie, or break that knot again, even to imprison him, for he never shall be free, unless God enslaves him, nor ever chaste, unless God ravishes him. Here Donne returns to the paradoxes of his idolatry when he was enslaved by passion.

Holy Sonnet XVI deals with man's inheritance under the Old and New Testament or Will. He addresses God the Father: Father, part of his double claim upon thy kingdom, thy Son gives to me, his share in the perplexed Trinity he keeps, and gives to me his conquest of death. This Lamb, whose death hath blest the world with life, was slain from the beginning of the world (Creation), and hath made two Wills, which do invest thy sons with the Legacy of his and thy kingdom. Yet such are these laws (Mosaic), that men argue yet whether a man can fulfil those statutes; None doth; but thy all-healing grace and spirit (John 1, 17) revive again what law and letter kill ("for the letter killeth, but the spirit giveth life," 2 Cor. 3, 6). The abridgment of thy law, and thy last command is only (nothing but) love (John 13, 34): Oh let this last Will stand!

Holy Sonnet XVII is related to the death of his wife. Since she whom he loved has paid her last debt to Nature and to her own, and his good is dead, and her Soul snatched early into heaven, his mind is seated wholly in heavenly things. Here the admiration of her did incite his mind to seek (thee) God; so streams do show the source; but though he has found God, and God has fed his thirst, a holy thirsty craving dissolves him yet. But why should he beg more love, since God does woo his soul, for lack of hers offering all his love: And dost not only fear lest I give my love to Saints and Angels, things divine (to which he has become susceptible), but in thy tender jealousy dost fear lest the World, Flesh, yea Devil displace you. These consequences suggest not only the possibilities of his loss, but also the extent of God's concern for him.

Holy Sonnet XIX defines the mercurial temperament that followed Donne from profane to sacred love. Involved is a distemper that disturbs or upsets the proportion of humours which determines the physical and mental constitution of a man. To vex him, contraries meet in one person: inconstancy has unnaturally produced its opposite by becoming a habit; so that when he would not change, he changes in vows and in devotion. As capricious (humourous) is his contrition as his profane love, and as soon forgotten: as enigmatically distempered, cold (dejected) and hot (elated), as praying as mute; as infinite as nothing. Yesterday I dare not look at heaven; and to-day I court God in prayers and flattering speeches: To-morrow I shiver with true fear of his rod. So my devout fits come and go away like a fantastic Ague (the basic metaphor): except that in my contrition my best days are those when I shake with fear of God. Thus religion adds another paradox to ague as well as to profane love.

Good Friday, 1613: Riding Westward. Written in a critical time, this poem develops a conflict of feeling about Good Friday in terms of eastward versus westward movement. In his *Letters* (p. 26) Donne applies the motions of spheres to the diversion of true friendship: "The first sphere only which is resisted by nothing, absolves his course every day . . . But as the lower spheres, subject to the violence of that, and yet naturally encouraged to a reluctation against it, have therefore many distractions, and eccentricities, and some trepidations, and so return but lamely, and lately to the same place, and office."

The first sphere or Primum Mobile moves daily from east to west against the natural yearly motion of the lower spheres from west to east, and so retards their proper motion. Thus on Good Friday let man's Soul be a Sphere, and then the Spirit (intelligence) that moves this Sphere is devotion; and as the other Spheres lose their own motion by becoming subject to outside motions, and being hurried every day by others, scarcely obey their natural orbit in a year: so our Souls admit pleasure or business (instead of devotion) for their first mover, and are whirled by it. Hence it is, that I am carried towards the West this day, when my Soul's form, as a Sphere moved by devotion, inclines toward the East. There I should see a Sun, by rising set (eclipsed at the crucifixion), and by that setting (in death) beget endless day (for man); except for the fact that Christ did rise and fall on this Cross, sin would have eternally benighted all of us.

Yet I dare almost be glad, that I do not see that spectacle, which is more than I could bear. Who sees God's face, which is life itself, must die (Exodus 33, 20); what a death then it would be to see God die? It made his own Lieutenant Nature recoil, it made his footstool (Isaiah 66, 1) crack, and the Sun wink (Matthew 27, 51; Luke 23, 45). Could I behold those hands which span the Poles, and tune (harmonize) all spheres at once, pierced with those holes? (On the next idea see his *LXXX Sermons*, p. 677: "To our Antipodes, to them that are under our feet, God is verticall, over their heads, then when he is over ours.") Could I behold that endless height which is Zenith to us and our Antipodes, humbled below us (like our Antipodes)? or that blood which is the seat or sanctuary of all our Souls, if not of us, made dirt (mud) of dust (out of which man was made), or that flesh which was worn by God, only as his apparel, ragged and torn? If I durst not look on these things, durst I cast my eye upon his miserable mother, who was God's partner here, and thus furnished half of that Sacrifice which ransomed us? (This adds an element of self-betrayal to the divine betrayal in which he is implicated.)

Though these things, as I ride, be away from my eye, they are still present to my memory, for that looks towards them; and thou look'st towards me, O Saviour, as thou hang'st upon the tree; I turn my back to thee, only to receive corrections, till thy mercies bid thee stop. O think me worth your anger, punish me, burn off my moral corrosion, and my deformity; restore thy Image enough, by thy grace, that thou may'st know me, and I'll turn my face. Thus he concludes that he is not prepared to turn eastward, and hence his westward movement becomes proper, not foreign. The latent mercy of Good Friday becomes active in his preparation to turn.

A Hymne to Christ, at the Authors last going into Germany, in which Father and Son are not kept apart, offers "this bill of my Divorce to All," his acceptance of the Gospel conditions for following the Cross (Matthew 16, 24; Mark 10, 21; Luke 14, 26): In whatsoever rent ship I embark, that ship shall be my emblem of thy Ark (of the Covenant); whatsoever sea swallow me, that flood shall be to me an emblem of thy blood (my second salvation); though thou do disguise thy face with clouds of anger; yet through that mask I know that those eyes, which, though sometimes they turn away, they never will despise. (Thus he enumerates the bases of his faith.) / I sacrifice this Island (Britain) unto thee, and all whom I loved there, and who loved me; when I have put our seas between them and me, put thou thy sea (his redeeming blood) between my sins and thee. As the tree's sap doth seek the root below in winter (cf. *Nocturnall*), in my winter now I go, where none but thee, the Eternal root of true love I may know. (This sacrifice and dedication to God reflects the recent death of his wife.) / Neither thou nor thy religion dost restrain the love of a consenting Soul (cf. "For love, all love of other sights controules"), but thou would have that love thy self: As thou art jealous, Lord, so I am jealous now; thou dost not love, until thou free my soul from loving more: whoever gives liberty, takes liberty away: O, if thou dost not care whom I love alas, thou dost not love me. (The Mosaic God is a jealous god and the Christ of the Gospels requires both love and detachment from others.) / Then seal this bill of my divorce to all, on whom those fainter beams of love did fall; marry those loves, which in youth are scattered on Fame, Wit, Hopes (false mistresses) to thee, Churches are best for Prayer, that have least light (symbols of his renunciation): To see only God, I go out of sight (of other things): And to escape stormy days (on the sea of life), I choose an Everlasting night (total exclusion of worldly light). Thus Donne sealed his bill of divorce to the world by translating the words, "If any man will come after me, let him deny himself, and take up his cross, and follow me."

A Hymne to God the Father is a vivid realization of the meaning of Romans vi, 23: "For the wages of sin is death; but the gift of God is eternal life through Jesus Christ our Lord." / Wilt thou forgive that sin where I begun (original sin), which is my sin, though it were done before? Wilt thou forgive those sins, through which I run, and do run still (present personal sins), though still I do deplore (them)? (Some texts prefer the weaker "do them" to the stronger "do run.") When thou hast done that, thou hast not done (or Donne), For, I have more (sins). / Wilt thou forgive that sin by which I have won others to sin (accessory sin)? and, made my sin their entrance into sin? Wilt thou forgive that (past) sin which I avoided a year or two, but wallowed in a score? When thou hast done that, thou hast not finished (or Donne), for I have more (sin). / I have a sin of fear, that when I have spun my last thread (of life), I shall perish on the shore (of death)—(his first definite sin is fear of the consequence of sin, which now becomes lack of faith)—Swear by thy self, that at my death thy son and sun (my redeemer from death) shall shine as he shines now, and heretofore (unclouded): And, having done that, Thou hast done (and Donne), I fear no more (the consequence of my sin). Thus he fulfils the Scriptural text by asking for the gift of life through Christ. The weaker close, "I have no more," substitutes the arithmetic of sin for relief from its consequence. Kinds of sin rather than numbers are emphasized throughout.

Hymne to God my God, in my Sicknesse is a preparation for death conceived in terms of a journey or voyage of discovery through the microcosmic figure of *Holy Sonnet V*. Thus he becomes a map and his physicians become cosmographers, and between them his course is charted. / Since I am coming to that Holy room (heaven or church), where, with thy Quire of Saints (Rev. xiv) for evermore, I shall be made thy Music; as I come I tune the Instrument (body and soul) here at the door (to that Holy room), and what I must do then, think here before (prepare myself for there). ("Door" is the first passage or strait in the poem.) / While my Physicians by their concern have become cosmographers, and I their Map (or instrument), who lie flat on this bed, so that by them I may be shown that this is my Southwest discovery through the strait of fever, by these hardships to die, / I joy, that in these straits, I see my West (death); for, though their currents yield return to none, what shall my West hurt me? As West and East in all flat Maps (and I am one) are one, so death doth touch the Resurrection. (In a letter, *Tobie Mathews Collection*, p. 305, Donne says: "But yet, *Oriens nomen ejus*, the East is one of Christ's names," and "if a flat Map be but pasted upon a round Globe, the farthest East and the farthest West meet, and are all one.") / Is the Pacific Sea my home? Or are the Eastern riches (East Indies)? Is Jerusalem? Anyan (Behring), and Magellan, and Gibraltar, all straits, and none but straits (hardships), are ways to them, whether where Japhet dwelt, or Cham, or Shem (Europe, Africa, or Asia). (The East as one of Christ's names appears in Donne's epitaph, translated as "Whose name is the Rising.") / We think that Paradise and Calvary, Christ's cross and Adam's tree, stood in one place; (as in his satire, *The Progresse of the Soule* [see stanza viii] is from Adam's tree to Christ's Cross, from Paradise to Calvary). Look Lord, and find both Adams met in me; as the first Adam's sweat (of labor—now fever) surrounds my face, may the last Adam's blood (of redemption) embrace my soul. / So, wrapped in his royal blood (not robe of mockery) receive me Lord, by these his crown of thorns (of Passion) give me his other Crown (of Resurrection). (In *Fifty Sermons*, No. 33, Donne says that the crown which Christ derived from his Mother or human nature "was his *passion*, his *Crown of thornes*"; and "the Crown wherewith his Father crowned his Humane nature, was the glory given to that, in his Ascension.") And as to others' souls I preached thy word, let this be my Text, my Sermon to my own soul, Therefore that he may raise the Lord throws down. In *LXXX Sermons* (No. 46) Donne says that in "a medicinal falling" God "throws him down therefore that he may raise him."

Thus Donne returns to the clerical role suggested at the beginning, as he completes the preparation of his own soul. In his paradoxical Text, which expresses the necessity of suffering, he summarizes the way in which God unites West and East, or Fall and Resurrection, in the little world of man.

V

George Herbert
1593-1633

George Herbert, according to Walton, dedicated his poetry to God in his first year at Cambridge by way of two sonnets sent to his mother as a New Year's gift. Subsequently he confirmed this act by his Dedication of *The Temple:* "Lord, my first fruits present themselves to thee." But for his earlier first fruits, he explains to his mother, a late ague has dried up the springs associated with the classical Muses: "However, I need not their help, to reprove the vanity of those many Love-poems that are daily writ and consecrated to *Venus;* nor to bewail that so few are writ, that look towards *God* and *Heaven.*" He is not going to follow the course of the sonnet-eers:

> *Leave me, O love, which reachest but to dust;*
> *And thou, my mind, aspire to higher things . . .*

"For my own part," he concludes, "my meaning (*dear Mother*) is in these Sonnets, to declare my resolution to be, that my poor Abilities in *Poetry* shall be all, and ever consecrated to Gods glory." The first sonnet may serve to characterize this early testimony:

> *My God, where is that ancient heat towards thee,*
>   *Wherewith whole shoals of Martyrs once did burn,*
>   *Besides their other flames? Doth Poetry*
> *Wear Venus Livery? only serve her turn?*
> *Why are not Sonnets made of thee? and layes*
>   *Upon thine Altar burnt? Cannot thy love*
>   *Heighten a spirit to sound out thy praise*
> *As well as any she? Cannot thy Dove*
> *Out-strip their Cupid easily in flight?*
>   *Or, since thy ways are deep, and still the same,*
>   *Will not a verse run smooth that bears thy name?*
> *Why doth that fire, which by thy power and might*
>   *Each breast does feel, no braver fuel choose*
>   *Than that, which one day, Worms may chance refuse.*

Most unexpected here perhaps is the opposition between depth of subject and smoothness of verse, a conflict that Carew felt in Donne.

But as a member of a proud family Herbert found it less easy to take holy orders than to follow the ways of the world that produce sources of tension in his poetry. At the end he sent the manuscript of *The Temple* to Nicholas Ferrar as "a picture of the many spiritual Conflicts that have past betwixt God and my Soul, before I could subject mine to the will of *Jesus my Master:* in whose service I have found perfect freedom." When he wrote *A Priest to the Temple, or The Country Parson* as "a Mark to aim at," he began by expressing the same intention for his parson: "A Pastor is the Deputy of Christ for the reducing of Man to the Obedience of God." This work has much in common with *The Temple;* for example, in "The Parson's Surveys" and *The Church-Porch.*

One of these common elements is the recollection of Donne's verses *To Mr. Tilman after he had taken Orders*, particularly on the state of the Gentry:

> Flie idlenesse, which yet thou canst not flie
> By dressing, mistressing, and complement.
> If those take up thy day, the sunne will crie
> Against thee: for his light was onely lent.
>> God gave thy soul brave wings; put not those feathers
>> Into a bed, to sleep out all ill weathers.

Moreover, according to Barnabas Oley, the feeling about taking orders that is described by Donne also affected Herbert: "I have heard sober men censure him as a man that did not manage his brave parts to his best advantage and preferment, but lost himself in an humble way; that was the phrase, I well remember it." In Walton's words, he "changed his sword and silk Cloaths into a Canonical Coat." His greatest distress, however, came from other reasons for feeling he had "lost himself in an humble way," especially in the period of futility between his ordination as deacon in 1626 and as priest in 1630, or before he finally committed himself to the priesthood. Then he felt lost to God's service by sickness and inadequacy, his own shortcomings; lost to a vocation, a loss from which Donne suffered at Mitcham, and by which Herbert is obviously moved in "The Parson's Surveys" when he insists on the necessity of a vocation: "And because idleness is twofold, the one in having no calling, the other in walking carelessly in our calling."

Biographers have found the first of Herbert's five poems on *Affliction* most revealing of his spirit in this time of trial. His character appears in the phrasing that God enticed him by his "service brave" and the "gracious benefits" which it could add to his "stock of naturall delights." God's furniture became fine to him, just as furniture meant something to him in "The Parson's Church" and *Jordan I*. The next stanza sug-

gests the service of a king that was lost to Herbert, whether
sought or not:

> *What pleasures could I want, whose King I served,*
> *Where joyes my fellows were?*
> *Thus argu'd into hopes, my thoughts reserved*
> *No place for grief or fear.*
> *Therefore my sudden soul caught at the place,*
> *And made her youth and fiercenesse seek thy face.*

The possible ambiguities of this stanza might reflect a secular
disappointment, but they do reveal some later disillusionment
in the conclusion that his hasty soul caught at a place where
"youth and fierceness" are not ready to serve.

At first he got what he expected: "There was no moneth
but May." But in time sorrow did combine and grow, and
made him unawares a party to woe. His flesh complained
against his soul in pain, that sicknesses cleave his bones, agues
dwell in his veins, and tune his breath to groans. Sorrow was
his whole soul; he hardly believed he was alive, until grief
reminded him sharply. When he recovered health, God took
away his life, and more; because his friends died, he lost his
mirth and edge, and became more useless than a blunted
knife. Thus thin and lean, without shield or friend, he was
blown through by every storm and wind.

Barnabas Oley, his first biographer, takes up the poem at
this point: "The memorials of him left in the orator's book,
show how he discharged the place: and himself intimates, that
whereas his birth and spirit prompted him to martial achieve-
ments, the way that takes the town; and not to sit simpering
over a book; God did often melt his spirit, and entice him
with academic honour, to be content to wear, and wrap up
himself in a gown, so long, till he durst not put it off, nor
retire to any other calling. However, probably he might, I
have heard (as other orators), have had a secretary of state's
place." Herbert makes the point thus:

I took thy sweetned pill, till I came where
I could not go away, nor persevere.

Yet lest he should find some happiness or strength in his purge, God throws him into more sicknesses: "not making / Thine own gift good, yet me from my wayes taking." Now that he is in this state, none of the books to which God betrayed him will show what God intends for him. If he were only a tree, he "should grow to fruit or shade," or at least some trust from a bird, to which he would be faithful. But while God troubles him, he must be meek; in weakness, strong. Well, he will change his service, and try to find another master. And he prays that, although he is entirely forgotten, let him not love God, if he really does not love him. It is a prayer for certainty in his own mind.

Desire for an active life appears under a significant title in *Employment* (II), even with a touch of scorn:

> *He that is weary, let him sit.*
>   *My soul would stirre*
> *And trade in courtesies and wit,*
>   *Quitting the furre*
> *To cold complexions needing it.*

Cold complexions include melancholy and phlegm, but the element that sat still, which is earth, makes it melancholy, and thus doubly appropriate to the fur of the academic gown. The strife of the elements is used to develop his theme. Man is not a star, but a live coal of mortal fire: who neither blows it, nor restrains a weak desire, lets his own ashes choke this coal. When the elements fought with fire for the highest place in the sublunary world, the earth sat still, and so is opprest by the others.

Life is a business, not a solace, but ever in strife. The sun shines whether visible or not, whereas the stars watch for a chance to appear. These are his most cutting words on his betrayal to a gown after he had been born to "the world of strife." If only he were busy like an orange-tree, then he should always be laden, and never lack some fruit for one who cultivated or tended him. But we are always either too young or too old; and the man is gone, before we produce anything: thus we freeze on in life, until the grave increases the cold that drew us to the furred gown. If the choice of vocation has seemed without spirit, it is still more painful to feel fruitless in that choice.

Herbert's literary achievements were threatened by division into piety and false wit. In Hobbes's *Answer to Davenant* (1650) Herbert's kind of wit was questioned: "In an Epigram or a Sonnet a man may vary his measures, and seek glory from a needlesse difficulty, as he that contrived Verses into the formes of an Organ, a Hatchet, an Egg, an Altar, and a paire of Wings; but in so great and noble a worke as is an Epique Poem, for a man to obstruct his own way with unprofitable difficulties is great imprudence." This was probably not Herbert's motive, but the criticism anticipates Addison. Dryden introduces this kind of wit into the satire of *Mac Flecknoe* in a passage that Addison recalls:

> *Thy Genius calls thee not to purchase fame*
> *In keen Iambicks, but mild Anagram:*
> *Leave writing Plays, and chuse for thy command*
> *Some peacefull Province in Acrostick Land.*
> *There thou maist wings display, and Altars raise,*
> *And torture one poor word Ten thousand ways.*

Addison begins his *Spectator* papers on wit (No. 58) with the false Wit of Figured Poems, found "among Mr. Herbert's Poems." He even suggests that Pindarick Writers "apply themselves to this kind of Wit without Loss of Time, as being provided better than any other Poets with Verses of all Sizes and Dimensions."

In his last paper (No. 62) Addison defines his basic terms:

"As *true Wit* generally consists in this Resemblance and Congruity of Ideas, *false Wit* chiefly consists in the Resemblance and Congruity sometimes of single Letters, as in Anagrams, Chronograms, Lipograms, and Acrosticks: Sometimes of Syllables, as in Ecchos and Doggerel Rhymes: Sometimes of Words, as in Punns and Quibbles; and sometimes of whole Sentences or Poems, cast into the Figures of *Eggs*, *Axes* or *Altars*." Such figures had been classified as examples of Geometrical proportion in Puttenham's *Arte of English Poesie* in 1589, where they were treated in the Chapter "Of Proportion in figure" (II, xi) and called "courtly trifles." And they were condemned as false wit in Ben Jonson's *Execration upon Vulcan.*

These verbal exercises in ingenuity are treated in Addison's preceding papers, and have their counterparts in Herbert's poetry. Lipogram, or letter-dropping, is found in the rhymes of *Paradise*, although it represents pruning. Variants of such word and picture forms as the Rebus and Figured Poem are found in such pictorial Conceits as *The Church-floore* and *The Windows*. The Anagram appears in the *Anagram of the Virgin Marie* and *Jesu*, the Echo in *Heaven*, and Rhyming point in the last line of *Deniall* and *Home*. More complex verbal artifice gives form to *The Call*, and in *Coloss. 3. 3.* runs an acrostic theme diagonally across ten lines from the first syllable to the tenth, which represents an obliquity or ecliptic in the annual motion of the sun. Thus Herbert complicates the two motions of Donne's *Good Friday* so as to make life lead to heaven. The pun, which Addison defines as "a Conceit arising from the use of two Words that agree in the Sound, but differ in the Sense," gives final point to "grace" in *The British Church*. Indeed, both conceits and verse that depend upon verbal ingenuity assume an unusual variety of forms in Herbert. The only way to test a Piece of Wit, says Addison, is to translate it into another language, the test that Dryden pre-

scribed in *An Essay of Dramatic Poesy*. But Herbert clearly
expected these devices to function as expression. Thus we are
left with the question of defining his theory of what is proper
to religious expression.

Walton tells us that Herbert delivered his first sermon
"after a most florid manner, both with great learning and elo-
quence," but promised his parishioners that "since Almighty
God does not intend to lead men to heaven by hard questions,
he would not therefore fill their heads with unnecessary no-
tions; but that for their sakes, his language and his expressions
should be more plain and practical in his future sermons."
Thus he passed from the University Orator to the "Country
Parson" of his own book. Thereafter he condescended to the
knowledge of rural life, but his chief storehouse was also that
of his Country Parson (IV), the Holy Scriptures. Yet how
was he to be effective? He opens *The Temple* with this invi-
tation:

> *Hearken unto a Verser, who may chance*
> *Ryme thee to good, and make a bait of pleasure.*
> *A verse may finde him, who a sermon flies,*
> *And turn delight into a sacrifice.*

Some of his verbal bait we have already noticed.

As a preacher Herbert found that exhortations often died
with the sermon, "especially with country people; which are
thick, and heavy, and hard to raise to a point of zeal, and
fervency, and need a mountain of fire to kindle them; but
stories and sayings they will well remember." After these
"heart-deep" words, he proceeds to his rhetoric (VII): "He
often tells them, that sermons are dangerous things, that none
goes out of church as he came in, but either better or worse;
that none is careless before his Judge, and that the word of
God shall judge us. By these and other means the parson pro-
cures attention; but the character of his sermon is holiness; he

is not witty, or learned, or eloquent, but holy." And surprising; with this mild approach to Chestertonian paradox, he abjures the "witty" mode of preaching then current.

Actually he seems to have found his mode of wit or rhetoric in the Bible, or its familiar illustration (XXI): "This is the skill, and doubtless the Holy Scripture intends thus much, when it condescends to the naming of a plough, a hatchet, a bushel, leaven, boys piping and dancing; showing that things of ordinary use are not only to serve in the way of drudgery, but to be washed, and cleansed, and serve for lights even of heavenly truths." In garden herbs and simples he found "nature serving grace both in comfort of diversion, and the benefit of application, when need requires: as also, by way of illustration, even as our Saviour made plants and seeds to teach the people: for he was the true householder, who bringeth out of his treasure things new and old; the old things of philosophy, and the new of grace; and maketh the one serve the other."

Christ's parables also supply the key to Herbert's poetry in method, imagery, and diction. His awareness is clear (XXIII): "And I conceive, our Saviour did this for three reasons: first, that by familiar things he might make his doctrine slip the more easily into the hearts even of the meanist. Secondly, that labouring people (whom he chiefly considered) might have every where monuments of his doctrine, remembering in gardens, his mustard-seed, and lilies; in the field, his seed-corn, and tares; and so not be drowned altogether in the works of their vocation, but sometimes lift up their minds to better things, even in the midst of their pains. Thirdly, that he might set a copy for parsons." And for sacred poets. Then he goes on to simples, and we remember that his roses are also cures. Certainly *The Temple* is full of monuments or reminders of Herbert's doctrine.

Puttenham's *Arte of English Poesie* (III, xix) had described this mode as follows: "But whensoever by your similitude ye will seeme to teach any moralitie or good lesson by speeches misticall and darke, or farre fette, under a sence metaphoricall applying one natural thing to another, or one case to another, inferring by them a like consequence in other cases the Greekes call it *Parabola*, which terme is also by custome accepted of us: neverthelesse we may call him in English the resemblance misticall: as when we liken a young childe to a greene twigge which ye may easilie bende every way ye list: or an old man who laboureth with continuall infirmities, to a drie and dricksie oke. Such parables were all the preachings of Christ in the Gospell, as those of the wise and foolish virgins, of the evil steward, of the labourers in the vineyard, and a number more." This figure also included fables.

For Hoskins (*Directions*, p. 10) the similitude "is the ground of all emblems, allegories, fables, and fictions." He distinguishes them as follows: "An emblem, an allegory, a similitude, a fable, and a poet's tale differ thus: an Emblem is but the one part of the similitude, the other part (viz., the application) expressed indifferently and jointly in one sentence, with words some proper to the one part, some to the other; a Similitude hath two sentences, of several proper terms compared; a Fable is a similitude acted by fiction in beasts; a Poet's Tale, for the most part, by gods and men." In the comparison of equal things, said Hoskins, "there are to be searched out all the several points of a consorted equality," as in the Conceit.

In 1605 Bacon's *Advancement of Learning* gave special emphasis to Allusive or Parabolical poetry as "a Narrative applied only to express some special purpose or conceit. Which latter kind of parabolical wisdom was much more in use in the ancient times, as by the fables of Aesop, and the brief sentences of the Seven, and the use of hieroglyphics may appear." After explaining why "parables were before arguments," he concludes, "and nevertheless now, and at all times, they do retain much life and vigour; because reason cannot be so sensible, nor examples so fit." But Poesy Parabolical also

had an opposite use: "for that tendeth to demonstrate and il-
lustrate that which is taught or delivered, and this other to
retire and obscure it: that is, when the secrets and mysteries
of religion, policy, or philosophy, are involved in fables or
parables. Of this in divine poesy we see the use is authorized."
Indeed, it becomes necessary: "For we see that, in matters of
Faith and Religion, we raise our Imagination above our Rea-
son; which is the cause why Religion sought ever access to
the mind by similitude, types, parables, visions, dreams." This
is why Sir Thomas Browne was "content to understand a
mystery without a rigid definition, in an easie and Platonick
description," in metaphors rather than metaphysics. Certainly
Herbert was not concerned with the esoteric use of parables
(although he had been a Latin scribe for Bacon), but with
their Biblical use; and there, rather than in the emblem tradi-
tion, he found his poetics.

Although *The Temple* begins by offering its poems to
God, and "a bait of pleasure" to the reader, Herbert occasion-
ally seems to feel uneasy about their dual audience. Although
his muse had turned from Helicon to Jordan, it felt the con-
flict of their rival claims, as in *Jordan* (I):

> *Who sayes that fictions onely and false hair*
> *Become a verse? Is there in truth no beautie?*
> *Is all good structure in a winding stair?*
> *May no lines passe, except they do their dutie*
>   *Not to a true, but painted chair?*
>
> *Is it no verse, except enchanted groves*
> *And sudden arbours shadow course-spunne lines?*
> *Must purling streams refresh a lovers loves?*
> *Must all be vail'd, while he that reads, divines,*
>   *Catching the sense at two removes?*
>
> *Shepherds are honest people; let them sing:*
> *Riddle who list, for me, and pull for Prime:*
> *I envie no mans nightingale or spring;*

> *Nor let them punish me with losse of rime,*
> *Who plainly say,* My God, My King.

Nevertheless, he is quarreling with the "Venus Livery" of the sonnet to his mother, and arguing that he can be plain without loss of rhyme; but not without drawing for a winning word, or making the reader "unriddle" his metaphor. It is with difficulty that his truth finally disengages itself from the fictions of verse enough to be plain to his shepherds.

In *Jordan* (II), where Herbert seems intent on outdoing the first sonnet of Sidney's *Astrophel and Stella*, no invention or expression seems equal to his feeling of heavenly joy, and so he is lavish in poetic fictions, until the climax:

> *As flames do work and winde, when they ascend,*
> *So did I weave my self into the sense.*
> *But while I bustled, I might heare a friend*
> *Whisper,* How wide is all this long pretence!
> There is in love a sweetnesse readie penn'd:
> Copie out onely that, and save expense.

But he still found its expression baffling in *Dulnesse*, or else "readie penn'd" only in terms that belonged to Venus, thus competing with the love sonnets. The problem becomes critical in *The Forerunners*, which is based on the conceit of a royal progress whose advance agents have required lodgings by chalking doors, in Herbert for God's progress. They have whitened his head, but must they oust his bright ideas and dull his wits? Yet they have left him one phrase of welcome. And they have left his best room, his heart. So long as his one phrase is out of danger, he does not care about the rest, for it will please God, and that is to "write fine and wittie."

Thus he says farewell to the enticing phrases of profane love that he had tried to turn to sacred use, believing like his Parson that they too could "be washed, and cleansed, and serve for lights even of heavenly truths." This infatuation with fine language or "sugar-cane" temptation costs him some luscious phrases as well as rude words before he concludes:

> *Yet if you go, I passe not; take your way:*
> *For,* Thou art still my God, *is all that ye*
> *Perhaps with more embellishment can say.*
> *Go birds of spring: let winter have his fee;*
>   *Let a bleak palenesse chalk the doore,*
> *So all within be livelier then before.*

If he accepts white hair, he tries to escape dullness in words of piety. Indeed, these poems on poetic wit in religion show a struggle between the University Orator and the Country Parson, or a conflict between pride and humility in expression. In short, the effort to humble himself may be seen in his language too: for Miss Tuve it is his poetics (*A Reading*, 194-95). *The Posie* rejects secular wit for that which is "readie penn'd" in the Bible:

> *Invention rest,*
> *Comparisons go play, wit use thy will:*
>   *Lesse then the least*
> *Of all Gods mercies, is my posie still.*

Yet a "posie" or motto is one of the forms of wit related to emblems and anagrams, and Herbert's motto in this setting expressed his final submission to the Divine Will. But its effectiveness depends upon the contrast between his secular idiom and the sacred idiom, as in this stanza; or upon the contest latent in the discordant union of the parables; that is, between the earthly and the heavenly, or the words of nature and the words of grace.

Herbert's sonnet *Redemption* may be compared with Donne's *Holy Sonnet XVI*, changing "Wills" to "leases," but not their end. Christ's redemption of man upon the Cross is put into terms closer to country people. The tenant cannot live on his old lease and so seeks a new one. The parallel of his rich master with Christ takes him to heaven, where he learns that Christ has gone to take possession of some land on earth which he had long ago bought dearly. So, knowing Christ's great birth, he looks for him in great places, without success until he hears a harsh sound and mirth of thieves and murderers: there he discovers Christ, who at once grants his petition and dies. Thus Herbert dramatizes Christ's crucifixion in more familiar but equally paradoxical terms, using his company on the cross to underwrite the manifestation of his mercy.

The Temper (I) depends upon various senses of tempering that connect steel, soul or mind, and music. How he should engrave his love if his soul always felt the same elation! But sometimes he rises higher than the highest heaven, sometimes falls as low as hell. O stretch me not, he exclaims, to such a vast extent; such distances belong to God: the world is too little for thy tent, but too big a grave for me when racked. Would God match arms with man, since he stretches a crumb of dust from heaven to hell? Will great God measure himself with a wretch? must he spell out God's stature? O let me, when my soul is exalted to thy roof, nestle there: then thou art free from a sinner, and I am free from hope and fear. Yet take thy way; for surely thy way is best: stretch or contract me, thy poor debtor: this is only tuning (tempering) my breast, in order to make the music better. Whether I fly with angels, or fall with dust, thy hands made both, and I am in them: thy power and love, my love and trust, make one place every where. Thus divine love transcends space or power, as in the secular love of Donne, and makes one place an everywhere.

The Windows or *Church-windows* poses a question of the Parson: how can man preach the eternal word? He is a brittle glass, full of cracks and flaws: yet God, by his grace, gives man the glorious and transcendent office of being a window in his church. / But when God burns his story into the glass, making his life shine within that of the preacher; then the light and glory that shines through grows more reverend, and wins more: which otherwise appears waterish, bleak, and thin. / Doctrine and life (in the preacher), colors and light (in the window), when they combine and mingle in one, bring a strong regard and awe: but speech alone vanishes like a flaring (showy but unsteady) thing, and rings in the ear, not conscience. The parson must live as well as preach the story.

Vanitie (I) suggests Bacon's use of Luke 24, 5, to distinguish between divinity and philosophy against the school of Paracelsus (*A. of L.* Ev. edn, 217). Man does not seek "the living among the dead," but searches for knowledge (death) and misses salvation (life). The fast Astronomer can penetrate the spheres and quickly calculate the value or meaning of their positions and aspects in their cosmic dance. / The nimble Diver also seeks his dearly-earned pearl, which God purposely hides from the daring wretch; so that he might save his life, and also hers who wears with fatal pride her own destruction and his danger. / The subtle Alchemist can undress and strip the created thing, until he finds the bare principles within their abode: there he studies them privately, before they appear in their proper dress to ordinary seekers. / What has man not sought out and found, except his dear God? who still embosoms his glorious law in us, mellowing the ground (heart) with showers and frosts, with love and awe, so that we need not ask, Where is this command? Poor man, he searches all round to find out death, but misses life or salvation at hand; hence the vanity of his search, which involves pride.

Vertue begins with the sweetness or odor that passes from the day to the rose, the spring, and the virtuous soul, where it does not die (2 Cor., 2, 15). In the day it marks the wedding of earth and sky, and its fall is wept by the dew. In the rose its angry red splendor bids the reckless gazer wipe his eye, for its root is always in its grave. In the spring it is full of sweet days and roses, all compacted into a box; his music shows they have their enclosures and cadences or "dying falls." Only the virtuous soul, like seasoned timber, never shrinks; but though the whole world turn to dead coal, then chiefly lives (glows).

The Pearl involves Matthew 13, 45-6: "Again, the kingdom of heaven is like unto a merchant man, seeking goodly pearls: Who, when he had found one pearl of great price, went and sold all that he had, and bought it." The poem itemizes what Herbert sold in order to buy the pearl. He knows the ways of Learning; as University Orator he knew the head and vocal pipes that feed the printing press; he knows what reason has borrowed from the observation of nature, or like a good housewife spun out of itself into laws and policy; what the stars plot in astrology, what nature reveals of her own accord, or when forced by the alchemist's fire; knows both the old discoveries, and the new voyages, the basic store and the excess, purpose (end) and record: all these ways are open, or he has the keys: Yet he loves God. The price of the pearl is measured by its cost, or an opposition in which the brevity of his divine choice is magnified by worldly amplitude.

He knows the ways of Honor or preferment, what continues the quick profits of courtesy and wit: in contests of favors which party gains, when ambition swells the heart, and shapes it to all expressions of hand and eye, which may tie a true-love knot on the world, and bear the bundle of favors thus gained, wherever it goes: he knows how many drams of spirit or courage are required to sell his life to his friends or foes: Yet he loves God. / He knows the ways of Pleasure, the sweet passages, soothings, and flavors of it (expressed in musical metaphor); the proposals of passion and thought; the meaning of mirth and music; what love and fancy have produced these two thousand years or more: he knows the schemes of ungoverned wealth: his stuff is flesh, not insensible matter; his senses live, and often complain that they have more invested in him than the Will that restrains them, being only one to five: Yet he loves God.

He knows all these, and has them at his disposal: therefore it is not with closed but with open eyes that he flies to God, and fully understands both the main exchange and the benefits involved; and at what rate and price he has God's love; with all the circumstances (conditions) that may prompt one: yet through these mazes, not his low intellect, but God's silk thread (like Ariadne's in the Labyrinth) let down from heaven to him, did both conduct and teach him (by grace), how by it to climb to God. To attain the pearl still required both grace and effort.

Man depends upon the chain of being and correspondences between the microcosm and the macrocosm. It begins with the proposition that no one builds a stately habitation unless he means to dwell in it. And proceeds to the question, what house is more stately than man? for whose creation all things disintegrate. / For Man is every thing, and more: a tree (vegetable), yet bears more fruit; a beast (animal), yet is, or should be more: only man has reason and speech (rational soul). If parrots have speech, they owe it to us. Each level on the scale of being is more than the level below it. / Man is all symmetry, all proportioned one limb to another, and to all the world besides: each part is related to the farthest: head has private concord with foot, and both with moons and tides. (Now correspondences of microcosm and macrocosm.) / Nothing has got so far away, but that man has caught and kept it as his booty. His eyes bring down the highest star: he is in little the whole world (microcosm). Herbs gladly cure our flesh; because they find their familiar (vegetable soul) there.

For us the winds blow, the earth rests, heaven moves, and fountains flow. We see nothing but what means our good, either as our delight, or as our treasure: the whole (everything) is either our cupboard of food, or cabinet of pleasure. / The stars put us to bed; night draws the curtain, which the sun withdraws; music and light wait on our head. All things are natural or akin to our flesh in their descent and being (on the scale of being); to our mind in their ascent and end (final cause) on that scale. / Each thing is dutiful in service: waters united provide our navigation; separated from land (Gen., 1, 9), our habitation; below, our drink; above (rain), our food; both waters give us cleanliness. Has one element such beauty? Then how nicely made or proportioned are all things!

More servants wait on Man, than he takes any notice of: in every path he treads down the herbs that befriend him, when sickness makes him pale and wan. Oh mighty love! that Man is one world, and has another to wait upon him. / Since then, my God, thou hast made so fine a Palace as man; O dwell in it, so that it may dwell at last with thee! (Cf. opening hypothesis.) Till then, grant us enough intelligence, so that we may serve thee, as the world serves us, and both be thy servants.

Life gives a moral twist to the *carpe diem* theme, and illustrates the place of sensuous perception in his religion. He tried to turn his time into a bouquet, so that he might smell his remnant out, and confine his life within the compass of flowers. But Time summoned them, and by noon they had withered in his hand. / His hand was nearest to them, and then his heart: without further thought, he took kindly Time's gentle reproof: who conveyed so sweetly death's sad taste, making his mind smell his fatal day, yet sweetening the apprehension. / Farewell dear flowers, you spent your time sweetly; while you lived, suitable for smell or ornament, and after death for cures (see *A Priest*, xxiii). I follow directly without complaint or grief, because if my scent is good, I care not if it be as short as yours. Thus scent may become moral.

Mortification develops the theme, "How soon doth man decay!" by finding reminders of death everywhere in life, and always related to the "breath" of Genesis. Each stage begins with "when," and rhymes "breath" with "death." When cloths are taken from a scented box to swaddle infants, whose young breath scarcely knows the way (to death); those cloths are little winding sheets, which do commit and send them unto death. / When boys first go to bed, they step into their voluntary graves, sleep binds them fast; only their breath makes them alive: successive nights, like rolling waves, carry them quickly, who are destined for death. / When youth is free and open, and calls for music, while his mood expands, exchanging mirth and breath all day in consort (concert); that music summons to the passing-bell, which shall bring the charitable to pray for him at the hour of death. / When man grows settled and wise, getting a house and home, where he may move within the compass (shortness) of his breath, disciplining his eyes; that mute enclosure manifests love for the coffin, that awaits his death. / When age grows low and weak, outlining his grave, and softening each year, until all do melt, and drown his breath when he would speak; a chair or litter represents the bier, which shall convey him to the house of death. / Man, before he is aware, has fashioned a solemn ceremony, and prepared his bier, while he still has breath to spare: Yet Lord, instruct us so to die, that all these dyings may become life in death.

The Quip opposes the worldly and the unworldly by a series of witty sarcasms in which the repartee is left to God. In the colloquy of *Love* (III) God gives the final answers for Herbert. Here the festive world with its trained bands and companions one day agreed to meet together, where he dwelt, and all in sport to scoff at him. / First, Beauty crept into a rose. . . . but although he prized beauty, he at last found it in "The British Church." / The temptation of Money plays upon his love of music by translating it into worldly terms. / Then came resplendent Glory puffing by, insolently making his silks whistle, who except he? He scarcely recognized me, half snubbed me. Family pride made this action the most cutting quip. / Quick Wit he is both exercising and denying himself in this poem, but he mocks himself as the Public Orator when he has this temptation, "And, to be short, make an Oration." / In the final stanza he caps this point by giving God the soul of wit or brevity: "Speak not at large; say, I am thine." If the hour of God's design has not yet come, then Herbert presumably has not yet committed himself finally.

Divinitie is treated here in the manner of the Country Parson. As men have supplied stars with spheres, for fear they should behave like country people; as if a star were duller than a ploughman, who knows his way without a guide: / Just so they treat the other heaven, the transcendent sky of divinity: which they cut and carve with the sharp edge of intellect. Reason triumphs, and faith remains unused. / Could not that Wisdom which first drew the wine, have thickened it with definitions? And slashed his seamless coat, had that been refined, with minute questions and distinctions? / But all the doctrine, which he gave and taught, was as clear as the heavens from which it came. At least those beams of truth which are necessary for salvation, surpass any flame in brightness. / The basic doctrines are then italicized, and ironically called "as dark as day." Who can undo these Gordian knots? / The next stanza begins with the Gordian knot of transubstantiation, of wine into blood. But whatever God bids, he is sure that to take and taste what God doth there designate, is all that is necessary, and not obscure. / Then burn your circular refinements (Epicycles), foolish man; break all your spheres, and save your head (reason). Faith needs no physical support, but alone can bravely both go and guide to heaven. In conclusion too, the answer is the same for both heavens.

The Collar might have prompted Hobbes to say: "In an Epigram or a Sonnet a man may vary his measures, and seek glory from a needless difficulty," except that it lacks the external constraint of the Figured Poem. Here the verse rather seeks freedom from the inner constraint symbolized by the collar, and so escapes all set patterns. The revolt is most open in the short lines or phrases; most covert in the widely spaced rhyme of pine-wine or the reiterated suit-fruit, fruit-dispute; most resolved in the concluding pattern.

He struck God's board or table, and cried, No more for him. He would be at liberty, free from restraint. Must he ever sigh and pine? His lot and life are free; free as the road, as loose as the wind, as liberal as plenty. Must he still be in service to another? Has he no harvest except a thorn to make him bleed, and not restore with heartfelt fruit what he has lost? Surely there was wine before his sighs dried it up: there was grain before his tears drowned it. Is the year lost only to him? Has he no laurels to crown it? No flowers, no gay garlands? all blasted? all wasted? It is not so, my heart: there is fruit, and you have hands. Recover all your sigh-blown time in double pleasures: leave your cold dispute of what is proper, and not. Forsake your constraint (cage), your flimsy bonds, which petty thoughts have made, and made to seem to you stout rope, to force and draw you, and be your law, while you shut your eyes and would not see. Away; take note: I will be free. Call in your death-warning there: tie up your fears (instead of yourself). He that forbears to follow and serve his own need, deserves his burden. But as he raved and grew more fierce and wild at every word (in growing stress of conscience), he thought he heard someone calling, Child! and he replied, My Lord, as he returned to God's suit and service. Thus revolt against conscience generated remorse of conscience.

The Pulley translates Pandora's box of blessings into a Christian myth. God pours upon man strength, beauty, wisdom, honor, and pleasure—all but rest. If he were to give man this jewel, man would adore the gifts and have no incentive to seek God. Thus if goodness does not lead man to God, then weariness or lack of rest may toss or hoist him to God as with a pulley. A verbal pulley is found in the play on "rest" by which the meaning turns to its conclusion.

The Flower images both spiritual and creative life in Herbert. How fresh, how sweet and clean, O Lord, are your returns of grace! even as the flowers in spring; to which the late frosts bring, besides their own mien, tributes of passing. Grief melts away like snow in May, as if such frost did not exist. / Who would have thought my withered heart could have recovered greenness? It had gone quite under ground; as flowers leave to see their mother-root, when they have bloomed; where they together during all the hard weather, dead to the world, keep house unseen. / These are your wonders, Lord of power, killing and quickning, bringing down to hell or up to heaven in an hour; softening the ring of the death-bell to a chime. We say wrongly, this or that is: thy word is all (law), if we could read. Nothing is self-existent; God confers the existence which things have.

O that I were once past changing, fast in thy Paradise, where no flower can wither! Many a spring I shoot up fair enough, aiming at heaven, growing and yearning towards it: nor doth my flower lack a spring shower, my sins and I joining in tears. / But while I grow in a straight line, still bent upwards, as if heaven were mine, thy anger comes, and I droop (sink): What frost compares to that? what frigid pole is not the torrid zone, where all things burn, when thou dost turn, and reveal thy least frown?

And now in age I bud again, after so many deaths I live and write; I once more smell the dew and rain (his senses live again) and relish versing: O my only light (illumination), it cannot be that I am he on whom thy tempests fell all night. / These are thy wonders, Lord of love (not of power), to make us see that we are only flowers that slip away: when we once discover and prove this by experience, thou hast a garden for us in which to abide (not glide). Who would be more than this, swelling through wealth (plenty), forfeit their Paradise by their pride. The Lord of power chastens man so that he may learn the humility through which he is saved by the Lord of love.

Aaron begins by naming the requirements of priestly dress (Exod. xxviii) in the first three lines: holiness of mind, love of light and perfection, harmony of spirit like bells raising the dead to life and rest. / On the contrary, he has profaneness in the head, defects and darkness in the breast, a clamor (not harmony) of passions ringing him dead to a place of no rest. (Yet he continues to be dressed in the same five rhymes throughout the poem.) / But he has another head, heart and breast, another music, making him alive not dead, without whom he could have no rest: in whom he is well dressed. / Christ is his sponsor, his only head, heart and breast, and music, ringing (striking) him even though dead; so that he may rest to the old Adam, and be regenerated in Christ. / Thus holy in head, perfect and light in breast, his doctrine tuned by Christ, (who lives in him while he rests in concord) Come people; Aaron is dressed for the priesthood.

Death attempts to show how Christ changed the image of death. In the Bible the change of resurrection (I Cor. xv) opposes the natural body and the spiritual body, or corruption and incorruption. But Herbert ventures to be more concrete, reducing the natural body to an "uncouth hideous thing," its mouth open but unable to sing, its bones turned to sticks. After this kind of image, "some blood" in the face, though put there by our Saviour's death, is not enough to make death "fair and full of grace," even if less alarming. Herbert's method is less effective in transforming death than in making death teach his body in *Church-monuments*, where death is less of a scarecrow. There both in rhythm and phrasing he brings "death's incessant motion" into being as it reduces the elements to quiet dust. He is less persuasive in taming death by wit, if this be wit, than by showing how "we shall all be changed" to dust.

Both religion and human nature are illuminated by the poetry of George Herbert. Religion is a subject which ought to evoke the deepest analysis of human nature and its needs. How it satisfied or failed to satisfy the whole personality of Herbert thus becomes something larger than a personal solution. T. S. Eliot has said that religious verse is bad poetry when it expresses, not what the author feels, but what he wants to feel. Yet tension between these two may also give power and intensity to religious verse, as when Herbert struggles with his own sincerity.

But religion also brings a metaphysical dimension to human nature. Religion not only introduces a definite scale of values; it moves the drama of human life to a larger stage, gives a different perspective; connects life with philosophy, modifies some emotions, intensifies others. It provides metaphysical connections which introduce strange vistas and surprising insights; it sets up tensions between this world and another world. Although Herbert generally avoids learning in his poetry, his world is the same as that of Donne, and exhibits, though less obtrusively, the same correspondences. Hence A. O. Lovejoy (1936, p. 60) finds the "Great Chain of Being" in his *Providence*. And thus Herbert is more like Donne than appears on the surface.

VI

Richard Crashaw
1613-1649

Crashaw began as a poet in the school of epigram and gradu-
ated in the school of music. In the first the temptation is to
glitter, in the second to indulge the ear; and Crashaw suc-
cumbed to both. More offensive to modern taste, however,
are his excesses in the expression of devotional love, or even
his feeling for the beauty of holiness. Herbert expressed this
aim of the Laudian church in these words: "And all this he
doth, not as out of necessity, or as putting a holiness in the
things, but as desiring to keep the middle way between super-
stition, and slovenliness, and as following the apostle's two
great and admirable rules in things of this nature: the first
whereof is, *Let all things be done decently and in order:* the
second, *Let all things be done to edification,* I Cor. xiv."
These two rules comprise our duty to God and man: "the
first being for the honour of God, the second for the benefit

of our neighbour." Crashaw was more concerned with the first object, and Herbert with the second.

Although Herbert's sensibility was also involved in his religion, it did not require so many avenues of expression as Crashaw's, nor was it so esthetic in nature. In *The British Church* Herbert said, "Beautie in thee takes up her place," and then particularized:

> *A fine aspect in fit aray,*
> *Neither too mean, nor yet too gay,*
> > *Shows who is best.*
> *Outlandish looks may not compare:*
> *For all they either painted are,*
> > *Or else undrest.*

The Roman extreme, to which Crashaw inclined, is the painted lady:

> *She on the hills, which wantonly*
> *Allureth all in hope to be*
> > *By her preferr'd,*
> *Hath kiss'd so long her painted shrines,*
> *That ev'n her face by kissing shines,*
> > *For her reward.*

Crashaw's esthetics were more High-Church than Herbert's, and yet his life was even more ascetic, if not devoid of wit. For Herbert, none the less, the "too mean" or Puritan church is so untidy "that her hair doth lie / About her eares."

Crashaw made his clearest profession of faith in a prefatory poem to Robert Shelford's *Five Pious and Learned Discourses* published in 1635. Although originally entitled "Upon the ensuing Treatises," it was called *On a Treatise of Charity* when its sharp conclusion against the "zealous ones" was deleted. They held the Pope to be Antichrist:

> *Why, 'tis a point of Faith. What e're it be,*
> *I'm sure it is no point of Charitie.*

> *In summe, no longer shall our people hope,*
> *To be a true Protestant, 's but to hate the Pope.*

The point is made again in *An Epitaph upon Mr. Ashton, a Conformable Citizen:*

> *He was a Protestant at home,*
> *Not only in despite of Rome.*
> *He loved his Father; yet his zeal*
> *Tore not off his Mother's veil.*
> *To th' Church he did allow her dress,*
> *True Beauty, to true Holiness.*

Crashaw's devotion to the "immortall maid, Religion," begins with the subject of the first treatise, the restoration of God's house: "Be what thy beauties, not our blots, have made thee," for Shelford would honor God with beauty and decorum.

But charity is the crown of the church:

> *Open this booke, faire Queen, and take thy crown.*
> *These learned leaves shall vindicate to thee*
> *Thy holyest, humblest, handmaid Charitie.*
> *Sh'l dresse thee like thy selfe, set thee on high*
> *Where thou shalt reach all hearts, command each eye.*
> *Lo where I see thy offrings wake, and rise*
> *From the pale dust of that strange sacrifice*
> *Which they themselves were; each one putting on*
> *A majestie that may beseem thy throne.*

By the fair laws of Shelford's firm pen,

> *Gods services no longer shall put on*
> *A sluttishnesse, for pure religion:*
> *No longer shall our Churches frighted stones*
> *Lie scatter'd like the burnt and martyr'd bones*
> *Of dead Devotion . . .*

No more shall one be thought upright because he will not kneel; no more shall disdainful eyes sacrifice scorn rather than

love upon the altar; henceforth the masculine theme of pen
and pulpit shall be

> *to redeem*
> *Vertue to action, that life-feeding flame*
> *That keeps Religion warme: not swell* a name
> *Of faith,* a mountaine word, *made up of aire . . .*

Shelford advanced charity above faith, hope, and knowl-
edge; Christian love was the root of the life of virtue, "the
form of vertues." For him, as for Crashaw, it was the meaning
of devotion: "Devotion, as hath been said, is the soul to
prayer and the rest of Gods service, because it is the daughter
of the mother-vertue Charitie: and this is a cheerfull and free
giving of our selves to Gods service, as his household servants.
Therefore this is the speciall act of religion." And this is why
Crashaw makes charity the crown of religion. For Shelford
"all other graces" without charity are like a body without a
soul. You may have "a bodie as well framed as Leanders and
Hero's," but without a spirit of charity it is dead. He points
to one of Crashaw's examples: "The blessed Marie Magdalene
washt our Saviours feet with her tears, and wiped them drie
again with the hairs of her head. Oh blessed charitie!" For
Shelford and Crashaw the esthetic grace of Herbert's *British
Church* is dead without moral grace, but it may also honor
God and contribute to the beauty of holiness. Even more
than for Herbert, purity of religion did not depend upon a
sluttish rejection of the arts that had been ancillary to reli-
gion. Saint Mary Magdalene is Crashaw's most beguiling fig-
ure of the graces.

The Weeper is Crashaw's hymn to the Magdalen as a con-
tradictory figure of devotion; it becomes an epiphany of her
most celebrated act of Christian love. Her beauty provides
symbols of Christian charity deriving from the use to which
her silver tears and golden hair were put. Even the picture of
"Sorrow's monument," as found in *The Maid's Tragedy* of

Beaumont and Fletcher, is raised to a new level by this queen of sorrow. Her devotion to Christ becomes the central motivation of the poem, but in its later version, as so often in Crashaw's revisions, it is given a more subtle and complicated integration. This is done by developing the "sweet contest" of contrarieties in the Magdalen as a figure of charity, or by making them "close in kind contrarieties," as he discovers more and more of the "wit of love." This was hinted by the epigraph added in 1648. The result is a chain of imagery leading from the Magdalen's eyes to the Lord's feet by way of earthly parallels to heavenly values. Each stanza provides a link with the next, beginning with "still spending, never spent."

Only in the later version does such an excess of devotional wit or feeling as the "walking baths" appear, and that is motivated by the central act of her devotion. This has also supplied the final line of the preceding stanza, though not regarded as a blemish: "The lamb hath dipp't his white foot here." Neither version alters the final destination of the tears: "We goe to meet / A worthy object, our lords Feet." But the alterations and additions or deletions in the later version do improve the cogency or force of the more integrated order leading to this object. Campion's "There is a garden in her face" has some of the imagery of *The Weeper*, but it lacks the complex similarities and contrarieties that produce the Metaphysical integration of later poetry. Even in revising his choral forms Crashaw seeks to tighten the texture of his poem by such means, to weave his similitudes and paradoxes more closely into his poetic structure. Dr. Johnson might call it "Subtlety" and say that he "broke every image into fragments."

In the Laudian movement Crashaw went beyond Herbert, toward Rome. He also went beyond Herbert in devotional life, by way of Little Gidding, the "Arminian Nunnery" of Nicholas Ferrar. Its conventual life is most nearly described

in Crashaw's *Description of a Religious House*. His own life is
described in the Preface to *Steps to the Temple*, probably
written by his friend and fellow poet, Joseph Beaumont, who,
like Milton and perhaps Crashaw himself, had written an
elegy on the death of Edward King: "Reader, we stile his
Sacred Poems, *Stepps to the Temple*, and aptly, for in the
Temple of God, under his wing, he led his life in St. *Maries*
Church neere St. *Peters* Colledge: There he lodged under
Tertullian's roofe of Angels: There he made his nest more
gladly than *David's* Swallow neere the house of God: where
like a primitive Saint, he offered more prayers in the night,
than others usually offer in the day; There he penned these
Poems, *Stepps* for happy soules to climbe heaven by." The
last phrase suggests the more devotional nature of Crashaw's
work; not Herbert's rhymes to catch him "who a sermon
flies," but rather steps to heaven for happy souls. His poetry
reveals opposition to the world rather than struggle with it,
the happiness of a settled faith, or rather of a faith constantly
enlivened by acts of Christian devotion, out of which he
made his poems.

Crashaw's personal asceticism is most vividly witnessed by
Thomas Car in his prefatory "Anagramme" to *Carmen Deo
Nostro*, which was published posthumously in 1652. He de-
scribes Crashaw as dead to the world, his thoughts wholly on
heaven:

> *A very bird of paradice. No care*
> *Had he of earthly trashe. What might suffice*
> *To fitt his soule to heavenly exercise,*
> *Sufficed him . . .*

Although thus assured of mind, he knew the discipline of as-
ceticism, of a self-denial that dedicated the sensuous life to
God. His devotional luxuriance is an expression both of this
self-denial and of honor to God. Carre describes what Cra-
shaw took from the world rather than what he gave to God:

What he might eate or weare he tooke no thought.
His needfull foode he rather found then sought.
He seekes no downes, no sheetes, his bed's still made.
If he can find a chaire or stoole, he's layd,
When day peepes in, he quitts his restlesse rest.
And still, poore soule, before he's up he's dres't.
Thus dying did he live, yet lived to dye
In th'virgines lappe, to whom he did applye
His virgine thoughtes and words, and thence was styld
By foes, the chaplaine of the virgine myld
While yet he lived without: His modestie
Imparted this to some, and they to me.

Crashaw died in the shrine of the Virgin at Loreto, and ani-
mus against his strictness is reflected in the last lines. Such
tension between heaven and earth is not reflected in his po-
etry; it appears as opposition. In his poetic devotion he ren-
ders unto God the things that are Caesar's, by indulgence
rather than denial. Both in his own asceticism and in the Lau-
dian beauty of holiness the sensuous world is sacrificed to
spiritual ends.

The Preface to *Steps to the Temple* in 1646 had already
separated Crashaw from his contemporaries: "Madrigall fel-
lowes, whose onely businesse in verse, is to rime a poore six-
penny soule, a Subburb sinner into hell;—May such arrogant
pretenders to Poetry vanish, with their prodigious issue of
tumorous heats and flashes of their adulterate braines . . ."
Crashaw crowned his qualifications with "his rare moderation
in diet (almost Lessian temperance), hee never created a
Muse out of distempers, nor (with our Canary scribblers)
cast any strange mists of surfets before the Intelectuall beames
of his mind or memory . . ." Even his *"Delights of the
Muses,* (though of a more humane mixture) are as sweet as
they are innocent." Altogether, "hee made his skill in Poetry,
Musicke, Drawing, Limming, graving, (exercises of his curi-
ous invention and sudden fancy) to bee but his subservient
recreations to vacant houres, not the grand businesse of his

soule." Thus we need not wonder if his curious invention was not always subservient to the grand business of his soul. Like Donne, he knew the temptation "to vent wit," in which his senses found their greatest temptation.

A shorter form of *Wishes to his (supposed) Mistress* was first published in the popular anthology *Witt's Recreations* in 1641. It is often regarded as lacking in general design, but in its final form it is not in fact amorphous. Rather it is ordered in this hypothetical fashion: "Whoever, wherever, she may be, until Fate produces her, incarnates this Platonic Idea, his Wishes must meet her, bespeak her, and kiss her: thus he wishes her Beauty of a certain kind; as of Face and Cheek; Looks that are best naked; special Eyes and Tresses; an obedient Heart; then Eyes in love, followed by Smiles, Blushes, Joys, Fears, Tears of love; then Days and Nights without regret; Life that can welcome its end; sweet talk like Sidney's, sunshine hours, delights that brighten and wing time; all the gifts of Nature that put art and ornament to shame; her flattery to be picture and poesy, her counsel her own virtue: he wishes her so much worth that she may be poor in wishes; he cannot wish more. Now if Time knows a Lady crowned by his wishes, who can claim his hopes as her trophy, who dares to be his Wishes, it is She. In her he can reveal the Character of his wishes. May she enjoy that which her merit deserves but Modesty denies. Such worth shall fix his wishes and end them in kisses. Let her full Glory surpass his fancies; let her be his fiction but her reality." The conclusion matches and exceeds the conditions of the beginning by realizing the portrait of the middle section and surpassing it. His *Wishes*, however, are countered by his epigram on marriage:

> *I would be married, but I'd have no Wife,*
> *I would be married to a single Life.*

Clearly in the mode of Donne is *Love's Horoscope*. By more complex argument it develops similar conclusions out of opposite propositions. The final paradoxes or alternatives conclude that his love can only live in her. Likeness in verse rhetoric ultimately triumphs over diversity in argument. A love related to virtue is born in his heart, which consults the omen of the Heavens to learn "If poor Love shall live or die." / But is that the way to find out? A beautiful face has brought a new astrology to determine his fortune. Whatever the Heavens may say, " 'Tis in the mercy of her eye, If poor Love shall live or die." / If her eye is adverse, no matter how favorable the Heavens may be, "Beauty frowns, and Love must die." / But if her aspect is beneficent, no matter how inauspicious the Heavens may be, "Beauty smiles, and Love shall live." / And if love shall live, where but in her eye, ear, breast, or breath can he hide Love from Death? Anywhere but in her, "Love shall die, although he live." / Or if love shall die, where but in her eye, ear, breath, or breast can he build Love's funeral nest? While thus entombed, "Love shall live, although he die." The horoscope of heaven is thus defeated by the horoscope of love.

Crashaw's poetry seldom lets us forget that he, like Donne, was proficient in the rhetoric of the epigram. In his *Divine Epigrams* none is more striking than that on Matthew 27, 12: "And when he was accused of the chief priests and elders, he answered nothing." Christ's refusal to defend himself evoked this response from Crashaw:

> *O Mighty Nothing! unto thee,*
> *Nothing, we owe all things that be;*
> *God spake once when He all things made,*
> *He saved all when He Nothing said.*
> *The world was made of Nothing then;*
> *'Tis made by Nothing now again.*

Thus Nothing made and saved everything, and became a magical concept for Crashaw.

Among the poetic modes affected by the epigram in his day

was the elegy, whether in the style of Jonson or in the style of Donne. In the unemphatic manner of Jonson we find Crashaw writing an elegy *Upon the Death of a Gentleman*, with touches here and there of his own more vivid phrasing. He begins in a chiding tone: "Faithless and foolish Mortality! who will ever trust you? That thus deceive us in our best hopes. What an account (reckoning) have you made of the hopes we put in him? Instead of a life lengthened by volumes, a line or two to declare him dead. Instead of the laurel in verse, the sullen cypress of the hearse. Instead of a head crowned with silver, a dirty pillow in Death's bed. Thus much dust is a sad return for so dear, so deep a trust! Now although the blow that snatcht him away stopped the mouth of Eloquence, although she be dumb ever since his death, unused to speak except in his breath, yet if at least she does not deny the sad language (tears) of our eyes, we are contented: for no language is more fluent than this. Nothing declares our grief so well as to say nothing. Come then, tell (reckon) thy mind in tears, whoever you are that owe (have to pay) a name to misery: eyes are vocal, tears have tongues, and there are words not made by lungs; (in more Crashavian idiom)

> *Sententious showers, O let them fall,*
> *Their cadence is rhetorical.*

For here is a theme that can drink all your watery eloquence; Weep then, only let us say this much: He is dead; and weep the rest."

The epigram on "Nothing" is not forgotten here; but the persistence of ambiguity, especially on reckoning, the absence of mythology, and the more vivid imagery of death are not Jonsonian. The language of tears is almost a trademark of Crashaw. From "nothing" as a mode of expressing grief, Crashaw turns to "nothing" as an epitome of mortality in *Death's Lecture at the Funeral of a Young Gentleman*. Although an

early poem, formerly *Upon Mr. Staninough's Death*, it never
lost its place in Crashaw's collections.

It is an elegy in the mode of Donne rather than of Jonson,
but as Crashaw does it: "Dear remains of a displaced soul,
whose lack makes many a note-paper put on the black edge of
mourning! O wait a while, before you draw in your head, and
wind your sheet up tight in your cold bed. Wait but a little
while, until I call an assembly worthy of your funeral. Then
come Youth, Beauty, and Blood, all the soft powers, whose
silken flatteries swell a few infatuated hours into a false eter-
nity. Come man, exaggerated Nothing! know your span
(grasp); take your own measure here: down, down, and bow
before your imagined self; you huge emptiness! contract
your bulk (self); and shrink all your wild circle (circuit) to a
point. O sink lower and lower still; until your thin size bid
Heaven to look on you with narrowed eyes (closely). Lesser
and lesser yet; until you begin to show a face, fit to reveal
your kinship, your proximity to Nothing. Proud looks, and
lofty eyelids, here put on your true aspect; here, gallant la-
dies! this impartial mirror shows you your true face through
all your painting. These death-sealed lips are they that dare
give the lie to the loud boasts of poor Mortality; these cur-
tained windows, this withdrawn eye out-stares the lids of
open-eyed (bold-faced) Tyranny: This posture is the brave
one; this that lies this low, thus stands up (methinks), and
defies the World. All-daring dust and ashes! of all interpreters
only you see Nature truthfully." The paradox of death is that
it alone dares to defy the World and tell the truth. In this
poem we finally perceive that the eyes of the dead are the
center of the circle or imagery described by this lecture.

Cowley entered Trinity College in Cambridge University
about the time Crashaw moved from Pembroke to Peter-
house. Sometime thereafter, time enough to become a "sweet
friend," Crashaw wrote *Upon two green Apricots sent to
Cowley by Sir Crashaw*, and presumably accompanied it with

two poetic apricots of the alleged variety. This poem is obviously a compliment to Cowley's precocious *Poetical Blossoms*, then in its third edition, and Crashaw's use of the title to which he was privileged by his B.A. may have been intended to emphasize the disparity between their respective fruits. At any rate, the light wit of this poem, from a dedicated man, makes a pleasant contrast to Milton's complaint about his lack of blossom on his twenty-third birthday. Moreover, the theme of the frustrated poet had entered into Crashaw's lament *Upon the Death of a Gentleman*.

If Crashaw regards his apricots as "Time's tardy truants," like Milton's "bud or blossom," he apologizes that despite all he could do they

> *Yet are scarce ripe enough at best to show*
> *The red, but of the blush to thee they owe.*

Apparently, even this year his fruit is late:

> *O had my wishes,*
> *And the dear merits of your Muse, their due,*
> *The year had found some fruit early as you;*
> *Ripe as those rich composures Time computes*
> *Blossoms, but our blest taste confesses fruits.*

Yet his wit can at least turn a compliment:

> *'Twas only Paradise, 'tis only thou,*
> *Whose fruit and blossoms both bless the same bough.*

The tardiness of his apricots he finally blames on his own character, unlike Milton, and turns it into a compliment to his rival:

> *Fain would I chide their slowness, but in their*
> *Defects I draw mine own dull character.*
> *Take them, and me in them acknowledging*
> *How much my Summer waits upon thy Spring.*

Cowley eventually returned the compliment in one of his most moving poems.

Their competition, however, produced a poetic debate. "On Hope, By way of Question and Answer, betweene A. Cowley and R. Crashaw," was published in *Steps to the Temple* in 1646, and Cowley's poem "Against Hope" appeared in *The Mistresse* in 1647. Crashaw followed the model set by Cowley in verse, theme, and imagery, improving the imitation in his later version. In style it is rather Senecan, an ejaculatory mode; quick, discontinuous phrases adumbrating a central idea or conceit. Cowley begins with Hope's relation to Fate: "Hope is ruined by realization, ceases to exist no matter what the outcome, regardless of the dilemma of Fate. It is a vain shadow that vanishes at midday and full night. The Fates cannot crown the fugitive. If things are judged by their ends, hope is the most hopeless thing of all."

To this Crashaw replies: "Dear Hope, the dowry of Earth, and the debt of Heaven, the entity of things not yet realized. Most rarefied but surest being! Thou by whom our Nothing has a determination. Fair cloud of fire [combining the two guides of Exodus 13, 21], both shade and light, whether in death or night. Against such abilities, the Fates cannot find the power to hurt you. From you their thin dilemma with its blunt horns shrinks, like the dying Moon at the healthy morn." In the later version Crashaw changed the "Faire cloud" lines to "Substantial shade! whose sweet alloy [composition] blends both the noons of night and day," thus bringing his answer closer to Cowley's lines.

Cowley then turns to Hope's relation to our estate in life: "Hope, you bold taster of delight, instead of tasting, you devour it completely. You bring us an estate, but leave us poor, by encumbering it with earlier bequests. The joys that we should wed intact, come like deflowered virgins to our bed. Good fortunes are imported without gain, because such large duty is paid to you. For joy, like Wine, tastes better when kept tight: if exposed to the air beforehand, its spirits waste."

To which Crashaw actually replies in two stanzas. First: "Thou art [later: Rich hope!] Love's legacy under lock of Faith, who is the keeper of our growing stock. Our Crownlands [inheritance] lie above, yet each meal [provided by our steward] brings a portion befitting the sons of kings. Nor will the virgin-joys we wed, come less unbroken to our bed, because you thus steal down a distant kiss from the bridal cheek of Bliss. Hope's chaste kiss no more wrongs Joy's maidenhead than spousal ceremonies prejudice the marriage-bed." / Second: "Fair Hope! our earlier Heaven! by you young time is taster to Eternity: your generous wine grows strong with age, not sour; nor need we kill your fruit in order to smell your flower. Your golden head never hangs down, until it falls in the lap of Love's full noon and dies. Oh no, it melts away as does the dawn into the day: As lumps of sugar lose themselves, and twine their subtle essence with the soul of wine."

Next Cowley turns to Hope's relation to Fortune: "Hope, the cheating lottery of Fortune, where, for one prize, there are a hundred blanks. Foolish archer, Hope! who takes aim so far that your arrows are still either short or wide [of the mark]. Your empty cloud deceives the eye itself with shapes that our own fancy gives: A cloud, which now appears gilt and painted, but soon must drop in tears. When your false beams prevail over Reason's light, we sail by *ignes fatui*, not North stars."

To which Crashaw responds: "Fortune, alas, wars above the world's law: Hope spurns the zodiacal signs of plotting stars. Her keel does not cut the waves [Cowley said "sail"], where our winds stir, and Fate's whole Lottery is one blank to her. Her rays and she fly far above, and search the fields of light and love. Sweet Hope! kind cheat! fair fallacy! because of you we are not where or what we are, but what and where we would be: thus you are our absent presence and our future now." Thus Hope is not our fortune, but our refuge.

Finally, Cowley turns to the motivation of Hope: "Brother of Fear! more gaily clad, the merrier Fool of the two, yet quite as mad. Father of Repentance! Child of foolish desire, that blows the Chymick's and the Lover's fire, still leading them unconsciously on, with the strange witchcraft of by and by. Because of you the one doth pursue changing Nature through her endless labyrinths, and the other chases woman, while she goes more ways and turns than hunted Nature knows."

To this motivation Crashaw retorts: "Sister of Faith! Nurse of fair desire! Fear's Antidote! a wise and well-regulated fire, tempered betwixt cold despair and torrid joy: acting ruler [Queen Regent] in young Love's minority. Though the vext Chymick vainly chases his fugitive gold through all her faces [phases], and Love's more fierce and fruitless fires assay [and essay] one face more fugitive than all those; true Hope is a glorious huntress, and her chase the God of Nature in the field of Grace." True Hope leads through both fields to God. Crashaw might persuade one here that he had known the more furious and fruitless fire.

Perhaps none of the Metaphysical Poets understood the rhetoric of contrariety better than Crashaw. His epigrams exhibit his talent, and a stanza of *The Weeper* expresses the peculiar appeal of this rhetoric:

> *O sweet contest; of woes*
> *With loves, of teares with smiles disputing!*
> *O fair and friendly foes,*
> *Each other kissing and confuting!*
> *While rain and sunshine, cheekes and eyes*
> *Close in kind contrarietyes.*

When Crashaw wrote *A Hymne of the Nativity, sung by the Shepheards*, he did not fully realize this principle, but in the version of 1652 it is completely worked out. Aside from his

concession to the choral form in the shape of choric repeti-
tions, his alterations result in a tighter and stronger develop-
ment of his theme.

First in importance is his deletion of a stanza from the Full
Chorus:

> *Shee sings thy Teares asleepe, and dips*
> *Her Kisses in thy weeping Eye,*
> *Shee spreads the red leaves of thy Lips,*
> *That in their Buds yet blushing lye.*
> *Shee 'gainst those Mother-Diamonds tryes*
> *The points of her young Eagles Eyes.*

These lines not only disperse the attention of the shepherds
from the object of their welcome, but distract and dissipate
the effect of the imagery related to this object. The basic
function of the Virgin is found in the sweet consent of con-
trarieties. But their "sweet contest" is significantly advanced
by the addition of these two stanzas:

> *Poor world (said I), what wilt thou do*
> *To entertain this starry Stranger?*
> *Is this the best thou canst bestow?*
> *A cold, and not too cleanly, manger?*
> *Contend, ye powers of Heaven and Earth,*
> *To fit a bed for this huge birth.*
>
> *Proud world, said I, cease your contest,*
> *And let the mighty Babe alone.*
> *The phoenix builds the phoenix' nest,*
> *Love's architecture is his own.*
> *The Babe whose birth embraves this morn,*
> *Made his own bed ere he was born.*

The contention of heaven and earth centers the poem more
subtly in the meaning of the Nativity and the imagery of its
circumstances. The second stanza asserts the divine answer to

this contention, but does not forestall its development. Both stanzas help Crashaw to organize more closely and emphasize more dramatically the natural and supernatural elements involved in the event. The Virgin resolves this contention, but Crashaw's alterations all contribute to a more integrated vision, which also improves the ironic contrast of his conclusion. The lack of focus in the first version, which begins by seeing "Dayes King deposed by Nights Queene," is removed in the final version by "love's Noon in Nature's night," which motivates the more integrated structure.

The final version begins with a paradoxical event: the shepherds have seen "Love's noon in Nature's night." They sing their hymn to wake the sun, to tell him where they have been and what they have seen, in paradoxes that define the king of heaven as opposed to the king of earth, the supernatural sun versus the natural sun. In gloomy night they saw a new day, winter turned to spring, their new sun in his balmy nest. Can the world provide no better than "A cold and not too cleanly manger"? But "Love's architecture is his own," and made his bed before he was born. Yet powers of heaven and earth contend to make him a bed. Nature offers snow: "Your fleece is white, but 'tis too cold." Heaven offers the rosy fleece of fiery Seraphim [of love]: "but are you sure / Your down so warm, will pass for pure?" (In Scripture white and red stand for purity and impurity.) How resolve the conflicting offers of earth and heaven? Where can the royal child repose his head? Only between the Virgin's breasts: "no way but so, / Not to lie cold, yet sleep in snow." Now the stanza of the "balmy nest," which summarized their "blest sight," is repeated with more realization of its meaning.

Then the full chorus of shepherds begins its welcome by recapitulating the paradoxes of this meaning, and welcomes the new king, not to the things that are Caesar's, but to the union of heaven and earth in the Virgin mother. And continues its welcome, not to the "gay flies" of earthly courts, whose God was Beelzebub, but to the poor shepherds themselves, who will bring their gifts

> *To thee, dread lamb! whose love must keep*
> *The shepherds, more than they the sheep.*

Until they feel the new love enough to repeat the phoenix motif:

> *Till burnt at last in fire of Thy fair eyes,*
> *Ourselves become our own best Sacrifice.*

The propriety of the imagery to shepherds is notable throughout.

A Hymne for the Epiphanie, Sung as by the three Kings shows how Crashaw could transform the imagery of the rival suns, or natural and supernatural light, into a truly metaphysical poem by using the *via negativa* of Dionysius the Areopagite, St. Paul's disciple. In the negative way to God the initiate "must leave behind all things both in the sensible and in the intelligible world, till he enters into the darkness of nescience that is truly mystical," a nothingness beyond sense and reason. Hence darkness becomes the way to true light in the poem, and the natural sun pays homage to the supernatural sun, particularly in the eclipse at the crucifixion, which converted Dionysius and is introduced by prophecy. Man, not the sun, is made responsible for sun worship, which becomes a cause of grief to the sun until the eclipse, when "The shutting of his eye shall open theirs." The three kings are delegates of the East bringing tribute to the new light or Sun, marking the end of the false worship that took the sun as a source rather than a symbol of light, and making the sun a guide to the new night through the eclipse that prefigures the mystical dark night of the soul.

In one way this darkness is Crashaw's supreme development of the concept of "nothing"; in another it produces his most brilliant unions of the Latin abstract word and the concrete word of the senses. For example:

> *Farewell, the world's false light!*
> *Farewell, the white*
> *Egypt! a long farewell to thee,*
> *Bright Idol, black Idolatry:*
> *The dire face of inferior Darkness, kist*
> *And courted in the pompous mask of a more specious mist.*

His idiom combines rather than rejects, as required, the sensible and intelligible worlds; fuses that which can be apprehended by the senses and that which can be apprehended only by the intellect; or else dissipates the concrete into the abstract:

> *Forcing his sometimes eclips'd face to be*
> *A long deliquium to the light of Thee.*

Since Crashaw's religious feeling is commonly expressed in a rapture of the senses, often unduly concrete, this more dissolved expression is a way of blurring the distinction between the concrete and the abstract, or these two worlds. The Latinism itself brings cadence and diffused connotation, and the metaphysical idea commonly entered poetry through the Latin abstract word.

Crashaw's *Hymn to the Name above Every Name*, despite its invocation of "more noble Architects of Intellectual Noise," is a good example of devotion as a rapture of the senses, in which the "name" is made "sweet" to as many senses as possible. The impulse to musical release prompts him to

> *traverse round*
> *The airy shop of soul-appeasing sound:*

> *And beat a summons in the same*
> > *All-sovereign name,*
> *To warn each several kind*
> *And shape of sweetness . . .*

Presently this mode becomes more imagistic:

> *And in the wealth of one rich word, proclaim*
> *New similes to Nature. May it be no wrong,*
> *Blest Heavens, to you and your superior song,*
> *That we, dark sons of dust and sorrow,*
> > *A while dare borrow*
> *The name of your delights and our desires,*
> *And fit it to so far inferior lyres.*

And finally reaches this excess in martyrdom:

> > *Fair, purple doors, of Love's devising;*
> *The ruby windows which enrich'd the East*
> *Of Thy so oft repeated rising!*
> *Each wound of theirs was Thy new morning,*
> *And re-enthroned thee in thy rosy nest,*
> *With blush of thine own blood thy day adorning:*
> *It was the wit of Love o'erflow'd the bounds*
> *Of Wrath, and made Thee way through all those wounds.*

In *The Weeper,* too, the "wit of love" carried Crashaw into extravagance. But here his rhapsody took one of the irregular ode forms that marked his maturity. His dithyramb reaches its greatest intensity, however, in the personal litany added to *The Flaming Heart* in 1652, beginning "O sweet incendiary!" and concluding in the vocabulary of mysticism with which Sir Thomas Browne ends his *Urn Burial.*

A Hymn to Sainte Teresa is one of Crashaw's finest achievements in a favorite meter. He uses the octosyllabic couplet with "the sense variously drawn out from one Verse into another," so that it often sinks the rhyme into a periodic rhythm before returning to the couplet emphasis. Thus he achieves a more undulating movement, broken for rhetorical effect, by the reassertion of couplet point. It is superbly adapted to his narrative vehicle for an exemplum or parable.

Saint Teresa is for Crashaw another figure of love, the basic Christian virtue; her life gave him a paradigm of its meaning. If love ends with marriage to the Lamb (Revelation 19), Teresa goes beyond the Song of Solomon (8, 6), "for love is strong as death," to show that it is stronger. The poem begins by addressing itself to prove this power by the example of Teresa:

> *Love, thou art absolute sole lord*
> *Of life and death. To prove the word,*
> *We'll now appeal to none of all*
> *Those thy old soldiers, great and tall,*
> *Ripe men of martyrdom, that could reach down*
> *With strong arms their triumphant crown.*

In developing the power of love by this contrast of soldier martyrs with a child—how love gives courage to the weakest —his emphasis on her weakness explains his use of the "mild and milky" phrase, just as the use of "reach down" as both to reach up and take down emphasizes the same disparity.

Although Teresa does not understand the relation of love and death, she has a sense that one gives value to the other, and feels capable of both. Although physically she is not ready for martyrdom, she may challenge the Song of Solomon:

> *Yet has she'a heart dares hope to prove*
> *How much less strong is Death than Love.*

For it is love, not maturity, that makes "the martyr, or the man." Love yearns to fulfil itself in death, and this is why she longs for martyrdom, which is not to be found at home; and why she wants to go to the Moors, among whom she may die for Christ. So farewell to the world and its pleasures, which she regards as toys.

But God intends her for a milder martyrdom—to prove that love is also "absolute sole lord of life." Hence she shall become Love's victim, not the Moors',

> *and must die*
> *A death more mystical and high:*
> *Into Love's arms thou shalt let fall*
> *A still-surviving funeral.*

Henceforth she shall be alive only to divine love, and shall continue to experience its martyrdom, its death in life, until

> *these thy deaths, so numerous,*
> *Shall all at last die into one,*

and exhale her to Heaven in a resolving sigh. There she will be greeted by Angels, her good works, her redeemed sufferings, and "shall leave writ / Love's noble history," as the inspiration of others. There she will see those who have been saved by her work, and with them about her will be married to the Lamb:

> *put on (He'll say), put on*
> *(My rosy love) that thy rich zone*
> *Sparkling with the sacred flames*
> *Of thousand souls, whose happy names*
> *Heaven keeps upon thy score (thy bright*
> *Life brought them first to kiss the light*
> *That kindled them to stars) . . .*

And wheresoever her Lord shall set his white steps, she will walk with him those ways of light,

> *Which who in death would live to see,*
> *Must learn in life to die like thee.*

Thus one may learn the ultimate meaning of love, and let fall another "still-surviving funeral." Crashaw's rhetoric does not confuse sacred and profane love any more than the Bible; nor is it effeminate to believe that love "can make the martyr, or the man."

If he seems to invite this charge upon occasion, he is misinterpreted upon other occasions. A case in point is the early ode that is finally called *Prayer*. Originally it was *On a prayer booke sent to Mrs. M. R.*, later a Young Gentlewoman. This is apt to be misinterpreted when detached from a later companion piece "To the Same Party. Counsel concerning her Choice." The persuasion in *Prayer* must not be confused with that sometimes found implicit in the *Hymn to Saint Teresa*, which consummates the marriage of the soul as found in Revelation. This persuasion to God is motivated by and opposed to a rival love on the part of the young gentlewoman, which is made clear by the *Counsel* added in 1652. There Crashaw speaks as a suitor, "Not for myself, alas! but for my dearer Lord." In arguing for "a braver love," he discovers God's stratagem to win her heart:

> *It was His heavenly art*
> *Kindly to cross you*
> *In your mistaken love . . .*

Thus deceived by sublunary love,

> *Your first choice fails; O when you choose agen*
> *May it not be amongst the sons of men!*

This is the situation that explains Crashaw's approach in *Prayer*, not his unconscious confusion of sacred and profane love. In the first version it was suggested by an odd turn on the Prayer Book, subsequently deleted:

> *(Fear it not, sweet,*
> *It is no hypocrite),*
> *Much larger in itself than in its look.*

In amplifying the value of the Prayer Book he does not disdain an old scholastic gambit:

> *It is in one choice handful, Heaven; and all*
> *Heaven's royal host; encamp'd thus small*
> *To prove that true, Schools use to tell,*
> *Ten thousand angels in one point can dwell.*

It is a great defense, but its use requires pure hands and a steady heart: "Dear soul, be strong, / Mercy will come ere long."

> *But if the noble Bridegroom, when he come,*
> *Shall find the loitering heart from home;*
> > *Leaving her chaste abode*
> > *To gad abroad*
> *Among the gay mates of the god of flies;*
> *To take her pleasure, and to play*
> *And keep the devil's holiday;*
> *To dance ith' sunshine of some smiling*
> > *But beguiling*
> *Spheres of sweet and sugar'd lies,*
> > *Some slippery pair*
> *Of false, perhaps as fair,*
> *Flattering but forswearing eyes;*

then no doubt some other heart will be favored with the

> *Amorous languishments, luminous trances;*
> *Sights which are not seen with eyes;*
> *Spiritual and soul-piercing glances,*
> *Whose pure and subtle lightning flies*
> *Home to the heart, and sets the house on fire*
> *And melts it down in sweet desire . . .*

The rival sensuousness of mystical love is dissipated into such abstractions as "Delicious deaths, soft exhalations / Of soul; dear and divine annihilations," which this love seemed to inspire. And all this rivalry of the senses is intended to justify the conclusion:

> *Happy proof! she shall discover*
> *What joy, what bliss,*
> *How many heavens at once it is*
> *To have her God become her Lover.*

But this apparent confusion or lapse of taste is a worldly strategy employed against a victim of sublunary love, for whom Crashaw was concerned enough to write two poems. And this is not the only evidence that he felt eyes could be as treacherous as they were faithful in the Magdalen, but he never made them quite so insidious, even in rhythm, as here.

In a later edition of *Witt's Recreations*, Crashaw's rather courtly poem *On Mr. G. Herberts booke intituled the Temple of Sacred Poems, sent to a Gentlewoman*, is used to introduce Henry Vaughan's *Silex Scintillans* to the reader:

> *There plumes from Angels wings, he'l lend thee,*
> *Which every day to Heaven will send thee.*

Aside from this use of Herbert, the chief sign of indebtedness in Crashaw is *Charitas Nimia, or the Dear Bargain*. No doubt it was inspired by the Psalmist's question (8, 4), "What is man, that thou art mindful of him?" But it ends in the more personal vein of Herbert, saying in effect, "What am I, that thou art mindful of me?" The simpler, more homely idiom of Herbert opens the poem, but soon finds itself in competition with the more splendid idiom of Crashaw. The dear bargain becomes witty in the second stanza:

> *Love is too kind, I see; and can*
> *Make but a simple merchant man.*
> *'Twas for such sorry merchandise*
> *Bold painters have put out his eyes.*

Love can make only a foolish businessman, and because of such poor bargaining, bold painters have made him blind. But soon the worms and flies of the poem are lost in a flaming imagery of light. And finally, "froward dust" and "peevish clay" acquire a personal voice which concludes with a petition:

> *O my Saviour, make me see*
> *How dearly thou hast paid for me;*
> *That lost again, my life may prove,*
> *As then in death, so now in love.*

Or make me realize the dearness of the bargain, so that my life, though lost again, may prove as worthy now in love as then in death. This is the inflection of Herbert in the voice of Crashaw.

The poetry of Crashaw might persuade one that he did not so much renounce "That not impossible She" as become her religious suitor. For his *Carmen Deo Nostro* contained a new persuasion to a gentlewoman, *To the Noblest and Best of Ladies, the Countess of Denbigh*, with an emblem of a heart drawn by him. Another, much altered, version was called *A Letter to the Countess of Denbigh* and published separately in 1653.

In his *Letter* love drops the quiver of darts and arrows for the semblance of Christ, and finds its pattern and pace in the course of nature. In fact, nature puts on a semblance closer to that of Solomon's Song, as Christ comes "Lightly as a lambent flame, / Leaping upon the hills," after the manner of the Song. But in neither vein of imagery do we find the sensuousness of the earlier Crashaw; indeed, the abstract vocabulary of the Metaphysical vein produces the most striking effects in both versions. Nothing in the poem is better than the opening definition of irresolution:

> *What heaven-entreated Heart is this,*
> *Stands trembling at the gate of bliss?*

> *Holds fast the door, yet dares not venture*
> *Fairly to open it, and enter;*
> *Whose Definition is a doubt*
> *Twixt life and death, twixt in and out.*

Or the passage that follows immediately in the later version, but in both exhibits the harmony of sound and symmetry peculiar to Crashaw's octosyllabic couplets:

> *Ah linger not, loved soul! a slow*
> *And late consent was a long no,*
> *Who grants at last, long time tried*
> *And did his best to have denied:*
> *What magic bolts, what mystic bars,*
> *Maintain the will in these strange wars!*

The heart at the gate of bliss is immobilized by a state of mind that cannot be defined without abstractions or wholly resolved within them. Delay could make a positive answer equivalent to a negative answer, if one tried and did his best to deny for a long time. What secret or hidden bolts and bars support the Will in these hidden wars? This question sends one back to the verse of the emblem, to which the first version of the poem keeps much closer than the second:

Non Vi

> *'Tis not the work of force but skill*
> *To find the way into man's will.*
> *'Tis love alone can hearts unlock.*
> *Who knowes the* Word, *he needs not knock.*

VII
Abraham Cowley
1618-1667

Cowley, already the precocious author of *Poetical Blossoms* when Crashaw sent him *Two Green Apricots*, was soon to declare his ambition to be Love's Columbus and the Muse's Hannibal. But even sooner the world learned from Crashaw's *Steps to the Temple*, as if prophetically, that Cowley was "Against Hope." His attempt to scale the Alps of religious epic ended in the unfinished *Davideis*, where, Dr. Johnson said, "as in all Cowley's works, we find wit and learning unprofitably squandered." Addison not only found wit out of place in the epic, but "mixt Wit" more abundant in Cowley "than in any Author that ever wrote." In this wit the resemblance is partly in the ideas and partly in the words, or dependent upon ambiguity, like the pun. Cowley's showcase of wit is *The Mistress*, his discovery of a New World of love, which Dr. Johnson found without "seduction" but Cowley a later cause for apology.

We shall not pursue Cowley's pioneering, however, in kinds of poetry like the Anacreontics or Pindarics, but shall limit ourselves to the kinds that relate him to the Metaphysical Poets. Dr. Johnson conceded that "where scholastick speculation can be properly admitted," as in Cowley's *Against Hope*, "their copiousness and acuteness may justly be admired." But the extreme example of this indulgence is found in his Pindarique Ode on *Life and Fame*, which points toward Rochester's *Upon Nothing*. And Johnson was prepared to admire the great variety of Cowley's achievement, though he thought him almost the last of the Metaphysical Poets rather than the first of the Neo-Classical. Yet no poet yearned more passionately to make the Age to come his own, or possessed it more immediately than Cowley.

The Motto is Cowley's answer to the desire that motivates Browne's *Urn Burial:* "What shall I do to be for ever known?" For any answer, he realizes, "Out of my self it must be strook." Now hope leads him on: "Yet I must on"; and cut through all that would stop "the Muses Hannibal." Books or learning will teach him how to conquer oblivion, by the example of Aristotle, Cicero, and Virgil:

> *Tell me, ye mighty Three, what shall I do*
> *To be like one of you.*

As he rejects all the flattering vanities that might distract him, he names one with which he flirted off and on:

> *Hence Love himself, that Tyrant of my days,*
> *Which intercepts my coming praise.*

This rejection probably led him to append *The Motto* to *The Mistress* as a last word. Certainly this Tyrant figured importantly in the poetic fortunes of Cowley.

Since the Muse had to be Cowley's way to fame—with others, "Their Mothers Labour, not their own"—he was concerned with the nature of Wit, and this concern was connected with the subject of his most famous elegy. *On the Death of Mr. William Hervey* reflects the same interests as *The Motto*, as well as the Cambridge days recalled in the essay *Of My self*, but all overwhelmed by a great loss. Here Cowley is no less committed to higher things than Milton in *Lycidas*, but his personal feeling has proved more eloquent to many readers. It begins in the vein of Donne's prose "for whom the bell tolls":

> *It was a dismal, and a fearful night,*
> *Scarce could the Morn drive on th'unwilling Light,*
> *When Sleep, Deaths Image, left my troubled brest,*
>   *By something liker Death possest.*
> *My eyes with Tears did uncommanded flow,*
>   *And on my Soul hung the dull weight*
>   *Of some Intolerable Fate.*
> *What Bell was that? Ah me! Too much I know.*

Henceforth Cambridge should be "Dark as the Grave" and "Mute as the Grave." Hervey's relation to Cowley's Muse is the subject of a special stanza both here and in the *Ode: Of Wit.*

> *To him my Muse made haste with every strain*
> *Whilst it was new, and warm yet from the Brain.*
> *He lov'd my worthless Rhimes, and like a Friend*
>   *Would find out something to commend.*
> *Hence now, my Muse, thou canst not me delight;*
>   *Be this my latest verse*
>   *With which I now adorn his Herse,*
> *And this my Grief, without thy help shall write.*

This more natural eloquence of grief has been preferred to that of the "uncouth" Muse of *Lycidas*. But Dr. Johnson was distressed by the figure with which Cowley now rejects the possible honor of the Bays:

> *Condemn it to the Fire, and joy to hear*
>   *It rage and crackle there.*
> *Instead of Bays, crown with sad Cypress me . . .*

The realism with which the Bays burn, however, emphasizes the nature of Cowley's grief and its sacrifice of honor.

The last stanza of his *Ode: Of Wit* finally relates its subject to the Wit that is saluted in his elegy on Hervey. Although the definition of wit was a common preoccupation of this time, it had a special importance to one who hoped to make his name by poetry. Whatever the value of his Ode to creation, its ideas were not soon forgotten as criticism. Cowley's method is that which was applied to subjects that elude definition, namely, scholastic definition by negatives. It has the advantage here of branding those things which cannot be regarded as wit. After the address to Hervey, we learn that wit loves variety; that wit is deceptive; that it is not levity, nor florid talk; nor the numbers of verse; nor ornament; nor puns, anagrams, acrostics, or bawdry; nor strong lines, hyperbole, Sentences, or odd similitudes; but variety united without discord or confusion, both animated and controlled. Lastly we are assured that if Hervey will answer the initial question, that will define Wit.

Concern with Wit, both as subject and as means, is also found in *An Answer to a Copy of Verses sent me to Jersey*. Wit helps to characterize the Island:

> *Alas, to bring your Tropes and Figures here,*
> *Strange as to bring Camels and Ele'phants were.*
> *And Metaphor is so unknown a thing,*
> *'Twould need the Preface of, God save the King.*
> *Yet this I'll say for th'honor of the place,*
> *That by Gods extraordinary Grace*
> *(Which shows the people'have judgment, if not Wit)*

The land is undefil'd with Clinches yet.
. . . . And so far
From th' Actual Sin of Bombast too they are,
(That other Crying Sin o'th' English Muse)
That even Satan himself can accuse
None here (no not so much as the Divines)
For th' Motus primò primi to Strong Lines.

Of the latter sin Dr. Donne had been accused and he was not innocent of the former. Both of these Cowley poems show what still passed for wit, if not with Cowley's approval. It may be added that rhetorical figures often provided Cowley with the substance as well as the form of wit.

In his schoolboy's *Vote* Cowley first revealed a bent of mind that made *The Wish* rather out of place in *The Mistress*, if not at odds with his life or fortune. Indeed, at times it seemed to conflict with his ambition. In *A Vote* he declared that he would not be a Puritan, School-master, Justice of Peace, or Courtier; would be innocent of the Lawyer's tongues, Usurer's conscience, eyes of Justice, Singing-men's Religion; and free "from too much Poetry," astronomy (astrology), or "from your Court-Madam's beauty." For example:

I would not be a Puritan, though he
Can preach two houres, and yet his Sermon be
*   But halfe a quarter long,*
Though from his old mechanicke trade
By vision hee's a Pastor made,
*   His faith was growne so strong.*
Nay though he thinke to gaine salvation,
By calling th' Pope the Whore of Babylon.

This bent of mind is most fully discussed in his essay *Of My self*, the last of the essays that justify his retirement. He explains: "As far as my Memory can return back into my past Life, before I knew, or was capable of guessing what the world, or glories, or business of it were, the natural affections of my soul gave me a secret bent of aversion from them, as some Plants are said to turn away from others, by an Antipathy imperceptible to themselves, and inscrutable to mans understanding." As evidence of this bent he quotes the last three stanzas of *A Vote*.

By this time, of course, he had emulated the Plants as well as written about them. In this essay he proceeds to describe his worldly "condition in banishment and publick distresses" before adding, "yet I could not abstain from renewing my old School-boys Wish in a Copy of Verses to the same effect," quoting the first two lines of *The Wish:*

> *Well then; I now do plainly see*
> *This busie World and I shall ne're agree, &c.*

He continues: "And I never then proposed to my self any other advantage from His Majesties Restoration, but the getting into some moderately convenient Retreat in the Country . . . But I had before written a shrewd Prophesie against my self, and I think Apollo inspired me in the Truth, though not in the Elegance of it.

> *Thou neither great at Court, nor in the War,*
> *Nor at th' Exchange shalt be, nor at the wrangling Bar;*
> *Content thy self with the small barren Praise*
> *Which neglected Verse does raise, &c."*

Thus the Muse pronounced his doom in the Pindaric ode *Destinie*, and he consoled himself thus:

> *No Matter, Cowley, let proud Fortune see,*
> *That thou canst her despise no less then she does Thee . . .*
> *Do Thou nor grieve nor blush to be,*
> *As all th' inspired tuneful Men,*
> *And all thy great Forefathers were from Homer down to Ben.*

In such poems Cowley was a son of Jonson rather than of Donne.

In renewing his schoolboy's *Wish*, however, Cowley added woman to his retreat, no doubt because it was included in *The Mistress*, but nevertheless posing a question about his diffidence on the subject of love in his Preface to the *Poems* of 1656. Pope connected the two subjects in his remarks quoted in Spence's *Anecdotes:* "When Cowley grew sick of the court, he took a house first at Battersea, then in Barnes; and then at Chertsey: always farther and farther from town. In the latter part of his life, he showed a sort of aversion for women; and would leave the room when they came in: 'twas probably from a disappointment in love. He was much in love with his Leonora; who is mentioned at the end of that good ballad of his, on his different mistresses. She was married to Dean Sprat's brother; and Cowley never was in love with any body after." We need not accept this identification to wonder if this consequence gave more point to the conclusion of *The Chronicle:*

> *But I will briefer with them be,*
> *Since few of them were long with Me.*
> *An higher and a nobler strain*
> *My present Emperess does claim,*
> *Heleonora, First o'th' Name;*
> *Whom God grant long to reign!*

At least, it might explain a remark in his essay *Of Greatness*, where he was under no compulsion to speak of love. Among the evidences that he is not inclined to greatness, he adds: "and if I were ever to fall in love again (which is a great Passion, and therefore, I hope, I have done with it) it would be, I think, with Prettiness, rather than with Majestical Beauty." Possibly Leonora taught him this moderation; certainly he suggests another reason for diffidence. In *The Chronicle*, however, the majestical had not dampened the gayest wit of love to be found in Cowley. But according to the essay *Of My self*, retirement was his first and last mistress: "Nothing shall separate me from a Mistress, which I have loved so long, and have now at last married; though she neither has brought me a rich Portion, nor lived yet so quietly with me as I hoped from Her." This must have added another irony to his conclusion *Against Hope:*

> *By Thee the one does changing Nature through*
> *Her endless Labyrinths pursue,*
> *And th'other chases Woman, whilst She goes*
> *More ways and turns than hunted Nature knows.*

The final poetic answer to *The Motto* and *Destinie*, however, is given in *The Complaint*. Returned to Cambridge in a vision, "the Melancholy Cowley" is chided by the Muse for his defection:

> *Art thou return'd at last, said she,*
> *To this forsaken place and me?*
> *Thou Prodigal, who didst so loosely waste*
> *Of all thy Youthful years, the good Estate;*
> *Art thou return'd here, to repent too late?*
> *And gather husks of Learning up at last,*
> *Now the rich harvest time of Life is past,*
> *And Winter marches on so fast?*

When she had meant to adopt him for her own:

> *Thou Changling, thou, bewitcht with noise and show,*
> *Wouldst into Courts and Cities from me go;*
> *Wouldst see the World abroad, and have a share*
> *In all the follies, and the Tumults there,*
> *Thou wouldst, forsooth, be something in a State,*
> *And business thou wouldst find, and wouldst Create:*
> *Business! the frivolous pretence*
> *Of humane Lusts to shake off Innocence;*
> *Business! the grave impertinence:*
> *Business! the thing which I of all things hate,*
> *Business! the contradiction of thy Fate.*

The vehemence may conceal Cowley's disappointment, for the poem is also an indirect complaint against his lack of reward by the King.

Cowley retorts that poetry made him what he is today; the Muse upbraids him for the ills which she has made; it was she who carried him off to "new-found Worlds":

> And ever since I strive in vain
> My ravisht freedom to regain;
> Still I Rebel, still thou dost Reign,
> Lo, still in verse against thee I complain.

As the conclusion makes clear, however, he is indirectly complaining against the Court and King. But in stanza 7 he indicts the Muse for making him unfit for the World, not without some Metaphysical wit:

> Thou slack'nest all my Nerves of Industry,
>   By making them so oft to be
> The tinckling strings of thy loose minstrelsie.
> Who ever this worlds happiness would see,
>   Must as entirely cast off thee,
>   As they who only Heaven desire,
>   Do from the world retire.

His schoolboy's *Vote* was also prophetic in the wish to be free "from too much Poetry," which now slackens his effort, turning nerves into tinkling strings.

If Love, "that Tyrant of his days," extracted the tribute of wit from Cowley in *The Chronicle* and *The Mistress*, as well as from Crashaw in his *Wishes*, Cowley took his revenge in the *Ode: Here's to thee Dick*. To this he gave his most cynical wit and an animus that carried it beyond Suckling toward Rochester. Here woman's rival is the bottle:

> Here's to thee Dick; this whining Love despise;
> Pledge me, my Friend, and drink till thou be'st wise.

> *It sparkles brighter far than she:*
> *'Tis pure, and right without deceit;*
> *And such no woman ere will be:*
> *No; they are all Sophisticate.*

This source of wisdom leads straight out of Cambridge into the Restoration Court, to vilify romantic myth:

> *With all thy servile pains what canst thou win*
> *But an ill-favor'd, and uncleanly Sin?*
>   *A thing so vile, and so short-liv'd,*
>   *That Venus Joys as well as she*
>   *With reason may be said to be*
>   *From the neglected Foam deriv'd.*

Here "neglected Foam" reduces the poetry of the sea, or the birth of Venus, to the level of worthless froth in a bottle, and the joys of love along with it. The figure is a damaging bit of Dr. Johnson's "discordia concors." After answering the question "Whom would that painted toy a Beauty move?" by reciting the follies and perfidies of women, he concludes:

> *Here's to thee again; thy senseless sorrows drown'd;*
> *Let the Glass walk, till all things too go round;*
>   *Again; till these Two Lights be Four;*
>   *No error here can dangerous prove;*
>   *Thy Passion, Man, deceiv'd thee more;*
>   *None Double see like Men in Love.*

This was not a way to truth for Donne as it was for Rochester, though it is another way of expressing the deception of the passions, or of translating their dangers.

The Mistress, which was published in 1647, has the marks of a virtuoso work: it begins by inviting the attack of Cupid, under a threat to teach more ways to defeat love than Ovid ever knew, and ends with a recital of reasons for "Love given over," asserting that he has had enough. In this rather formal framework Cowley exhibits his virtuosity. For example, *The Given Love* argues by proper consequences that love should be given and not bought. This is the preferred course:

> *But rather thus let me remain,*
> *As Man in Paradise did reign;*
> *When perfect Love did so agree*
> *With Innocence and Povertie.*
> *Adam did no Joynture give,*
> *Himself was Joynture to his Eve:*
> *Untoucht with Av'arice yet or Pride,*
> *The Rib came freely back to'his side.*

The development is commonly pointed by epigrammatic turns, sometimes at the expense of other subjects:

> *Bestow thy Beauty then on me,*
> *Freely, as Nature gave't to Thee;*
> *'Tis an exploded Popish thought*
> *To think that Heaven may be bought.*

And he concludes in obvious rivalry with Waller as a poet of love:

> *I'll fix thy title next in fame*
> *To Sacharissas well-sung name.*
> *So faithfully will I declare*
> *What all thy wondrous beauties are,*
> *That when at the last great Assise,*
> *All Women shall together rise,*
> *Men strait shall cast their eyes on Thee*
> *And know at first that Thou art She.*

He will triumph over Waller at the last judgment when men shall identify the real Sacharissa by his description. Cowley still finds a metaphysical background useful in the definition of love.

His supreme effrontery appears in *The Prophet:*

> *Teach me to Love? go teach thy self more wit;*
> *I chief Professour am of it.*

It begins in the style of Donne's *Will* and develops the boast of being Love's Columbus, which magnified *The Mistress* but invited Walsh's attack. It openly scorns the God of Love,

> *He who does boast that he has bin*
> *In every Heart since Adams sin,*

as Cowley asserts that he is more knowing. His last stanza really tempts providence:

> *'Tis I who Love's Columbus am; 'tis I,*
>   *Who must new Worlds in it descry:*
>   *Rich Worlds, that yield of Treasure more,*
>   *Than all that has bin known before.*
> *And yet like his (I fear) my Fate must be,*
> *To find them out for others; not for Me.*
>   *Me Times to come, I know it, shall*
>   *Loves last and greatest Prophet call.*
>   *But, ah, what's that, if she refuse,*
> *To hear the wholesome Doctrines of my Muse?*
> *If to my share the Prophets fate must come;*
>   *Hereafter Fame, here Martyrdome.*

Whatever his present, it did not buy this future, but another verdict from Walsh and Dryden, who would find poetic justice in her refusal to hear his doctrines. Whether or not to make his claim more secure, Cowley added seven poems in the 1656 edition of *The Mistress*, from "The Gazers" to "Bathing in the River" inclusive. For some this addition will make his double talk about love in the Preface seem more disingenuous.

Many of the poems in *The Mistress* involve themes, imagery, or cosmological background like those found in Donne, but Cowley was no doubt admired rather for his novelty or difference. He gives a novel turn to the use of nature, for example, in *The Spring*:

> *Though you be absent here, I needs must say*
> *The Trees as beauteous are, and flowers as gay,*
>> *As ever they were wont to be;*
>> *Nay the Birds rural musick too*
>> *Is as melodious and free,*
>> *As if they sung to pleasure you:*
> *I saw a Rose-Bud o'pe this morn; I'll swear*
> *The blushing Morning open'd not more fair.*

Poets had conditioned the reader to expect the following question, "How could it be so fair, and you away?" But poets had not prepared the reader for the answer to come. If only they could remember last year "How you did Them, They you delight"!

> *Where ere you walk'd trees were as reverend made,*
> *As when of old Gods dwelt in every shade.*

Although Pope remembered this passage (*Pastorals*, ii, 73), the trees do not, and so earn this rebuke:

> *Dull Creatures! 'tis not without Cause that she,*
> *Who fled the God of wit, was made a Tree.*

In ancient times they were wiser when, against Nature, they followed Orpheus. She would have drawn those trees as well as their poet. Another unexpected turn is provided by the reason for their conduct now:

> *But who can blame them now? for, since you're gone,*
> *They're here the only Fair, and Shine alone.*

For their poet, however, there is another Spring:

> *When e're then you come hither, that shall be*
> *The time, which this to others is, to Me.*
>> *The little joys which here are now,*
>> *The name of Punishments do bear;*
>> *When by their sight they let us know*

> *How we depriv'd of greater are.*
> *'Tis you the best of Seasons with you bring;*
> *This is for Beasts, and that for Men the Spring.*

Even as a rivalry between woman and nature, the opening stanza might have taken a less flattering turn; but nature remains a ground of hyperbole, not antithesis, for it never escapes the wit of Cowley.

On the other hand, love and woman are given a macrocosmic dimension in *The Change*, after an attractive opening:

> *Love in her Sunny Eyes does basking play;*
> *Love walks the pleasant Mazes of her Hair;*
> *Love does on both Lips for ever stray;*
> *And sows and reaps a thousand kisses there.*
> *In all her outward parts Love's always seen;*
> *But, oh, He never went within.*

Here love is like the sun, but leads to its antithesis:

> *Within Love's foes, his greatest foes abide,*
> *Malice, Inconstancy, and Pride,*
> *So the Earths face, Trees, Herbs, and Flowers do dress,*
> *With other beauties numberless:*
> *But at the Center, Darkness is, and Hell;*
> *There wicked Spirits, and there the Damned dwell.*

The microcosmic figure is less well pursued in man's relationship and the final exchange of hearts.

In *Love and Life* Cowley uses the double motion of the Ptolemaic spheres, which Donne used in *Good Friday, Riding Westward*. Here it is to explain the double time of life and love:

> *Yet Love, alas, and Life in Me,*
> *Are not two several things, but purely one,*
> *At once how can there in it be*
> *A double different Motion?*

> *O yes, there may: for so the self same Sun,*
> *At once does slow and swiftly run.*

The daily journey and the annual journey within the same sphere make it possible for him to distinguish between life and love:

> *When Soul does to my self refer,*
> *'Tis then my Life, and does but slowly move;*
> *But when it does relate to her,*
> *It swiftly flies, and then is Love.*
> *Love's my Diurnal course, divided right*
> *'Twixt Hope and Fear, my Day and Night.*

This is why, like the sun, "He runs the Day, and Walks the year," and thus his psychological time may make him the "Methusalem of Love."

Clad all in White is a persuasion to a lady that turns upon her dress:

> *Fairest thing that shines below,*
> *Why in this robe dost thou appear?*

The answer leads by devious flattery through a course that seems to glorify but finally compromises the lady. If she would show the most perfect white, she must wear nothing at all. Then she will be whiter than Winter clad in snow. / It is not the linen of her dress that shows so fair, but the skin that shines through it; so the sun shines through clouds, so lilies turn a glass white. / Undressed she is nothing but a pile of beauty, every part made of condensed beams; her body clothed like her soul, her soul displayed like a star in the Milky Way. / Such robes are worn by departed Saints, woven of divine light; such are their exalted bodies, and shine with such glory:

> *But they regard not mortals pain;*
> *Men pray, I fear, to both in vain.*

The equation of her beauty with her virtue has landed him in
a quandary: saints are not likely to pity mortal weakness. But
when he returns to the significance of her robe, he discovers
hope:

> *Yet seeing thee so gently pure,*
> *My hopes will needs continue still;*
> *Thou wouldst not take this garment sure,*
> *When thou hadst an intent to kill.*
> *Of Peace and yielding who would doubt,*
> *When the white Flag he sees hung out?*

Thus gentle purity may translate a white dress into a white
flag and expand into acquiescence, at least for the wit of Cow-
ley. The poem combines beauty and wit as unexpectedly as
Donne.

The Wish introduces Cowley's earliest mistress, retirement,
into an amatory context. It provides many parallels to Mar-
vell's *Garden* without opposing nature and woman. Cowley
will not go to the bee for wisdom; rather he rejects the busy
world and its honey, and pities its bees:

> *Who for it can endure the stings,*
> *The Crowd, and Buz, and Murmurings*
> *Of this great Hive, the City.*

His requirements are modest, showing his moderation even in
"A Mistress moderately fair"; his wealth is found in nature:

> *Oh, Fountains, when in you shall I*
> *My self, eas'd of unpeaceful thoughts, espy?*
> *Oh Fields! Oh Woods! when, when shall I be made*
> *The happy Tenant of your shade?*
> *Here's the Spring-head of Pleasures flood;*

> *Here's wealthy Natures Treasury,*
> *Where all the Riches lie, that she*
>   *Has coyn'd and stampt for good.*

Here Pride and Ambition produce only farfetched Metaphors (like his); only winds scatter "hurtful Murmurs"; only Echo flatters. The Gods, when they descended from Heaven, always came here, and this shows "That 'tis the way too thither." His conclusion, however, magnifies the reason for including *The Wish* among his love poems:

> *How happy here should I,*
> *And one dear She live, and embracing dy?*
> *She who is all the world, and can exclude*
>   *In desarts Solitude.*
> *I should have then this only fear,*
> *Lest men, when they my pleasures see,*
> *Should hither throng to live like me,*
>   *And so make a City here.*

If she is his microcosm, or world enough for him, still she does not include, by his argument, all the pleasures that might turn his retreat into its opposite.

The Thief names a lovely thief who transforms love into an idolatry from which he cannot escape. She robs his days and nights, and threatens to rob him of Heaven:

> *Even in my prayers thou hauntest me.*
>   *And I, with wild Idolatry,*
> *Begin, to God, and end them all, to Thee.*

Thus love becomes a sin that tortures his conscience, haunts him in her face, pursues him in her shape, as if she were his victim. / When he tries to escape in books, everywhere the letters make her name; and he perishes, like Midas, by turning everything to gold (into her). He cannot avoid the feeling of damnation:

> *What do I seek, alas, or why do I*
>   *Attempt in vain from thee to fly?*
>   *For making thee my Deity,*
>   *I gave thee then Ubiquity.*
>   *My pains resemble Hell in this;*
>   *The Divine presence there too is,*
> *But to torment Men, not to give them bliss.*

The ambiguities of the final lines point the transformation of love into a torment, which can be interpreted only by the consequences of idolatry in religion.

The Soul in Dryden's view no doubt brought Cowley into competition with Donne. But Cowley professes to be stumping the Philosopher rather than the lady by having his soul flee into the body of another

> *That neither Is, nor will be I,*
> *As a Form Servient and Assisting there* . . .

That is, as a subservient form, not a determining form or principle of her being. / Since the soul is the form of life in the body, the Philosopher will ask, how can he live? But syllogisms depend on "weak Natures Law" (reason), and philosophies do not comprehend the mysteries of love and religion. / The answer to the mystery is a paradox:

> *Her Body is my Soul; laugh not at this,*
>   *For by my Life I swear it is.*
> *'Tis that preserves my Being and my Breath,*
>   *From that proceeds all that I do,*
>   *Nay all my Thoughts and speeches too,*
> *And separation from it is my Death.*

Her body is his soul because it is his determining form or principle, the life that preserves his being, the cause of all he does, thinks, or says, and separation from it, as from the soul, is death to him. No soul can be a more determining form than that. In love and religion it is a mystery; in philosophy it is sophistry. But in Cowley it is a paradox of causation.

The rich Rival is couched in a colloquial style that scorns the social mode of Restoration lyric as it raises love above the vanities of the world. So much depends upon its unique tone that it must be quoted rather than resolved into prose:

> *They say you're angry, and rant mightilie,*
> *Because I love the same as you;*
> *Alas! you're very rich, 'tis true;*
> *But prithee Fool, what's that to Love and Me?*
> *You'have Land and Money, let that serve;*
> *And know you'have more by that than you deserve.*
>
> *When next I see my fair One, she shall know,*
> *How worthless thou art of her bed;*
> *And wretch, I'll strike thee dumb and dead,*
> *With noble verse not understood by you;*
> *Whilst thy sole Rhetorick shall be*
> *Joynture, and Jewels, and Our Friends agree.*
>
> *Pox o' your friends, that dote and Domineere:*
> *Lovers are better Friends than they:*
> *Let's those in other things obey;*
> *The Fates, and Stars, and Gods must govern here.*
> *Vain names of Blood! in Love let none*
> *Advise with any Blood, but with their own.*
>
> *'Tis that which bids me this bright Maid adore;*
> *No other thought has had access!*
> *Did she now beg I'd love no less,*
> *And were she'an Empress, I should love no more;*
> *Were she as just and true to Me,*
> *Ah, simple soul, what would become of Thee!*

Despite the final turn, his rhetoric brings him more than a Pyrrhic victory over his rival. The vanity of birth or blood touched even *The Motto*, but the social obstacles of this poem become more formidable in *Looking on, and discoursing with his Mistress:*

> *Ah wretch! I seem to touch her now; but, oh,*
>   *What boundless spaces do us part?*
> *Fortune, and Friends, and all earths empty show,*
>   *My Lowness, and her high Desert:*
>   *But these might conquerable prove;*
>   *Nothing does me so far remove,*
> *As her hard Souls aversion from my Love.*

In *Love undiscovered,* on the other hand, he does not disclose his love

> *Lest too much goodness make her throw*
> *Her Love upon a Fate too low.*

The Mistress might persuade Pope that Cowley had been unhappy in love, or others that he was indeed "Against Hope," and often felt like a squire of low degree.

Cowley's *For Hope* is not less disillusioned than *Against Hope,* for it seems to leave one in possession of less. Its themes are similar, but not ordered the same, except to end with love. A summary will expose more of the melancholy Cowley: "Hope, the only cheap and universal cure of all the ills that men endure: the freedom of the captive, health of the sick man, victory of the loser, wealth of the beggar. The Manna given by Heaven, to every taste a different meat; the strong retreat, the inalienable estate; the pleasant, honest flatterer, for only hope flatters unhappy men. / Hope, the first offerings of happiness, the quiet dawning of success, the good preparatory to joy, lest it prove too strong; which is out of reach of Fortune, and a blessing still in hand. While we have it as a presage (down-payment), we are certain to gain, whether Fortune keeps her bargain or not. Only hope is good, not worse, for ending ill. / Brother of Faith, between you two the joys of Heaven and Earth are divided. Though Faith is heir and has the fixed property, your portion in movable property is great. Happiness is the same whether in hope or in possession, the future is yours, the present his. Yours is the more hard and noble bliss; you are the best apprehender of our joys, because you have so long a reach and can hold so fast. / Hope, the sad lover's only friend, the Way that may compete with the End. For love, I fear, is a fruit that delights the taste less than the smell and sight. Fruition is more deceitful than hope when it misses; men lose hope by obtaining it, and straight flee some other way to it again."

> And that's a pleasant Country, without doubt,
> To which all soon return that travel out.

The conclusion rather disguises hope as the refuge from all the ills that men endure. But the passage from Cowley's Hope to Marvell's Despair in *The Definition of Love* is not great.

The Frailty is a lyrical treatment of the mortal frailty of man. The repetitions in the first stanza emphasize how little moral awareness avails against it:

> I know 'tis sordid, and 'tis low;
> (All this as well as you I know)
> Which I so hotly now pursue;
> (I know all this as well as you)
> But whilst this cursed flesh I bear,
> And all the Weakness, and the Baseness there,
> Alas, alas, it will be always so.

This is his inheritance from Adam. And if the despotic flesh even hurt Christ, how can he expect to break his bonds?

> In vain, exceedingly in vain
> I rage sometimes, and bite my Chain;
> For to what purpose do I bite

> *With Teeth which ne're will break it quite?*
> *For if the chiefest Christian Head,*
> *Was by this sturdy Tyrant buffeted,*
> *What wonder is it, if weak I be slain?*

Thus the highest example shows how difficult is the conquest of the flesh; but its difficulty, though offered as an excuse, cannot exempt the sons of Adam from mortality.

Various learning is used to convey the feeling in *My Fate:* "When the needle of the compass, the stone, and the flame prove false to their old motions, then he will cease to love her alone. / Everlasting Fate ties nothing more strongly than him to her. His fixt love does not depend on her love or hate. She cannot kill his love with disdain, but she may wound it and make it live in pain. / Let the Stoics use his example to maintain their sad and cruel doctrine; let Predestinators produce him in struggling to explain eternal bonds. This fire he is born to, but she must tell whether it be beams of Heaven or flames of Hell." His fate is one thing, but his feelings are another, and they depend upon her:

> *You, who mens fortunes in their faces read,*
> *To find out mine, look not, alas, on Me;*
> *But mark her Face, and all the features heed;*
> *For only there is writ my Destiny.*
> *Or if Stars shew it, gaze not on the Skies;*
> *But study the Astrol'ogy of her Eyes.*
>
> *If thou find there kind and propitious rays,*
> *What Mars or Saturn threaten I'll not fear;*
> *I well believe the Fate of mortal days*
> *Is writ in Heav'en; but, oh my heav'en is there.*
> *What can men learn from stars they scarce can see?*
> *Two great Lights rule the world; and her two, Me*

First, he identifies his fate with her face, and then the influence of the stars with that of her eyes. Next, if they are beneficent, he will fear no readings of the stars. Finally, he trumps the metaphor of the stars by the two great lights that rule the world, and him. Thus he magnifies both her beauty and his fate as he propitiates one by his praise of the other.

Cowley, like Donne, sometimes regarded love as a devil. In *The Dissembler*, by feigning love too well, he was caught by his own fancy: "Ah, there's no fooling with the Devil!" But perhaps the God is rather stupid:

> *Dull, sottish God of Love, and can it be*
> *Thou understand'st not Raillery?*

Thus he is forced into an explanation:

> *Darts, and Wounds, and Flame, and Heat,*
> *I nam'd but for the Rhime, or the Conceit.*
> *Nor meant my Verse should raised be,*
> *To this sad fame of Prophesie;*
> *Truth gives a dull propriety to my stile,*
> *And all the Metaphors does spoil.*

This wit could have a more serious application to the style of his friend Crashaw. But in *The Inconstant* he proves a more willing victim of the devil Cupid:

> *I never yet could see that face*
> *Which had no dart for me;*
> *From fifteen years, to fifties space,*
> *They all victorious be.*
> *Love thou'rt a Devil; if I may call thee One,*
> *For sure in Me thy name is Legion.*

And he proceeds to prove it by itemizing the colors, shapes, and sizes that have led him down the primrose path of inconstancy.

The Separation evokes a response of puzzled melancholy: "Ask me not what will happen to my love, which is my soul, when I am separated from you. I could show as easily what the soul will do after death, which is a separation of body and soul. It will last, I am sure, and that is all we know. / The thing called Soul will neither stir nor move in separation, but prove a lifeless shell, only the body of my love; not that my love will fly away, but still continue as, they say, sad troubled ghosts linger about their graves." Thus love in separation continues to have a kind of ghostly existence that is sad and troubled rather than triumphant.

When Gildon defended the Moderns against the charges of Walsh, he argued "that there are a great many very tender and soft Thoughts, and passionate Expressions in Cowley's *Mistress*, as in this one, that now occurrs to my Mind"; and he quoted the first line of

> *Then like some wealthy Island thou shalt ly;*
>   *And like the Sea about it, I;*
> *Thou like fair Albion, to the Sailors Sight,*
> *Spreading her beauteous Bosom all in White:*
>   *Like the kind Ocean I will be,*
> *With loving Arms for ever clasping Thee.*

If this poem (earlier "The Injoyment") ends on a Restoration note, it is not for a Restoration reason, but because its joys are above expression. In it, moreover, "the softnesses of love" are carried by a very ingratiating rhythm, which helps to vindicate Gildon.

We should recall that the Sacred Muse also attracted Cowley. Since both Hervey and Crashaw were inclined to religion, their influence may appear in the *Davideis*, which Cowley finally lacked the appetite to finish. At least, the invocation to *Davideis* expresses the opposition of the sacred and the profane that inspired his elegy on Crashaw and his Preface to the *Poems* of 1656. It seems opposed to *The Mistress:*

> *Lo, with pure hands thy heav'enly Fires to take,*
> *My well-chang'd Muse I a chast Vestal make!*
> *From earths vain joys, and loves soft witchcraft free,*
> *I consecrate my Magdalene to Thee!*
> *Lo, this great work, a Temple to thy praise,*
> *On polisht Pillars of strong Verse I raise!*
> *A Temple, where if Thou vouchsafe to dwell,*
> *It Solomons, and Herods shall excel.*
> *Too long the Muses-Land have Heathen bin;*
> *Their Gods too long were Dev'ils, and Vertues Sin;*
> *But Thou, Eternal Word, hast call'd forth Me*
> *Th' Apostle, to convert that World to Thee;*
> *T' unbind the charms that in slight Fables lie,*
> *And teach that Truth is truest Poesie.*

Perhaps a more lasting consequence of this change was the serious dedication of his muse to the advancement of learning in his time. If this was how he once proposed to redeem poetry, it did in fact add to his appreciation of Crashaw and to the range of feeling in his other great elegy.

On the Death of Mr. Crashaw hails both "Poet and Saint."

> *Long did the Muses banisht Slaves abide,*
> *And built vain Pyramids to mortal pride;*

but Crashaw, like Moses, brought them back to their Holy Land. He united Earth and Heaven:

> *Ah wretched We, Poets of Earth! but Thou*
> *Wert Living the same Poet which thou'rt Now.*

And poets of earth unfortunately still have their way:

> *Still the old Heathen Gods in Numbers dwell,*
> *The Heav'enliest thing on Earth still keeps up Hell.*
> *Nor have we yet quite purg'd the Christian Land;*
> *Still Idols here, like Calves at Bethel stand.*
> *And though Pans Death long since all Oracles breaks,*
> *Yet still in Rhyme the Fiend Apollo speaks.*

In poetry pagan mythology is still mixed with Christian elements.

> *Nay with the worst of Heathen dotage We*
> *(Vain men!) the Monster Woman Deifie;*
> *Find Stars, and tye our Fates there in a Face,*
> *And Paradise in them by whom we lost it, place.*
> *What different faults corrupt our Muses thus?*
> *Wanton as Girles, as old Wives, Fabulous!*

If we had not seen Cowley do these things, we might think that Walsh should have accused him of a lack of gallantry.

Crashaw, on the contrary, devoted himself to the Virgin:

> *How well (blest Swan) did Fate contrive thy death;*
> *And made thee render up thy tuneful breath*
> *In thy great Mistress Arms? thou most divine*
> *And richest Off'ering of Loretto's Shrine!*

And this leads Cowley to indulge in some poetic license that brings him into conflict with religious license:

> *Pardon, my Mother Church, if I consent*
> *That Angels led him when from thee he went,*
> *For even in Error sure no Danger is*
> *When joyn'd with so much Piety as His.*
> *Ah, mighty God, with shame I speak't, and grief,*
> *Ah that our greatest Faults were in Belief!*
> *And our weak Reason were ev'en weaker yet,*
> *Rather then thus our Wills too strong for it.*
> *His Faith perhaps in some nice Tenents might*
> *Be wrong; his Life, I'm sure, was in the right.*
> *And I my self a Catholick will be,*
> *So far at least, great Saint, to Pray to thee.*

And so he asks Crashaw to bestow some care on the earthbound poets below, whose faults go beyond belief:

> *Oppos'ed by our old En'emy, adverse Chance,*
> *Attacqu'ed by Envy, and by Ignorance,*

Enchain'd by Beauty, tortur'd by Desires,
Expos'd by Tyrant-Love to savage Beasts and Fires.

And this leads him to a personal petition (as in 2 Kings 2):

Lo here I beg (I whom thou once didst prove
So humble to Esteem, so Good to Love)
Not that thy Spirit might on me Doubled be,
I ask but Half thy mighty Spirit for Me.

The conclusion to this elegy might persuade us that Cowley had not yet given up the prospect of finishing the *Davideis*. But in general it relates his experience to some of the deeper issues of his time as well as to a friend, and to the wit, of his precocious youth.

So far as Cowley's learning led him into more philosophical poems, a brief comparison with Donne may be in order. The metaphysical background of Donne's *Anniversaries* is the decay of the world. Their humanistic wisdom is the wisdom of Ecclesiastes. The metaphysical background of Cowley's odes *To Mr. Hobs* and *To the Royal Society* is the idea of progress. Their humanistic wisdom is liberal and utilitarian. In life Cowley's *Wish* seeks not so much freedom from worldly values as moderation of them. Donne and Cowley might be distinguished by the attitudes for and against learning found in Book I of Bacon's *Advancement of Learning*. The pioneer attitude of Bacon emerges in our survey, perhaps unconsciously, in such boasts as "Love's Columbus" and "the Muse's Hannibal." Although Cowley began poetry in Spenser, he ended in a new world.

When Spenser wrote his melancholy *Cantos of Mutabilitie*, he expressed one of the dominant moods of the age to come; and when he gave Nature the office of replying to the Titaness, he indicated the power which was to dissolve the mood that rose out of the idea of a decaying world. Even the answer which he gave to Nature may be said to anticipate the greatest paradox of the seventeenth century, the idea of "circular change" rather than decay, which George Hakewill set forth in his *Apologie for the Providence of God* in 1627. Bacon, of course, laid the broad foundations for advancement through power acquired over nature, and round this idea grew up the "climate of opinion" which eventually subdued the vapors of melancholy. If any mood can be said to be fundamental to significant trends of thought in the first half of the seventeenth century, it is the melancholy associated with mutability and aspects of a decaying world. Emotionally Jacobean stoicism, skepticism, and religion are rooted in mutability.

It will not do to object that mutability has always moved the poets, preachers, and philosophers, for Jacobean literature is there to show how Ezekiel's "valley of dry bones" compelled their imagination. If we follow this theme from Spenser to the Restoration, we shall know that when cosmological "inconstancy" fails to sustain either levity or melancholy in the poet, we have arrived at the reign of progress and the Royal Society. For Cowley this theme no longer has reverberations in a decaying world, and therefore it fails to stir the depths of his imagination. Cowley marks the end of the sensibility best described by Jacobean melancholy; his own melancholy is more personal and less metaphysical in its roots. The story is told more fully in the first essay of my *Seventeenth Century Contexts*.

Yet we are wrong to deny Cowley more esteem than has been our custom. When the precocity of Cowley is crowned by the variety of his achievement, it is difficult to deny him the prominence he assumed in his own time. But these advantages finally denied him the fame they sought, for they spread his gifts thin and sacrificed experience to versatility. Only a few passions compelled his imagination to depth or resonance, though many subjects provoked him to wit or magniloquence. Seldom, however, did he synthesize experience into the more complicated expression of the Metaphysical imagination. His wit had a more limited range of feeling, and his learning, though various, more limited systems of invention. Despite his enthusiasm, he was most conscious of the license and extravagance of Pindar. Though a Baconian in science, he became less willing to shape poetry to the desires of men's minds. In him the Metaphysical complex begins to break up: wit begins to be separated into the Anacreontic or satiric poem, passion transformed into the magniloquence of the Pindaric ode, argument into public discourse. In verse, even in the Pindaric ode, principles of balance exert themselves more and more, and imagination gradually submits to decorum. But Cowley also translates elements of wit and speech into Neo-Classical verse that endured. His love poetry is located somewhere between the Metaphysical Donne and Waller's muse of gallantry.

VIII
Henry Vaughan
1621/2-1695

In 1646, or one year before Cowley's *Mistress*, Vaughan pub-
lished his *Poems, with theTenth Satyre of Juvenal Englished.*
There he shows his admiration for Jonson and Randolph, ex-
presses a wish to meet them in the Elysian fields, imitates
Donne in a few poems and is a tavern poet like Jonson in
others. Anthony Wood tells us that he was taken from col-
lege by his father and sent to London to study law: "But soon
after, the Civil War beginning, to the horror of all good men,
he was sent for home, followed the pleasant paths of poetry
and philology, became noted for his ingenuity, and published
several specimens thereof, of which his *Olor Iscanus* was most
valued." His Preface to the *Poems* seems to reflect this im-
plied criticism "amidst the common noise" or "distractions,"
and to explain his ambition: "you have here a flame, bright
only in its own innocence, that kindles nothing but a gener-

ous thought: which though it may warm the blood, the fire at highest is but Platonic; and the commotion, within these limits, excludes danger." If the allusion is not both civil and moral, then his courage is daring to be moral in an age of coarse taste.

The first poem in the volume, *To my Ingenuous Friend, R.W.*, passes from the atmosphere of taverns and law to the Elysian fields, where, after listening to Jonson and Randolph,

> *They'll come into the drowsy fields*
> *Of Lethe, which such virtue yields,*
> *That if what poets sing be true,*
> *The streams all sorrow can subdue.*
> *Here, on a silent, shady green,*
> *The souls of lovers oft are seen,*
> *Who, in their life's unhappy space,*
> *Were murder'd by some perjur'd face.*
> *All these th'enchanted streams frequent,*
> *To drown their cares, and discontent,*
> *That th'inconstant, cruel sex*
> *Might not in death their spirits vex.*

At this point one is not sure whether this natural solace is purely mythological or already biographical. However, one soon discovers that Vaughan united nature with love before he united it with religion. Indeed, "To Amoret, Walking in a Starry Evening," he first offered his most famous image:

> *If, Amoret, that glorious eye,*
> *In the first birth of light,*
>   *And death of Night,*
> *Had with those elder fires you spy*
>   *Scatter'd so high,*
>   *Received form and sight;*
>
> *We might suspect in the vast ring,*
> *Amidst these golden glories,*
>   *And fiery stories;*

> *Whether the sun had been the king*
> *And guide of day,*
> *Or your brighter eye should sway.*

It may have been even closer to *The World* if he wrote the manuscript lines:

> *We may suspect in the vast ring,*
> *Which rolls those fiery spheres*
> *Thro' years and years . . .*

At least, the Vaughan we admire was already stirring.

In *To Amoret Gone from Him* he treats absence with an idea from Donne and the commerce between different parts of creation effected by sympathy or the "tye of bodies." We might call it the pathetic fallacy, but to Vaughan it was an idea of the Hermetic philosophy or alchemy cultivated by his brother Thomas.

> *Fancy and I, last evening, walk'd,*
> *And Amoret, of thee we talk'd;*
> *The West just then had stolne the sun,*
> *And his last blushes were begun:*
> *We sate, and mark'd how everything*
> *Did mourn his absence: how the spring*
> *That smil'd and curl'd about his beams,*
> *Whilst he was here, now check'd her streams:*
> *The wanton eddies of her face*
> *Were taught less noise, and smoother grace;*
> *And in a slow, sad channel went,*
> *Whisp'ring the banks their discontent:*
> *The careless ranks of flowers that spread*
> *Their perfum'd bosoms to his head,*
> *And with an open, free embrace,*
> *Did entertain his beamy face,*
> *Like absent friends point to the West,*
> *And on that weak reflection feast.*

Nature now points clearly to the theme, and we are ready for the application:

> *If creatures then that have no sense,*
> *But the loose tie of influence,*
> *Though fate and time each day remove*
> *Those things that element their love,*
> *At such vast distance can agree,*
> *Why, Amoret, why should not we?*

Thus the creatures that fall below the level of sense on the scale of being sympathize through the tie of influence, and have this advantage over Donne's dull sublunary lovers, or the sensual "things that element their love." Meanwhile, nature makes love to Amoret for Vaughan. Although he borrows ideas, he contrives new situations in which to use them.

A Rhapsodie reflects his London days, being "Occasionally written upon a meeting with some of his friends at the Globe Tavern," probably with Ben Jonson in mind. It offers a less Platonic scene:

> *Should we go now a-wand'ring, we should meet*
> *With catchpoles, whores and carts in ev'ry street:*
> *Now when each narrow lane, each nook and cave,*
> *Sign-posts and shop-doors, pimp for ev'ry knave,*
> *When riotous sinful plush, and tell-tale spurs*
> *Walk Fleet Street and the Strand, when the soft stirs*
> *Of bawdy, ruffled silks, turn night to day;*
> *And the loud whip and coach scolds all the way;*
> *When lust of all sorts, and each itchy blood*
> *From the Tower-wharf to Cymbeline, and Lud,*
> *Hunts for a mate, and the tir'd footman reels*
> *'Twixt chairmen, torches, and the hackney wheels.*

This poem seems to give a coarse sense to his words in the Preface: "and revel it thus in the dregs of an age." But Vaughan did not have to be ashamed of the bite of such verse.

In *To Amoret: of the Difference 'twixt him and other Lovers, and what True Love is*, the sunset is again put to the service of love, but with a difference; and this provides a Vaughan context for a borrowing from Donne: "Mark, when the evening's cooler wings fan the afflicted air, how the faint sun, leaving his work undone, resigns and brings those spurious flames, sucked up from slime and earth, back to their first, low birth. / They shoot their tinsel beams and vanities, threading their way with those false fires; but as you stay and see them scatter (disperse), you lose the flaming track, and subtly they fade away, and cheat your eyes." A similar exhalation of water is later employed in *The Showre*. Then comes the adaptation from Donne:

> *Just so base, sublunary lovers' hearts*
>   *Fed on loose profane desires,*
>   *May for an eye*
>   *Or face comply:*
> *But those remov'd, they will as soon depart,*
>   *And show their art,*
>   *And painted fires.*
>
> *Whilst I by pow'rful love, so much refin'd,*
>   *That my absent soul the same is,*
>   *Careless to miss*
>   *A glance or kiss,*
> *Can with those elements of lust and sense*
>   *Freely dispense,*
>   *And court the mind.*

Where before he had gone below sense to express his love, now he goes above it more completely than Donne. Finally, he returns to the subsensate level on the scale of being:

> *Thus to the North the loadstones move,*
>   *And thus to them th'enamour'd steel aspires:*
>   *Thus, Amoret,*
>   *I do affect;*
> *And thus by winged beams, and mutual fire,*
>   *Spirits and stars conspire:*
>   *And this is Love.*

Thus by another species of the opening metaphor his love and true love are defined: the false is visible, the true invisible. If

Vaughan is less compelling than Donne, his metaphorical system is more subtle than some of his critics.

Upon the Priory Grove, his Usual Retirement is his finest union of nature and love, in which his feeling for one intensifies the other. The grove and love are interwoven in their fortune and future because he first confessed his love there.

> *Hail, sacred shades! cool, leavy house!*
> *Chaste treasurer of all my vows*
> *And wealth! on whose soft bosom laid*
> *My love's fair steps I first betray'd.*

Then the consequences of this love are suggested in terms of his retreat:

> *Henceforth no melancholy flight,*
> *No sad wing, or hoarse bird of night,*
> *Disturb this air, no fatal throat*
> *Of raven, or owl, awake the note*
> *Of our laid echo, no voice dwell*
> *Within these leaves, but Philomel.*
> *The poisonous ivy here no more*
> *His false twists on the oak shall score;*
> *Only the woodbine here may twine,*
> *As th'emblem of her love, and mine.*

Henceforth let such negative aspects give way to happier emblems.

> *The amorous sun shall here convey*
> *His best beams, in thy shades to play;*
> *The active air, the gentlest show'rs,*
> *Shall from his wings rain on thy flowers;*
> *And the moon from her dewy locks*
> *Shall deck thee with her brightest drops:*
> *Whatever can a fancy move,*
> *Or feed the eye, be on this grove!*

At this point one is almost persuaded that his love is the grove. But they become distinct again in the last part of his vision:

> *And when at last the winds and tears*
> *Of heaven, with the consuming years,*
> *Shall these green curls bring to decay,*
> *And clothe thee in an aged gray:*
> *(If ought a lover can foresee,*
> *Or if we poets prophets be)*
> *From hence transplanted, thou shalt stand*
> *A fresh grove in th' Elysian land;*
> *Where (most bless'd pair!) as here on earth*
> *Thou first didst eye our growth, and birth;*
> *So there again, thou'lt see us move*
> *In our first innocence and love:*
> *And in thy shades, as now, so then,*
> *We'll kiss, and smile, and walk agen.*

When the storms of life have done their work, after the "green curls" have turned to gray, both love and grove are to be restored in heaven to youth and innocence. The metaphorical unity of the two enables him to intimate with delicate ambiguity his love of both.

Vaughan was "Olor Iscanus," the swan of Usk, until God struck sparks from his flint, *Silex Scintillans*. He called himself the Silurist after the ancient inhabitants of his part of Wales, and he became a physician of the alchemical persuasion. The first book of *Silex Scintillans* was published in 1650, with the emblem of a celestial hand shaking a thunderbolt at a stone heart. *Olor Iscanus* came out in 1651, with a Dedication by the author dated 1647, but the Preface says that it was published without Vaughan's consent, after being consigned to oblivion. Vaughan explains why in his Preface to *Silex Scintillans* (1655). The poems of *Olor Iscanus* are primarily occasional, in the mode of Jonson, some of which crowd the date of publication.

One of the later poems is *To his Retired Friend, an Invitation to Brecknock*, inviting him to "a revel in the town" some time after the demise of Charles I: "They have not seen thee here since Charles, his reign." And it does not suggest Vaughan's conversion; certainly not in his attempts to explain his friend's retirement:

> *Hadst thou been bach'lor, I had soon divin'd*
> *Thy close retirements, and monastic mind;*
> *Perhaps some nymph had been to visit, or*
> *The beauteous churl was to be waited for,*
> *And like the Greek, ere you the sport would miss,*
> *You stay'd, and strok'd the distaff for a kiss.*
> *But in this age, when thy cool, settled blood*
> *Is ti'd t'one flesh, and thou almost grown good,*

he finds it difficult to understand. And more to the point:

> *Or is't thy piety? for who can tell*
> *But thou may'st prove devout, and love a cell,*
> *And (like a badger) with attentive looks*
> *In the dark hole sit rooting up of books.*
> *Quick hermit! what a peaceful change hadst thou,*
> *Without the noise of haircloth, whip, or vow!*
> *But is there no redemption? must there be*
> *No other penance but of liberty?*

Then he addresses his friend in a more positive vein:

> *Come! leave this sullen state, and let not wine*
> *And precious wit lie dead for want of thine.*

And he deplores the dull wits of the rural rout that come to drink:

> *O let not such prepost'rous tippling be*
> *In our metropolis; may I ne'er see*
> *Such tavern-sacrilege, nor lend a line*
> *To weep the rapes and tragedy of wine!*

Even if this were no more than a Jonsonian disdain of the dull, his conversion renounced the consequence of the next lines:

> *Here lives that chymic, quick fire which betrays*
> *Fresh spirits to the blood, and warms our lays.*
> *I have reserv'd 'gainst thy approach a cup*
> *That were thy Muse stark dead, shall raise her up,*
> *And teach her yet more charming words and skill*
> *Than ever Cælia, Chloris, Astrophil,*
> *Or any of the threadbare names inspir'd*
> *Poor rhyming lovers with a mistress fir'd.*

Although Vaughan makes his wine alchemical and sacrifices a lady for a rhyme, he does not prepare us for his conversion by such offerings of the muse, or by finally leaving the obtuse

> *Rout to their husks; they and their bags at best*
> *Have cares in earnest; we care for a jest.*

With this sacrifice to the wit of the time, he concluded his care for what he now called "innocent spenders" of "our short lease."

In 1655 *Silex Scintillans* appeared as a second Edition in two Books, with a Preface dated September 30, 1654. As "The Author's Preface to the Following Hymns," it suggests the solemn dress that he now assigns to these "Sacred Poems," dedicated to Christ more urgently because, as he says, "I was nigh unto death, and am still at no great distance from it." Between Books I and II of *Silex Scintillans* he had published translations of various devotional works, and he now explains his change of heart. He shows a sense of the past with respect to the profanation of the Muse, remarking, "for the complaint against vicious verse, even by peaceful and obedient spirits, is of some antiquity in this kingdom." In short, by other than Puritan spirits. Those without the talent for verse now translate, and nothing takes like a French romance. And he makes his own free confession: "I myself have, for many years together, languished of this very sickness; and it is no long time since I have recovered."

By God's grace he has suppressed his greatest follies, and those which escaped from him, he does "here most humbly and earnestly beg that none would read them." Then he gives the immediate cause of his change: "The first, that with any effectual success attempted a diversion of this foul and overflowing stream, was the blessed man, Mr. George Herbert, whose holy life and verse gained many pious converts, of whom I am the least, and gave the first check to a most flourishing and admired wit of his time." It was a fashion of profane wit rather than of Donne that Herbert sought to check. But those who followed Herbert, says Vaughan, "had more of fashion than force." No better reason can be found for the decline of mere imitators. Aside from Herbert, the emblem of *Silex Scintillans* and the poem on "Affliction" describe the "great Elixir" that converted this alchemical physician.

Although the debt of *Silex Scintillans* to Herbert is large, it does not prove that Vaughan also owed more to fashion than to force. If his poems related to the Church calendar are inferior, he was a country philosopher rather than a country parson. The revolt against profane love poetry described in his Preface is now echoed in *Idle Verse* after the fashion of Herbert:

> *Go, go, queint folies, sugred sin,*
> *Shadow no more my door!*

Their products now seem to him

> *Blind, desp'rate fits, that study how*
> *To dresse and trim our shame,*
> *That gild rank poyson, and allow*
> *Vice in a fairer name;*

> *The Purles of youthfull bloud and bowles,*
> * Lust, in the Robes of Love,*
> *The idle talk of feav'rish souls*
> * Sick with a scarf or glove;*

> *Let it suffice my warmer days*
> * Simper'd, and shin'd on you;*
> *Twist not my Cypresse with your Bays,*
> * Or Roses with my Yewgh.*

Purles may be glossed as the commotion of youthful blood and bowels. But in *Isaac's Marriage*, especially in 1650, this theme is not treated in the fashion of Herbert:

> *But being for a bride, sure, prayer was*
> *Very strange stuffe wherewith to court thy lasse;*
> *Had'st ne'r an oath, nor Complement? thou wert*
> *An odde, coarse sutor; Had'st thou but the art*
> *Of these our dayes, thou couldst have coyn'd thee twenty*
> *New sev'rall oathes, and Complements (too) plenty.*

Here his new faith is emphasized by his unregenerate wit, which gave pointed ambiguity to his opening:

> *Praying! and to be married? It was rare,*
> *But now 'tis monstrous . . .*

Vaughan also found Biblical opportunity to echo his theme of artistic responsibility in *The Daughter of Herodias:*

> *Vain, sinful Art! who first did fit*
> *Thy lewd loath'd Motions unto sounds,*
> *And made grave Musique, like wilde wit,*
> *Erre in loose airs beyond her bounds?*

> *What fires hath he heap'd on his head!*
> *Since to his sins, as needs it must,*
> *His Art adds still, though he be dead,*
> *New fresh accounts of blood and lust.*

But Nature gave a new and positive dimension to his religion, significantly in the poem called *Religion:*

> *My God, when I walke in those groves,*
> *And leaves thy Spirit doth still fan,*
> *I see in each shade that there growes*
> *An Angell talking with a man . . .*
>
> *Nay thou thy selfe, my God, in fire,*
> *Whirle-winds, and Clouds, and the soft voice,*
> *Speak'st there so much, that I admire [wonder]*
> *We have no Conf'rence in these daies.*

Thus Vaughan returns to Eden. In *The Tempest* he tells what man could learn from nature:

> *O that man could do so! that he would hear*
> *The world read to him! all the vast expence*
> *In the Creation shed, and slav'd to sence*
> *Makes up but lectures to his eie and ear.*
>
> *Sure mighty Love, foreseeing the descent*
> *Of this poor Creature, by a gracious art*
> *Hid in these low things snares to gain his heart,*
> *And layd surprizes in each Element.*

Vaughan found love in nature, and how to interpret the book of God's word by the book of God's works.

Vaughan opens *Silex Scintillans* with a poem on his own pilgrim's progress, *Regeneration*. As often in his Sacred Poems, it has an epigraph from the Bible, in this instance from the Song of Solomon (iv): "Arise, O North, and come thou South-wind, and blow upon my garden, that the spices thereof may flow out." This is a prayer for regeneration, and its imagery introduces the nature imagery of the poem, specifically wind and a garden. Vaughan's title also suggests another Biblical passage, John iii, where Nicodemus learned about regeneration, and in terms that supply the rest of Vaughan's nature imagery, especially in these verses:

> "Jesus answered, Verily, verily, I say unto thee, Except a man be born of water and of the Spirit, he cannot enter into the kingdom of God . . .
>
> "The wind bloweth where it listeth, and thou hearest the sound thereof, but canst not tell whence it cometh, and whither it goeth: so is every one that is born of the Spirit."

A ward of the world as opposed to God, and still in bonds to sin, he stole abroad one day and found the semblance of spring:

> *It was high-spring, and all the way*
> *Primros'd, and hung with shade . . .*

"Primrosed" is used again in the opening poem of Book II, and is a feature of spring in Wales. But it is not spring within him:

> *Yet was it frost within,*
> *And surly winds*
> *Blasted my infant buds, and sinne*
> *Like clouds eclips'd my mind.*

Thus regeneration is to be described as a progress towards spring or rebirth, and it begins by contrasting his external and internal weather, or appearance and reality. "Storm'd thus," he saw that his spring was only an appearance, and his walk in reality "a monstrous, mountain'd thing," a hard and frosty way. In grief and between steps and falls, he struggled upwards, and at the top found a pair of scales, which weighed his "late paines" against "smoake and pleasures" and proved them lighter. With that he heard the command, "Away," which he obeyed, and was led "full East" to holy land.

Here he found a grove of stately height:

> *I entred, and once in,*
> *Amaz'd to see't,*
> *Found all was chang'd, and a new spring*
> *Did all my senses greet.*

Instead of the primroses, "The unthrift Sunne shot vitall gold," the elixir of life. Now the Biblical passages begin to impinge upon his experience:

> *The aire was all in spice,*
> *And every bush*
> *A garland wore; Thus fed my Eyes,*
> *But all the Eare lay hush.*

Here again the opposition of the seen and unseen, which was introduced at the beginning, appears in the opposition of eye and ear, organs of the seen and unseen but heard. Although the spice now flows out, St. John had said that one hears the wind of regeneration. And so the poem emphasizes hearing:

> *Only a little Fountain lent*
> *Some use for Eares,*
> *And on the dumbe shades language spent,*
> *The Musick of her teares;*
> *I drew her neere, and found*
> *The Cisterne full*
> *Of divers stones, some bright and round,*
> *Others ill-shap'd and dull.*

Thus hearing leads him to St. John's other requirement for regeneration, water, and to two kinds of stones.

The next stanza turns the stones into positive and negative responses to water:

> *The first (pray marke,) as quick as light*
> *Danc'd through the floud;*
> *But th'last more heavy than the night*
> *Nail'd to the Center stood;*
> *I wonder'd much, but tyr'd*

> *At last with thought,*
> *My restless Eye, that still desir'd,*
> *As strange an object brought.*

By his perplexity Vaughan makes the reader infer the lesson
of the stones, but he repeats it for the eye:

> *It was a banke of flowers, where I descried*
> *(Though 'twas mid-day,)*
> *Some fast asleepe, others broad-eyed,*
> *And taking in the Ray . . .*

Here we have response and apathy to the "vital gold" of the
sun; but now his meditation is broken by another appeal to
the ear:

> *Here musing long I heard*
> *A rushing wind,*
> *Which still increas'd, but whence it stirr'd*
> *No where I could not find.*

This is how St. John's wind of regeneration enters the
poem, and Vaughan looks for any response in nature, thus
evoking the lesson he has refused to draw:

> *I turn'd me round, and to each shade*
> *Dispatch'd an Eye,*
> *To see if any leafe had made*
> *Least motion, or Reply;*
> *But while I listning sought*
> *My mind to ease*
> *By knowing, where 'twas, or where not,*
> *It whisper'd: Where I please.*

Remembering the sign of St. John, "The wind bloweth where
it listeth," Vaughan utters the prayer of his epigraph:

> *Lord, then said I, On me one breath,*
> *And let me dye before my death!*

Thus, by God's grace, he too may die to the world and be "born of the Spirit." As we have seen, the wind and garden of the Song of Solomon unite with the water and wind of St. John to develop this parable of regeneration. And in its poetic integration the opposition of the seen and unseen, which served to state the conflict, also leads to the resolution.

The Showre involves one of the ways by which Nature teaches man the way to heaven in *The Tempest:* "Mists of corruptest foam / Quit their first beds and mount." In *The Showre* its lesson takes a negative form:

> *'Twas so, I saw thy birth: That drowsie Lake*
> *From her faint bosome breath'd thee, the disease*
> *Of her sick waters, and Infectious Ease.*
> > *But now at Even,*
> > *Too grosse for heaven,*
> *Thou fall'st in teares, and weep'st for thy mistake.*

Its analogy with the speaker is made obvious in the second stanza, but the points of comparison are more subtle. The "faint bosome" of the lake passes into the speaker and its action becomes fruitless; only love can open the way; "smoke and exhalations of the breast" are like the "corruptest foam" of the lake. Where sickness and slackness and grief appeared in the first stanza, only the last, as rain or tears, provides a way out of this moral state; and this is developed in the last stanza as a possible way to "Sun-shine after raine."

Distraction begins with the body and moves to the mind, but involves various meanings like scatter, disperse, divert, or confuse. Its remedy is to knit, contract, restrict, or unite the mind. "O unite me, that am pulverized earth! the heap is all scattered and cheap; for a handful give only a thought, and its attention is bought. If you had made me a star, a pearl, or a rainbow, the beams [thoughts] I had shot then would not have lessened my light [mental]; but now the more I grow in knowledge the less I become. The world is full of voices [attractions]; man is called and thrown by each; he answers all, knows every note and call of temptation; hence fresh infatuation still tempts, or old usurps his will. Yet if you had clipt my wings, when I was coffined in this quickened mass of sin [the flesh], and had saved that light [of the mind], which you then freely bestowed, I am afraid I should have spurned you, and said you neglected me, or that your stock was less. But now since you blessed me so much, I grieve, my God! that you have made me such. I grieve? O, yes! you know I do. Come, and relieve, and tame, and keep down with thy [divine] light, earthly dust that would rise and dim my sight! Lest left alone too long amidst the noise and throng [of things], overwhelmed I, striving to save [keep] everything, die by parts [particles]." Hence his opening prayer to knit his scattered dust or being.

The Incarnation, and Passion plays upon the paradoxical union of opposites implicit in the religious events of its title. The union of divine and human nature in the Incarnation looks at once to its no less paradoxical end in the Passion:

> *Lord! when thou didst thy selfe undresse,*
> *Laying by thy robes of glory,*
> *To make us more, thou wouldst be lesse,*
> *And becam'st a wofull story.*

The wonder of the Incarnation is then magnified by two stanzas that exploit both the translation and the union of opposites:

> *To put on Clouds instead of light,*
> *And cloath the morning-starre with dust,*
> *Was a translation of such height*
> *As, but in thee, was ne'r exprest.*

> *Brave wormes and Earth! that thus could have*
> *A God Enclos'd within your Cell,*
> *Your maker pent up in a grave,*
> *Life lockt in death, heav'n in a shell!*

Others could glorify mortality by such means, but only Vaughan could express this union by such a translation as "clothe the morning star with dust." Then the mystery of the "woeful story" is explored:

> *Ah, my deare Lord! what couldst thou spye*
> *In this impure, rebellious clay,*
> *That made thee thus resolve to dye*
> *For those that kill thee every day?*

Now the Incarnation adds to the wonder of the martyrdom until only the ultimate cause can answer the riddle.

> *O what strange wonders could thee move*
> *To slight thy precious bloud, and breath?*
> *Sure it was Love, my Lord; for Love*
> *Is only stronger far than death.*

The motive thus becomes the means to the end of the Passion, and the means now surpasses its power in the Song of Solomon (8, 6): "for love is strong as death." In love and religion, paradox reached beyond logic.

Vaughan's search was not a matter of one poem, but was continual. In *Vanity of Spirit* he begins:

> *Quite spent with thoughts I left my Cell, and lay*
> *Where a shrill spring tun'd to the early day.*
>   *I beg'd here long, and gron'd to know*
>   *Who gave the Clouds so brave a bow,*
>   *Who bent the spheres, and circled in*
>   *Corruption with this glorious Ring,*
>   *What is his name, and how I might*
>   *Descry some part of his great light.*

After this anticipation of his famous image, he searched Nature, and came at last

> *To search my selfe, where I did find*
> *Traces, and sounds of a strange kind.*
> *Here of this mighty spring, I found some drills [rills]*
> *With Ecchoes beaten from th' eternall hills.*

But his little light gave out, and he concluded:

> *Since in these veyls my Ecclips'd Eye*
> *May not approach thee, (for at night*
> *Who can have commerce with the light?)*
> *I'le disapparell, and to buy*
> *But one half glaunce most gladly dye.*

Another attempt to find the answer among the Creatures is found in *Cock-crowing*. This title is related to his epigraph for *The Lampe*, Mark xiii, 35: "Watch you therefore, for you know not when the master of the house cometh, at Even, or at mid-night, or at the Cock-crowing, or in the morning." Another Hermetic idea of Thomas Vaughan was that the soul is guided by "a seed or glance of light . . . descending from the first Father of Lights," which is in some measure shared by the rest of Creation. Hence the poem begins:

> *Father of lights! what Sunnie seed,*
> *What glance of day hast thou confin'd*
> *Into this bird? To all the breed*
> *This busie Ray thou hast assign'd;*
>   *Their magnetisme works all night,*
>   *And dreams of Paradise and light.*

But again as in *Vanity of Spirit* he finds

> *Onely this Veyle which thou hast broke,*
> *And must be broken yet in me,*
> *This veyle, I say, is all the cloke*

> *And cloud which shadows thee from me.*
> *This veyle thy full-ey'd love denies,*
> *And onely gleams and fractions spies.*

And this time he concludes with a touch of depreciative wit:

> *O take it off! make no delay,*
> *But brush me with thy light, that I*
> *May shine unto a perfect day,*
> *And warme me at thy glorious Eye!*
> *O take it off! or till it flee,*
> *Though with no Lilie, stay with me!*

No lily of purity, or lily of the field? In his devotional *Mount of Olives* he puts the Song of Solomon (2, 16-17) into this context: "Thou that feedest among the Lilies untill the day breaks and the shadows flee, what is there in my heart where onely tares and thistles grow, that thou canst feed upon?"

The Dwelling-place returns to Christ as the Light, and particularly his answer to the question in John i, 38, "where dwellest thou?" Vaughan's answer is now more confident:

> *What happy, secret fountain,*
> *Fair shade, or mountain,*
> *Whose undiscover'd virgin glory*
> *Boasts it this day, though not in story,*
> *Was then thy dwelling? did some cloud,*
> *Fix'd to a Tent, descend and shrowd*
> *My distrest Lord? or did a star,*
> *Beckon'd by thee, though high and far,*
> *In sparkling smiles haste gladly down*
> *To lodge light, and increase her own?*
> *My dear, dear God! I do not know*
> *What lodged thee then, nor where, nor how;*
> *But I am sure, thou dost now come*
> *Oft to a narrow, homely room,*
> *Where thou too hast but the least part,*
> *My God, I mean* my sinful heart.

With these allusions to Christ's coming to dwell among men, the poem descends from Vaughan's sublime imagery of light to his homely imagery of the heart. It is easy to see why his most splendid imagery was related to light.

The Morning-watch shows with what elation Vaughan could greet the return of light; it is like a release from death. At least it is pointed by such a contrast at the end, and may be appreciated by a comparison with the Body's response to the Soul in *Death: A Dialogue*. The Body cannot tell how he will stand it:

> *But if all sence wings not with thee,*
> *And something still be left the dead,*
> *I'le wish my Curtaines off, to free*
> *Me from so darke and sad a bed;*
>
> *A nest of nights, a gloomie sphere,*
> *Where shadowes thicken, and the Cloud*
> *Sits on the Suns brow all the yeare,*
> *And nothing moves without a shrowd.*

In *The Morning-watch* all nature worships the return of light, and even for the pious soul it is like a return to life:

> *The Pious soul by night*
> *Is like a clouded starre, whose beames, though sed*
> *To shed their light*
> *Under some Cloud,*
> *Yet are above,*
> *And shine and move*
> *Beyond that mistie shrowd.*
> *So in my Bed,*
> *That Curtain'd grave, though sleep, like ashes, hide*
> *My lamp and life, both shall in thee abide.*

It is from this that his soul rises to the glory of light and life.

The Retreate regrets the effects of the soul's incarnation in the world of time. Likewise in *Childe-hood*, but there he begins:

> *I cannot reach it; and my striving eye*
> *Dazzles at it, as at eternity.*

Here his longing for the realm of eternity makes him differ from other men:

> *Some men a forward motion love,*
> *But I by backward steps would move . . .*

Unfortunately he can now go backward only by going forward:

> *And when this dust falls to the urn,*
> *In that state I came return.*

Nothing but death can release the soul from time back to eternity, its home. This poem deals with the soul's longing for its origin and its sense of alienation by the sinful flesh. Critical is the time before he had lost sight of his first love,

> *When on some gilded Cloud or flowre*
> *My gazing soul would dwell an houre,*
> *And in those weaker glories spy*
> *Some shadows of eternity;*

and before he lost this sense of eternity,

> *Or had the black art to dispence*
> *A sev'rall sinne to ev'ry sence,*
> *But felt through all this fleshly dresse*
> *Bright shootes of everlastingnesse.*

Eternity and time, light and shadow, backward and forward, these are the polarities that define Vaughan's feeling in this poem.

> *But ah! my soul with too much stay*
> *Is drunk, and staggers in the way!*

Only the separation of body and soul can restore his soul to sobriety or the right path.

Peace has Vaughan's most lilting tune; but peace, like his *Retreate*, leads "Afar beyond the stars." Paradoxically it is defined by metaphors of war. It is guarded by "a winged Sentrie" and "Beauteous files," but commanded by "one born in a Manger." Thus it becomes a refuge or fortress for those who will leave the "foolish ranges" or ranks of this world. It is also a flower because love brought peace, the only security to man.

"Silence, and stealth of dayes!" is without title, but a moving poem on death which laments a personal loss. It presents death in terms of a light gone out and the subsequent darkness, but the loss is registered in terms of days, the product of light and the measure of time. The "silence and stealth of dayes" is multiplied into "Twelve hundred houres," before the light becomes a lamp "To brave the night," and finally "his Sun." Then time is multiplied into smaller parts:

> *So o'er fled minutes I retreat*
> *Unto that hour*
> *Which shew'd thee last, but did defeat*
> *Thy light and pow'r.*

Until he is conscious of nothing but the lamp gone out:

> *I search, and rack my soul to see*
> *Those beams again,*
> *But nothing but the snuff to me*
> *Appeareth plain.*

Then the lamp is translated into body and soul, or "snuff" and light:

> *That, dark and dead, sleeps in its known,*
> *And common urn,*
> *But those, fled to their Makers throne,*
> *There shine and burn.*

Yet this flight deepens his sense of separation:

> *O could I track them! but souls must*
> *Track one the other,*
> *And now the spirit, not the dust,*
> *Must be thy brother.*

But he has a final recourse, which is the Gospel:

> *Yet I have one Pearle, by whose light*
> *All things I see,*
> *And in the heart of Earth and night*
> *Find Heaven, and thee.*

He finds consolation in a spiritual source of light, leading from earth and night to heaven and thee, or to a resolution of the basic imagery of the poem.

Among various poems contrasting man and nature, or the different levels of being, often to nature's advantage, a good example is the one on Romans 8, 19: "And do they so?" In such poems Vaughan commonly gives the lowest orders an Hermetic sense like the magnetism of the loadstone. One of the sharpest examples of this contrast is "Sure, there's a tye of Bodyes!" And "as the bodies dissolve with the bond into clay, love languishes, and memory rusts, covered by that cold dust; for things thus centered in earth, without beams [light] or action [influence], neither give, nor take contact; and man is such a marigold, that without beams, he shuts up and hangs his head [like the flower]. / Absent things join within the equator, being equidistant from the poles, and Sense unites distant things; herbs sleep toward the

East, and some fowls watch thence the return of light. But hearts are not so kind [by nature]: deceptive and short delights tell us the world is splendid, and wrap us in flights of fancy wide of a trustworthy grave. / Thus Lazarus was removed; for it is our foe's chief art first to drown all good objects by distance, and then besiege the heart [with others]. But I will be my own death's-head; and though the flatterer say, *I live*, be sure not to believe, because we cannot know uncertainties." Thus Vaughan reveals the weakness of man.

Vaughan's most famous poem, *The World*, derives both title and substance from his Scriptural epigraph, I John ii, 16-17:

"All that is in the world, the lust of the flesh, the lust of the Eyes, and the pride of life, is not of the Father, but is of the world.

"And the world passeth away, and the lusts thereof; but he that doth the will of God abideth for ever."

Vaughan constructs his poem upon this opposition between the world and God. First as the realms of time and eternity, by the splendid antithesis which makes time the shadow of eternity in Plato's *Timaeus*, as the Ring of light is translated into shadow by the spheres. These opposites become the poles of being for man:

I saw Eternity the other night
Like a great Ring of pure and endless light,
    All calm, as it was bright;
And round beneath it, Time in hours, days, years,
        Driv'n by the spheres
Like a vast shadow mov'd, In which the world
    And all her train were hurl'd.

The epithets given to the Ring suggest the attractions of eternity as opposed to the pressures of time in which the world moves. Then he begins to describe the train of lusts in which the world is hurled; first in the "doting Lover," who provides a contrast to the conclusion. Appropriately his gaze is not directed towards the Ring: "while he his eyes did pour / Upon a flowr." Upon "his dear Treasure" Vaughan seems to lavish his new scorn for the Wits of profane love.

The lust of the Statesman is much more oppressive and also the most devious of all. Here the dark side of the antithesis multiplies its effects:

> *The darksome States-man hung with weights and woe,*
> *Like a thick midnight-fog, mov'd there so slow*
>   *He did not stay, nor go;*
> *Condemning thoughts like sad Ecclipses scowl*
>   *Upon his soul,*
> *And Clouds of crying witnesses without*
>   *Pursued him with one shout.*
> *Yet digg'd the Mole, and lest his ways be found,*
>   *Workt under ground . . .*

The description dwells upon privations of light and underground ways to project this pillar of state. He got his prey, "but one did see / That policie," while he consumed churches, perjury, blood, and tears. Vaughan now employs the rhetoric of dispraise as he exhibits comparable power to depreciate the lusts of the world.

Avarice is a more sordid vice than power, but the miser lives in apparent straits and will not trust any of his treasure to heaven (Matthew 6, 20):

> *The fearfull miser on a heap of rust*
> *Sate pining all his life there, did scarce trust*
>   *His own hands with the dust,*
> *Yet would not place one peece above, but lives*
>   *In feare of theeves.*

The Epicure has another heaven:

> *The down-right Epicure plac'd heav'n in sense,*
>   *And scorn'd pretence;*

> *While others, slipt into a wide Excesse,*
>   *Said little lesse.*

Still others are more contemptible:

> *The weaker sort slight, triviall wares Inslave,*
>   *Who think them brave,*
> *And poor, despised truth sate Counting by*
>   *Their victory.*

The neglected accountant sat reckoning by their victory the consequences (of his defeat).

The last stanza turns from the dark side of the antithesis to the light side, or back to the original image:

> *Yet some, who all this while did weep and sing,*
> *And sing and weep, soar'd up into the Ring;*
>   *But most would use no wing.*
> *O fools, said I, thus to prefer dark night*
>   *Before true light!*

Then as he rebukes this preference for the dark night of the world, he hears another voice:

> *But as I did their madnes so discusse*
>   *One whisper'd thus,*
> This Ring the Bride-groome did for none provide
>   But for his bride.

And this is the voice of Revelation (19) making the Ring a sign of marriage with the Lamb. Altogether, the passage from darkness to light, from the world to God, is dependent both on our "wing" or effort and on the "Bridegroom" Christ.

In *The Pulley* Herbert had given "rest" a Pandora-box turn; in *Man* Vaughan relates it to his philosophy. He begins by observing some habits of nature that excite his envy; he finds "stedfastness" and "staidness" in nature as opposed to motion and restlessness in man. His dialectic between man and nature produces the answer, and it arises from a comparison of their activities, beginning with birds, bees, and flowers, and is related to time. First, nature shows its qualities with respect to time:

> *Where birds like watchful Clocks the noiseless date*
> *And Intercourse of times divide . . .*

Nature is faithful "To His divine appointments" and its peace is not broken by worldly concern (Matthew 6).

Then man's activities are contrasted in two parallel stanzas, beginning with his distractions:

> *Man hath still either toyes or Care;*
> *He hath no root, nor to one place is ty'd,*
> *But ever restless and Irregular*
> *About this Earth doth run and ride;*
> *He knows he hath a home, but scarce knows where,*
> *He sayes it is so far*
> *That he hath quite forgot how to go there.*

Man lacks nature's attributes, but he knows he has a home, as in *The Retreate*, even if he has lost his way. Indeed, his restlessness suggests that his home is not here, that he cannot rest in nature:

> *He knocks at all doors, strays and roams;*
> *Nay hath not so much wit as some stones have,*
> *Which in the darkest nights point to their homes*
> *By some hid sense their Maker gave.*

The comparison appears to leave the advantage with nature and to rebuke man for having less wit than loadstones.

We must observe, however, that the final lines remove the blame and find purpose in man's restlessness:

> *Man is the shuttle, to whose winding quest*
>   *And passage through these looms*
> *God order'd motion, but ordain'd no rest.*

Thus man is not governed by the law of nature, but obeys an impulse of the soul, his own sanction. Man's resolving difference is related to "these looms" of time as nature is related to the "Intercourse of times" in the first stanza. Nothing could be more fundamental, since the poem is concerned with a contrast between the powers of man and nature in the world of time.

One of the first poems in Book II of *Silex Scintillans* is haunted by the same vision that we found in *The World*. It is one of his finest poems on death, and again without title:

> *They are all gone into the world of light!*
>   *And I alone sit lingring here;*
> *Their very memory is fair and bright,*
>   *And my sad thoughts doth clear.*

The attraction of this world of light beautifies death itself:

> *Dear, beauteous death! the Jewel of the Just,*
>   *Shining nowhere but in the dark;*
> *What mysteries do lie beyond thy dust,*
>   *Could man outlook that mark!*

Usually death is a jewel only to the just and shines only in the darkness of life. But a feeling of transcendence often produces a sense of frustration in Vaughan, and then he seeks reassurance:

> *If a star were confin'd into a Tomb,*
>   *Her captive flames must needs burn there;*
> *But when the hand that lockt her up, gives room,*
>   *She'll shine through all the sphære.*

This image connects the soul with his vision, and is elaborated in *The Bird:*

> *For each inclosed Spirit is a star*
> *Inlightning his own little sphære,*
> *Whose light, though fetcht and borrowed from far,*
> *Both mornings makes, and evenings there.*

Such Hermetic overtones pass into allusions to Romans 8, 21, in his concluding prayer:

> *O Father of eternal life, and all*
> *Created glories under thee!*
> *Resume thy spirit from this world of thrall*
> *Into true liberty.*

> *Either disperse these mists, which blot and fill*
> *My perspective still as they pass;*
> *Or else remove me hence unto that hill,*
> *Where I shall need no glass.*

But this frustrating physical veil, which he often laments in his poetry, is a limitation that he discovers in the book of God's works. This poem, like *The World*, sustains its power and builds to a conclusion appropriate to his feeling about death.

The Night is given a religious context by its epigraph, John 3, 2, which concerns Nicodemus: "The same came to Jesus by night, and said unto him, Rabbi, we know that thou art a teacher come from God: for no man can do these miracles that thou doest, except God be with him." And the fifth stanza has two references to define "Christ's progress, and his prayer time": Mark 1, 35, "And in the morning, rising up a great while before day, he went out, and departed into a solitary place, and there prayed." Luke 21, 37, "And in the day time he was teaching in the temple; and at night he went out, and abode in the mount that is called the mount of Olives."

These passages suggest the central opposition of the poem: night versus day as ways to God. But they also suggest where Nicodemus found him, where the poem finds him: for not Solomon's temple (2 Chronicles 3),

> *But his own living works, did my Lord hold*
> *And lodge alone;*
> *Where trees and herbs did watch and peep*
> *And wonder, while the Jews did sleep.*

Of course Nicodemus had the vision of faith, which shall see (Malachi 4, 2) "the Sun of righteousness arise with healing in his wings."

> *Most blest believer he!*
> *Who in that land of darkness and blinde eyes*
> *Thy long expected healing wings could see,*
> *When thou didst rise;*
> *And what can never more be done,*
> *Did at mid-night speak with the Sun!*

Thus is the Son to be found at night. Vaughan had felt the wings of evening in his *Amoret* poems.

Then Vaughan salutes night with something like the thesaurus wit of Cowley. First as a refuge from the diurnal round of the world:

> *Dear night! this world's defeat;*
> *The stop to busie fools; care's check and curb;*
> *The day of Spirits; my soul's calm retreat*
> *Which none disturb!*
> *Christ's progress, and his prayer time;*
> *The hours to which high Heaven doth chime.*

And then in terms of "his own living works" amplified by the Song of Solomon (v):

> *God's silent, searching flight:*
> *When my Lord's head is filled with dew, and all*
> *His locks are wet with the clear drops of night;*
> *His still, soft call;*
> *His knocking time; The soul's dumb watch,*
> *When Spirits their fair kindred catch.*

He concludes that if all his "loud, evil days" were "Calm and unhaunted as is thy dark Tent," then he would lodge in Heaven all the year long, and never stray here.

However, his life is not so blessed, and must be lived in the diurnal world of the sun:

> *But living where the Sun*
> *Doth all things wake, and where all mix and tyre*
> *Themselves and others, I consent and run*
> *To ev'ry myre;*
> *And by this world's ill-guiding light,*
> *Erre more than I can do by night.*

It is in the daylight that he goes astray, not in the "dark Tent," whose peace is rent only by "some Angel's wing or voice," and where he, like Nicodemus, came to God:

> *There is in God, some say,*
> *A deep, but dazzling darkness; As men here*
> *Say it is late and dusky, because they*
> *See not all clear;*
> *O for that night! where I in him*
> *Might live invisible and dim.*

After his own paradoxical progress, this petition unites for Vaughan both nature and night as the devotional haunt of the Lord.

In *The Water-fall* Vaughan finds a parable of man's destiny; it lends a voice to "time's silent stealth." Description leads to the slow emergence of the parallel. The waters flow with "deep murmurs," then "chide and call" as if afraid of this steep place. Here death comes to the surface:

> *The common pass,*
> *Where, clear as glass,*
> *All must descend*
> *Not to an end,*
> *But quickned by this deep and rocky grave,*
> *Rise to a longer course more bright and brave.*

As the grave becomes obvious, the water is ambiguously quickened, and rises to a longer and brighter course.

Now Vaughan draws inferences from the waterfall to man's fate, based on parallels between them. While it had pleased his "pensive eye," it had taught him Christian answers to the fear of death. The analogy provokes him to reflect upon water as a religious symbol leading into the mysteries of baptism and Creation:

> *O useful Element and clear!*
> *My sacred wash and cleanser here,*
> *My first consigner unto those*
> *Fountains of life, where the Lamb goes!*
> *What sublime truths, and wholesome themes,*
> *Lodge in thy mystical, deep streams!*
> *Such as dull man can never finde*
> *Unless that Spirit lead his minde,*
> *Which first upon thy face did move,*
> *And hatch'd all with his quickning love.*

Thus religious vision is required for the interpretation of nature. Now the parallel is completed, but this "restagnates" the "quickened":

> *As this loud brook's incessant fall*
> *In streaming rings restagnates all,*
> *Which reach by course the bank, and then*
> *Are no more seen, just so pass men.*

This passage discovers the limitation of his visual symbol, and obliges him to reject it:

> *O my invisible estate,*
> *My glorious liberty, still late!*
> *Thou art the Channel my soul seeks,*
> *Not this with Cataracts and Creeks.*

Thus his governing figure leads to its rejection because the natural ultimately fails to express the supernatural or Christian.

In *Quickness*, one of his most characteristic poems, Vaughan employs the neatness of form that is admired in Herbert. He contrasts false life and true life in two pairs of symmetrical stanzas, and then opposes their quickness in a final stanza. The conclusion seems to reflect the contrast between the natural state and the state of grace found in Ephesians 2, 4-5, where God "for his great love wherewith he loved us, / Even when we were dead in sins, hath quickened us together with Christ."

The main antithesis is detailed in the poem: "False life! a flattering contrast, and no more, when will you be gone? You foul sham of all men, who would not have true life come on them. / You are a Moon-like toil [false, chargeable, etc.], a blind self-puzzling state; a dark contest of waves and wind; merely a stormy debate; [all associated with the moon]. / Life is a fixed, penetrating light [unlike the moon], a conscious Joy; no fortune, or caprice; but ever bright and calm and full, yet doth not surfeit; [oppositions to the moon]. / It is such a blissful thing, that it constantly animates, and shines and smiles, and has the ability [art] to please without Eternity [only found in heaven]." The conclusion opposes two forms of the illusive:

> *Thou art a toylsom Mole, or less,*
> *A moving mist;*

> *But life is, what none can express,*
> A quickness, which my God hath kist.

A working mole and a moving mist produce the illusion of life or movement. True life or the state of grace cannot be expressed, except in metaphor. It is life quickened by divine love or God's mercy.

The basic contrast has turned on the opposition between false and true life or light, centered in associations of the moon. Vaughan's last line would lose the force of its "quickness" if it did not rest on the contrast between appearance and reality that is elaborated in the poem. The quick and the dead have seldom been distinguished more paradoxically or more neatly.

In closing *Silex Scintillans* we may recall the words of the Preface: "By the last Poems in the book, were not that mistake here prevented, you would judge all to be fatherless, and the Edition posthume; for, indeed, I was nigh unto death, and am still at no great distance from it." His sign of departure is clear in *L'Envoy:*

> *Arise, arise!*
> *And like old cloaths fold up these skies,*
> *This long worn veyl.*

IX

Andrew Marvell
1621-1678

Andrew Marvell had been at Cambridge in the time of Crashaw and Cowley, had been rescued from the Jesuits by his father, and had gone on a foreign tour during the Civil War before he showed real signs of becoming a poet. In 1645 he was demonstrating his wit in Rome to one whom Dryden later celebrated for his lack of wit, Flecknoe. Possibly Flecknoe was already a Catholic acquaintance as well as a priest. Marvell returned to England in 1646, and made his presence known by an elegy for Lord Hastings in 1649, which associated him with Dryden, Herrick, and Denham. At the same time he appeared in an edition of *Lucasta*, prepared by Lovelace in prison, to defend "his noble Friend, Mr. Richard Lovelace, upon his Poems." This is not the sort of company that finally made him a colleague of Milton. Indeed, Marvell was never really involved in the Civil War. And his poems, with few exceptions, were published posthumously, in 1681, and then incompletely. This reticence was unusual for one who became a noted Restoration satirist.

In his satire, *Fleckno, an English Priest at Rome*, Marvell begins in a familiar way:

> *Oblig'd by frequent visits of this man,*
> *Whom as Priest, Poet, and Musician,*
> *I for some branch of Melchizedek took,*
> *(Though he derives himself from my Lord Brooke),*
> *I sought his Lodging, which is at the Sign*
> *Of the sad Pelican; Subject divine*
> *For Poetry . . .*

Then he caricatures Flecknoe in this triple capacity, but makes him as thin as Dryden makes Shadwell fat, and almost starved:

> *Nor was I longer to invite him Scant:*
> *Happy at once to make him Protestant*
> *And Silent. Nothing now Dinner stay'd*
> *But till he had himself a Body made.*
> *I mean till he were drest: for else so thin*
> *He stands, as if he only fed had been*
> *With consecrated Wafers: and the Host*
> *Hath sure more flesh and blood than he can boast.*
> *This Basso Relievo of a Man,*
> *Who as a Camel tall, yet easly can*
> *The Needles Eye thread without any stich,*
> *(His only impossible is to be rich) . . .*

This kind of Biblical wit (Luke 18, 25) and play with the Eucharist is not the reform sought by the sacred poets. But Flecknoe is not yet dressed:

> *Lest his too suttle Body, growing rare,*
> *Should leave his Soul to wander in the Air,*
> *He therefore circumscribes himself in rimes;*
> *And swaddled in's own papers seaven times,*

> *Wears a close Jacket of poetick Buff,*
> *With which he doth his third Dimension Stuff.*

We may notice that Marvell's geometrical wit is already at play. However, a visitor interrupted their departure, down the staircase from Flecknoe's confined chamber, and became quarrelsome:

> *He gathring fury, still made sign to draw;*
> *But himself there clos'd in a Scabbard saw*
> *As narrow as his Sword's; and I, that was*
> *Delightful, said there can no Body pass* [delighted]
> *Except by penetration hither, where*
> *Two make a crowd, nor can three Persons here*
> *Consist but in one substance. Then, to fit*
> *Our peace, the Priest said I too had some wit:*
> *To prov't, I said, the place doth us invite*
> *By its own narrowness, Sir, to unite.*
> *He ask'd me pardon; and to make me way*
> *Went down, as I him follow'd to obey.*

To prove his wit he adds to the "penetration" metaphor of the *Horatian Ode* a profane application of the "trinity."

But his poetic torture was not over. After dinner "the waxen Youth" insisted on reading Flecknoe's poems:

> *Yet he first kist them, and after takes pains*
> *To read; and then, because he understood*
> *Not one Word, thought and swore that they were good.*

This had been the test of "strong lines" for their enemies.

> *But all his praises could not now appease*
> *The provok't Author, whom it did displease*
> *To hear his Verses, by so just a curse,*
> *That were ill made condemn'd to be read worse:*
> *And how (impossible) he made yet more*
> *Absurdityes in them than were before.*
> *For he his untun'd voice did fall or raise*

> *As a deaf Man upon a Viol playes,*
> *Making the half points and the periods run*
> *Confus'der than the atomes in the Sun.*

The disdainful poet left in a rage, and the rebellious youth

> *Wept bitterly as disinherited.*
> *Who should commend his Mistress now? Or who*
> *Praise him? both difficult indeed to do*
> *With truth. I counsell'd him to go in time,*
> *Ere the fierce Poets anger turn'd to rime.*

No one else came as close to Donne's satires as this, or contradicted the modernizations of Pope more effectively. For *Fleckno* is in the satiric mode of Donne: events expressed in narrative rhyme; not verse pointed by rhyme, but rather by metaphoric wit or odd similes; the couplets lost in syntactic involution, not articulated by parallelism and balance, but achieving a more dramatic movement.

Yet Marvell could also achieve the antithetic mode of Jonson and Waller, or the gallantry desired by Walsh. His eulogy of Lovelace begins in this manner:

> *Our times are much degenerate from those*
> *Which your sweet Muse, which your fair Fortune chose;*
> *And as complexions alter with the Climes,*
> *Our wits have drawne th'infection of our times.*
> *That candid Age no other way could tell*
> *To be ingenious, but by speaking well.*
> *Who best could prayse, had then the greatest prayse,*
> *Twas more esteemd to give, than weare the Bayes.*

Wit then was a mode of civility; but "the infection of our times" embraces more than wit:

> *These vertues now are banisht out of Towne,*
> *Our Civill Wars have lost the Civicke crowne.*
> *He highest builds, who with most Art destroys,*
> *And against others Fame his owne employs.*

If the first couplet has lost the oak-garland of Roman citizen-
ship, one wonders whether the second couplet might include
Cromwell. Certainly, so far as Lovelace is concerned,

> *The barbed Censurers begin to looke*
> *Like the grim consistory on thy Booke;*
> *And on each line cast a reforming eye,*
> *Severer than the yong Presbytery.*

Literary criticism has become a branch of religious reforma-
tion. But the Parliamentary forces forgot to reckon with the
ladies:

> *Lovelace that thaw'd the most congealed brest,*
> *He who lov'd best, and them defended best;*
> *Whose hand so rudely grasps the steely brand,*
> *Whose hand so gently melts the Ladies hand;*
> *They all in mutiny, though yet undrest,*
> *Sally'd, and would in his defence contest.*

And then Marvell, not to be outdone, would join the ladies:

> *And one, the loveliest that was yet e're seen,*
> *Thinking that I too of the rout had been,*
> *Mine eyes invaded with a female spight,*
> *(She knew what pain 'twould be to lose that sight.)*

And thus defends himself with compliment against Lucasta
herself:

> *O no, mistake not, I reply'd, for I*
> *In your defence, or in his cause would dy.*
> *But he secure of glory and of time,*
> *Above their envy, or mine aid doth clime.*

Moreover, Marvell had proved that he too knew how to be
ingenious by speaking well, in the more urbane couplets of his
time.

Yet the infection of the times had put the poet out of court, and Marvell turns in the *Horatian Ode* to its larger civil manifestation. This ode is not merely a political poem but a transition from his view of the times to the new order, which must be explained metaphysically. For the *Ode* raises the problem of fate in Marvell, especially as it involves the providential view of history current in his time. History was a kind of national drama determined by men under the providence of God, of which "the usual order of nature" was the ordinary law, as Milton said in *The Christian Doctrine*.

In *The Rehearsal Transprosed* Marvell later distinguished fate into "several families of the necessities." He accused Parker of deriving "that imaginary absolute government, upon which rock we all ruined," or one like it, from the original necessity "that was pre-eternal to all things, and exercised dominion not only over all humane things, but over Jupiter himself and the rest of the Deities, and drove the great iron nail through the axletree of nature" (ed. Thompson, II, 364). The necessity of God is described thus: "beside all other the innumerable calamities to which human life is exposed, he has in like manner distinguished the government of the world by the intermitting seasons of discord, war, and public disturbance. Neither has he so ordered it only (as men endeavour to express it) by meer permission, but sometimes out of complacency" (ibid., II, 367). Sometimes God does not simply permit it, but takes satisfaction in it. In *De Constantia* Justus Lipsius had provided a popular Neo-Stoic formulation of mutability and decay related to "the wonderful and incomprehensible Law of Necessity," which included the Mathematical among the different kinds of fate.

Thus fate may appear in the order of nature and the providence of God, or in the geometry that measures or describes earth and space. These are important clues to Marvell's use of nature as metaphysical imagery, the metaphor of extension in space, or physical properties for metaphysical realities. There could also have been an element of fashion. In 1654 Thomas Blount borrowed his popular *Academie of Eloquence* largely from Hoskins, but he made some attempt to bring the *Directions* up to date. A passage I have quoted appears with some alterations: "We study now-a-days according to the predominancy of Criticall fancies. Whilst Moral Philosophy was in request, it was rudeness, not to be sententious; whilst Mathematics were of late in vogue, all similitudes came from *Lines*, *Circles* and *Angles;* But now that Mars is predominant, we must *recruit* our wits, and give our words a new *Quarter*" (p. 34). Blount changes the arbiter of fashion from "Courtly inclinations" to "Criticall fancies," reverses the order of the sententious and the mathematical vogue, and adds a martial vogue. In 1667 when Thomas Sprat outmoded metaphysical wit in his *History of the Royal Society*, he rejected "Mathematical Comparisons" more reluctantly: "The Sciences of mens Brains are none of the best Materials for this kind of Wit. Very few have happily succeeded in Logical, Metaphysical, Grammatical, nay even scarce in Mathematical Comparisons; and the reason is, because they are most of them conversant about things removed from the Senses, and so cannot surprise the *fancy* with very obvious, or quick, or sensible delights" (III, xxxv). But Marvell was enamored with mathematics as a handmaid to metaphysical wit.

The beginning of *An Horatian Ode upon Cromwell's Return from Ireland* is certainly unusual: Cromwell did not forsake poetry; therefore it must reflect the poet's feeling. The ambitious youth now has to give up poetry and take up arms, which Marvell did not. So Cromwell had to give up "the inglorious Arts of Peace" and turn to War, but "inglorious" by now is tinged with irony. Certainly "restless" sounds like undirected energy. Then he urged his star of destiny into activity like that of lightning, a force of nature, cutting his way through rivals and enemies alike, and destroying Church and State, until a Caesar's head blasted through his laurels.

> *'Tis Madness to resist or blame*
> *The force of angry Heavens flame:*
>   *And, if we would speak true,*
>   *Much to the Man is due.*

It is useless to blame Providence or fate, and candor obliges us to give the devil his due.

We must give credit to a man who could leave a reserved life in his private gardens, and by industrious valor climb high enough to pull down "the great Work of Time" and cast the old kingdom into a new mold, even though justice complain against fate, and plead for the ancient rights. But (in the providential view of history) they depend upon the strength or force of men. And in natural necessity, although nature abhors a vacuum, it tolerates even less two bodies in the same place at the same time. *Fleckno* had proved satirically this family of necessity. Cromwell, like a Roman, could show the deepest scars of war, and had the political guile to inveigle Charles into a trap. Against war, "wiser Art" here seems invidious.

As an actor in this drama of fate Charles plays his part with regal decorum, makes no vulgar appeal to the Gods to defend his helpless right, but accepts his fate with dignity. To emphasize this act of insurance (the regicide), Marvell repeats "memorable" and makes "forced" carry the implication both of force and of fate. The Roman parallel conveys a mixed reaction to the event. The "happy Fate" is then extended into the fortunate consequences of the event, and the virtues of the new instrument of fate, who pays his rents or royalties in kingdoms, and as far as possible makes his fame theirs.

As a servant of the Commons, he is given a new similitude, which resumes the celestial figure of power in a more obedient form, that of a falcon. As a bird of prey he may be directed to enhance the national prestige. Now the Pict or Scot shall find no cover in his variegated mind, but from this sober-colored valor shrink underneath the plaid, happy if he can

escape physical detection. In conclusion Marvell mixes admo-
nition with praise: because Cromwell owes his power to war
and fate, his virtues must maintain his destiny; his sword must
be kept upright both as a force to ward off evil (because the
cross-hilt suggests the crucifix) and in the arts to sustain its
power.

In *Tom May's Death* Marvell chastises a poet as an apostate
who abandoned the Royalist cause when he lost the laureate-
ship to Davenant. It is appropriate that he be judged by the
poet he hoped to succeed, Ben Jonson. For Marvell as for
Vaughan, Jonson is in the Elysian fields, where May is hur-
ried drunk and tries to locate himself by familiar taverns:

> *At last while doubtfully he all compares,*
> *He saw near hand, as he imagin'd Ares.*
> *Such did he seem for corpulence and port,*
> *But 'twas a man much of another sort;*
> *'Twas Ben that in the dusky Laurel shade*
> *Amongst the Chorus of old Poets laid,*
> *Sounding of ancient Heroes, such as were*
> *The Subjects Safety, and the Rebel's Fear.*

Mars (Ares) would have been kinder to May than Marvell's
spokesman:

> *But Ben, who knew not neither foe nor friend,*
> *Sworn Enemy to all that do pretend,*
> *Rose more than ever he was seen severe,*

and berated May in no uncertain terms:

> *Far from these blessed shades tread back agen*
> *Most servil' wit, and Mercenary Pen . . .*
> *Go seek the novice Statesmen, and obtrude*
> *On them some Romane cast similitude,*
> *Tell them of Liberty, the Stories fine,*
> *Until you all grow Consuls in your wine.*

Presumably Marvell was not such a pen in the *Horatian Ode*, for he makes Jonson emphasize the error of May:

> *Foul Architect that hadst not Eye to see*
> *How ill the measures of these States agree.*
> *And who by Romes example England lay,*
> *Those but to Lucan do continue May.*

Then Jonson gives eloquent voice to the whole duty of the poet:

> *When the Sword glitters ore the Judges head,*
> *And fear has Coward Churchmen silenced,*
> *Then is the Poets time, 'tis then he drawes,*
> *And single fights forsaken Vertues cause.*
> *He, when the wheel of Empire, whirleth back,*
> *And though the World's disjointed Axel crack,*
> *Sings still of ancient Rights and better Times,*
> *Seeks wretched good, arraigns successful Crimes.*

Readers may ponder whether Marvell lived up to this credo in the *Horatian Ode*, when the whole order of things seemed to crack, or whether his conscience was stirred by the condemnation that follows:

> *But thou base man first prostituted hast*
> *Our spotless knowledge and the studies chast,*
> *Apostatizing from our Arts and us,*
> *To turn the Chronicler to Spartacus.*

The poet's party is found in the moral tradition of the classics, and an Horatian ode was responsible to that tradition.

Marvell does not omit a gibe at the arrangements for May's funeral made by the Council of State:

> *Poor Poet thou, and grateful Senate they,*
> *Who thy last Reckoning did so largely pay;*
> *And with the publick gravity would come,*
> *When thou hadst drunk thy last to lead thee home.*

But not where Spenser and Chaucer lie: "Nor here thy shade must dwell," in the realm of the Blessed; "return, return," to Hades and its tortures. After that "irrevocable Sentence . . . straight he vanished in a cloud of pitch." Marvell's view of May is unequivocal enough to make one reread *An Horatian Ode*. As satire the verse and rhetoric are moving toward the Neo-Classical mode; more intricate figures give way to the sharp metaphor and the mocking ambiguity; the method is more sententious and less narrative. But its subject is really the Civil War and May simply offers another approach to it.

After the *Horatian Ode* Marvell's career led from tutor to the daughter of Lord Fairfax, the Parliamentary general, and then tutor to a ward of Cromwell, to assistant to Milton in the Latin Secretaryship, and finally to Member of Parliament for Hull from 1659 to his death. In life the poet was submerged in the politician as he reversed the course of Fairfax and moved from retirement to involvement. *Upon Appleton House*, which was dedicated to Lord Fairfax, reveals a formative influence upon Marvell's poetry. Although the tradition of moralized nature or country life represented by Jonson, and carried on by Denham, is found in *Upon Appleton House*, it is amplified historically by Marvell.

For Marvell it is an experimental piece or thesaurus of his poetic motifs, having manifold relations with his other work. A few excerpts will suggest some of them. In imagery, humility alone can "immure / The Circle in the Quadrature," or square the circle. Of art and nature:

> *Art would more neatly have defac'd*
> *What she had laid so sweetly wast.*

When he says that a Fairfax "would respect / Religion, but not Right neglect . . . / For Justice still that Courage led," one may contrast the *Horatian Ode*. Or says of his own relation to nature:

> *Thus I, easie Philosopher,*
> *Among the Birds and Trees confer . . .*
> *Thrice happy he who, not mistook,*
> *Hath read in Natures mystick Book.*

And here suggestive of his poem *The Garden:*

> *How safe, methinks, and strong, behind*
> *These Trees have I incamp'd my Mind;*
> *Where Beauty, aiming at the Heart,*
> *Bends in some Tree its useless Dart;*
> *And where the World no certain Shot*
> *Can make, or me it toucheth not.*

But his moral view is most striking in his treatment of Fair-fax's relation to his garden. In 1650 Fairfax had left the command of the Parliamentary army for retirement at Nunappleton because of disagreement with Cromwell. In his *Second Defence of the English People*, which Marvell delivered to Bradshaw, Milton excuses Fairfax's retirement on the ground that he knew liberty would be safe with his successor, Cromwell. Here Marvell presents his view of Cromwell's rival in contrast to his *Horatian Ode:*

> *Who, when retired here to Peace,*
> *His warlike Studies could not cease;*
> *But laid these Gardens out in sport*
> *In the just Figure of a Fort;*
> *And with five Bastions it did fence,*
> *As aiming one for ev'ry Sense.*

In the moral war also, Marvell learned about defense against the batteries of sense as he extended this martial metaphor over the garden. But the extension is also historical:

> *Oh Thou, that dear and happy Isle,*
> *The Garden of the World ere while,*
> *Thou Paradise of four Seas,*

> *Which Heaven planted us to please,*
> *But, to exclude the World, did guard*
> *With watry if not flaming Sword;*
> *What luckless Apple did we tast,*
> *To make us Mortal, and Thee Wast?*

Thus the Civil War finds its parallel only in the loss of Eden. Now Fairfax enters into the destruction of their garden world:

> *And yet there walks one on the Sod,*
> *Who, had it pleased him and God,*
> *Might once have made our Gardens spring*
> *Fresh as his own and flourishing.*

And why did this fail to happen? Because it had to please both God and man, and Fairfax preferred otherwise:

> *But he preferr'd to the Cinque Ports*
> *These five imaginary Forts:*
> *And, in those half-dry Trenches, spann'd*
> *Pow'r which the Ocean might command.*
> *For he did, with his utmost Skill,*
> *Ambition weed, but Conscience till;*
> *Conscience, that Heaven-nursed Plant,*
> *Which most our Earthly Gardens want.*

However devoted Marvell was to gardens, the Cinque Ports still seemed more important to him, and Fairfax's choice a waste of ability. If conscience is a sensitive plant, it is not always an undivided blessing:

> *A prickling leaf it bears, and such*
> *As that which shrinks at ev'ry touch;*
> *But Flowrs eternal, and divine,*
> *That in the Crowns of Saints do shine.*

Yet the saint's way seems not to have pleased God in this case, because one earthly garden needed something more than what earthly gardens usually lack. If this example influenced Marvell's future career, it did not exhibit for the first time the delicate balance of his judgment; and it also involved Providence.

Bermudas may have been inspired by John Oxenbridge, in whose house Marvell tutored Cromwell's ward; at least, it is Marvell's most vivid reflection of the religious aspect of the Civil War. Here Marvell shows the benevolence of Providence in contrast to its stern necessity in the Civil War. It is presented as a song of thanksgiving by English pilgrims to an island "far kinder" than their own, where nature exhibits the difference in kindness. By his details Marvell shows how benevolence appears in the guidance of Providence, in the exotic bounty of nature, and in the religious fortunes of the voyagers:

> *He cast (of which we rather boast)*
> *The Gospels Pearl upon our Coast;*
> *And in these Rocks for us did frame*
> *A Temple, where to sound his Name.*

They dare boast a little because they have bought the Gospel's pearl, freedom of worship, by their sacrifices and efforts. Their song and rowing unite to point the final rhyme of their deliverance.

The Coronet deserts simple octosyllabics for a complex form combining lyric and heroic measures with intermixed rhyme, ending with interlocking triplets and a couplet. Its pastoral background can extend to Eden. The speaker feels that he has added too long to the crown of thorns that Christ derived from his humanity, and wants to redeem himself with a crown of flowers. His good intentions are never realized. In gathering flowers he dismantles the high head-dresses (towers) he has given to his shepherdess (profane love). And now presumes (so he deceives himself) that he can make a crown such as the King of Glory has never worn. Here the Serpent of Eden entwines worldly motives of fame and self-interest into his floral offering. Thus foolish man would debase, with flowers bound by mortal glory, the diadem already given by Heaven. In chagrin he appeals to the conqueror of the Serpent either to disentangle his worldly motives or to shatter his crown with them. Thus his efforts will not be entirely lost, for the spoils of his flowers and snake (its skin) while Christ treads on them, "May crown thy Feet, that could not crown thy Head." Crashaw's *Weeper* gave the paradox another form:

> Crown'd heads are Toyes; We goe to meete
> A worthy object: our Lord's feet.

Eyes and Tears is Marvell's revision of Ecclesiastes, the vanity of life translated into the wisdom of Nature. He sees more than Virgil's "*lacrimae rerum*," he sees their wisdom. The same eyes do not weep and see for reasons of economy, but tears correct the errors of sight, measure the deceits and vanities of the world, and make pity the basis of wisdom. How tears correct the measurements of eyes is expressed in geometrical imagery; how they weigh things, in terms of scales. What appears most fair, even laughter, turns to tears; likewise "all the Jewels which we prize." We may begin to suspect that the eyes see only vanity:

> I have through every Garden been,
> Amongst the Red, the White, the Green;
> And yet, from all the flow'rs I saw,
> No Honey, but these Tears could draw.

If this sounds like disillusionment, the "all-seeing Sun" teaches us understanding when it distills the world and finds its essence to be showers. Those "that weep the more, and see the less" are fortunate, because that is the way "to preserve their

Sight more true." The Magdalen's wisdom in tears enabled her "to fetter her Redeemer's feet." Nothing looks so fair "As two Eyes swoln with weeping" (and no sentiment is more paradoxical to the world); moreover, they make desire lose its fire; even Jupiter often slakes his lightning in the waves produced by the waxing moon (Cynthia). No incense is more precious to heaven:

> *The Incense was to Heaven dear,*
> *Not as a Perfume, but a Tear.*
> *And Stars show lovely in the Night,*
> *But as they seem the Tears of Light.*

And no beauty could seem more satisfying to eyes. So open your eyes and practice their noblest use; other eyes can see or sleep, but only human eyes can weep. Weep until eyes and tears are the same:

> *And each the other's difference bears;*
> *These weeping Eyes, those seeing Tears.*

Until sight is qualified by weeping, and tears qualified by seeing; or sight corrected by tears, and tears enabled to see. Then both the vanity and the wisdom of life will become perceptible.

Clorinda and Damon opposes in dialogue pagan and Christian pastoralism. The shepherdess expresses the *carpe diem* philosophy of classical poetry, enjoy today; the shepherd responds in Christian terms. His lack of gallantry is a moral attitude. At the beginning his flock has gone astray, but he has resolved not to. He is quite brusque in rejecting her offerings of grass for his sheep and flowers for his temples. Clorinda replies with her form of *carpe diem* before it passes. Each suggestion she makes belongs to pastoral love poetry, and he denigrates each one by giving it a Christian turn. He quite baffles her when he relates her pretty fountain to a baptismal font. When he explains what has changed him, he speaks of the shepherd's god Pan, but makes his words transcend a shepherd's understanding, although Pan now fills Damon's songs. When each agrees the other can make Pan sound sweet, they join in a chorus of praise to Pan, and thus resolve their differences. Throughout this dialogue the antithesis in feeling has been magnified by the common imagery but divergent associations which it provokes in the lovers.

A Dialogue between the Soul and Body might be taken as another conflict with natural necessity or the order of nature. Fulke Greville had expressed the rival claims on man in the "Chorus Sacerdotum" of his *Mustapha:*

> *Oh wearisome Condition of Humanity!*
> *Borne under one Law, to another bound:*
> *Vainely begot, and yet forbidden vanity;*
> *Created sicke, commanded to be sound:*
> *What meaneth Nature by these diverse Lawes?*

Donne had written of the soul imprisoned in the body and obliged to use the organs of the body, but not of the complaint of the body against the soul. In this poem the soul speaks as the rational or immortal soul, the body as a physical structure that is informed by the souls or faculties of growth and sense. Hence the Soul first complains of the disabilities that the anatomy of the body imposes on it. The Body retorts with the constraints which it suffers from the soul. It is impaled by the upright soul (like a skewer) so that it becomes its own vertical hazard; out of spite the soul animates and moves this useless form only to let it die after a life of agitation. The Body's riposte to rectitude is partly to Auden's "vertical man."

The Soul then complains of the pains and ills of the body that it is obliged to endure by its connection with the body;

and, what is worst of all, the cure, which only delays its re-
lease. The Body retorts with the psychic maladies which the
soul teaches it, hope, fear, love, hatred, joy, sorrow, or the
passions of the mind that are forced upon it.

> *What but a Soul could have the wit*
> *To build me up for Sin so fit?*

Marvell's conclusion reverses the verdict of Donne's *To the
Countess of Salisbury*. Donne is grateful to his souls of
growth and sense:

> *I owe my first souls thanks that they*
> *For my last soul did fit and mold my clay.*

In the body and soul dichotomy such things could be said
without prejudice to either side, but Marvell allows the Body
more lines in which to conclude by charging the Soul, appro-
priately enough, with a triumph of wit (or ability) that is not
in its best interest.

A Dialogue between the Resolved Soul and Created Pleasure
is often related to Ephesians 6, 16-17, which will supply the
shield, helmet, and sword that arm the Resolved Soul. But for
Created Pleasure we need to return, possibly to Cowley's *Soul*
(I), and certainly to the garden of *Appleton House*. When
Fairfax retired there, he did not cease his warlike studies, as
we know,

> *But laid these Gardens out in sport*
> *In the just Figure of a Fort;*
> *And with five Bastions it did fence,*
> *As aiming one for ev'ry Sense.*

There flowers "Their Silken Ensigns each displays," and

> *See how the Flow'rs, as at Parade,*
> *Under their Colours stand displaid.*

Here they have become the enemy or Created Pleasure:

> *See where an Army, strong as fair,*
> *With silken Banners spreads the air.*

Then Earth's garden tempts the Resolved Soul through the senses, one by one, taste, touch, smell, sight, and hearing. For the first the Soul cannot stop so long; for the second he finds easier rest in rectitude; for the third he would not be guilty of arrogance; for the fourth he admires nothing in man's image but God's art; for the fifth he would give any time he could spare, but when musical chords cannot bind him, temptation is useless. This point is emphasized by the contrasting meters of the Soul and Pleasure. The Chorus recalls Fairfax's moral garden:

> *Earth cannot show so brave a Sight*
> *As when a single Soul does fence*
> *The Batteries of alluring Sense,*
> *And Heaven views it with delight.*

But the war is not over. The senses combine their attack in sensuous beauty. Next, wealth is offered, then glory, and last, knowledge. To the first the Soul opposes heavenly beauty, to the second the worth that is above price, to the third the glory of moral conquest, to the last the achievement of humility. The Chorus now sings the triumph of the soul, for all other pleasures lie beyond the pole of the world, where they are in store for him. Thus Marvell imitates the moral garden of *Appleton House*, which was laid out by a warfaring Christian:

> *For he did, with his utmost Skill,*
> *Ambition weed, but Conscience till;*
> *Conscience, that Heaven-nursed Plant,*
> *Which most our Earthly Gardens want.*

Here its "prickling leaf" is more evident in the path of virtue, and ambition is more strictly weeded.

The Nymph complaining for the Death of her Faun is a song of innocent love disguising a song of betrayed love. The fawn is both a gift of and a substitute for her deceiver. Now wanton men have shot her fawn; its death is also wanton. Yet if her prayers may prevail with Heaven to forget its murder (as she regards it), she will add her tears rather than fail in charity. But she fears it cannot die forgotten, for God keeps a register of everything, and nothing may be used in vain; even beasts must be slain with justice, otherwise men become forfeits to God. But to wash in this red will not turn them white (Rev. 7, 14); their stain is too deep. There is not such another fawn in the world to offer for their sin (and then she tells why).

Her lover gave it to her before she had found him false. She remembers only too well what he said:

> *Said He, look how your Huntsman here*
> *Hath taught a Faun to hunt his Dear.*

This is how the fawn became Sylvio's substitute. The fawn grew tame and Sylvio wild; he beguiled her, and without regard for her pain, left her his fawn but took his heart. / Thenceforth she devoted her solitary and idle life to the fawn, which proved "full of sport" (potentially wanton). She implies her story in an exclamation: "O I cannot be / Unkind, t' a Beast that loveth me."

She wonders whether the fawn in time might have acted like Sylvio, whose gifts might prove as false, or more, than he. But she feels sure, though she is now cautious, that

> *Thy Love was far more better then*
> *The love of false and cruel men.*

It is now her substitute love, but not a religious symbol. Under her loving care the fawn grew more white and sweet every day. Significantly, she blushed to see its foot more soft and white than—the hand that fed it. (Her hesitant question is suggestive, and is answered competitively.) / Yet it was wonderfully fleet and graceful, and could run away from her, but always waited.

She has a garden of her own so overgrown with roses and lilies that you would think it wild, and all spring the fawn only wanted to be there. Lying among the lilies, it was hard to distinguish (her nursing had contributed to its whiteness). But now, instead of milk and sugar, it fed on roses (and gave vicarious love):

> *Upon the Roses it would feed,*
> *Until its Lips ev'n seem'd to bleed:*
> *And then to me 'twould boldly trip,*
> *And print those Roses on my Lip.*

"Boldly" tells much. The fawn's chief delight was to fill itself with roses and fold its pure virgin limbs in lilies. If it had lived long, it would have been lilies without, roses within—passion enfolded in innocence, like her song and story.

It dies like a saint (not like a lustful faun), its slow tears suggesting wounded balsam turning into holy frankincense, and finally tears of the sisters of Phaëthon, which the gods in compassion turned into amber. The male loss seems to express the nymph. / As mementos, however, the two tears become crystal in a golden vial, to be filled by hers and placed in Diana's shrine, virgin goddess of the chase. The fawn has gone to the Elysium of whiteness, where swans, turtle doves, lambs, and ermines go. The nymph will select its grave and die.

First, her unhappy statue shall be cut in marble, and weeping too (like Niobe, who had offended Diana). At her feet, the fawn shall be laid, made of purest alabaster:

> *For I would have thine Image be*
> *White as I can, though not as Thee.*

She cannot achieve the whiteness of the fawn, which might also have become "roses within." This is Marvell's greatest poem of implication, where the feelings of the nymph are conveyed and developed largely by suggestion and association. If the nymph were not complaining about Sylvio, the poem would lose its resonance, and exceed its motive.

To his Coy Mistress is more than a *carpe diem* poem because it exhibits man's race with time, which can make coyness in a lady a crime, especially if it is artful. The hyperbole in the poem is not a technique of seduction but an unreal extension of time. The macrocosmic background gives perspective to human action, or an aspect of eternity that measures time and its values; just as much in the first section as in the second, whether values of vanity or nature, or their conflict. In the macrocosm, time and space become dimensions of fate for the microcosm.

Beginning with a hypothesis of enough space and time, the witty hyperbole of the first part magnifies the space and time the lover would be willing to extend into their "long Loves Day," from the Ganges to the Humber, from ten years before the Flood till the conversion of the Jews (just before Judgment Day). His vegetable love (like that soul) should grow vaster than empires and more slow. He measures the rate by the requirements of her vanity:

> *For Lady you deserve this State;*
> *Nor would I love at lower rate.*

She deserves this pomp and ceremony, and he would not love more cheaply. Compliment now verges on mockery.

But this is not reality. The sun's chariot is always at our heels; all that lies before us is deserts of vast eternity, the opposite of our imagined space and beyond time. Our time and space are real between these limits; and when they meet, your beauty shall be found no more, nor shall my song echo in your marble vault (her final pomp). Her "long preserv'd Virginity" is suggested by the first section; her nice honor and his lust shall turn to dust and ashes with the body. The grave might satisfy her scruples (the epithets define them), but it is not a place for love.

Now therefore, while you are young, and while your sensitive soul is responsive, now let us enjoy ourselves while nature permits; and like amorous birds of prey, devour our time at once rather than languish in its slow-jawed power (seems slow to love). (So caught in natural necessity,) Let us roll up all our strength and sweetness into one ball (as in a game), and tear our pleasures by force through the iron gates of life (or fate). Thus, though we cannot make our time stand still, yet we will make it run. Thus "will" may conquer "cannot" or fate. And since her "coyness" did not owe its scruples to morality, it became a crime against nature.

The Fair Singer combines eyes and voice in a beauty, a Created Pleasure, that is mortal to him, a "fatal Harmony." We may recall that *The Resolved Soul* found music's "sweet Chordage" the greatest temptation, and that *Eyes and Tears* revealed "those captivating Eyes,"

> *Whose liquid Chaines could flowing meet*
> *To fetter her Redeemers feet.*

Here he might have fled from beauty of a single kind, "Breaking the curled trammels of her hair," but not from one whose art could also wreathe "My Fetters of the very Air I breathe." / It would have been an easy fight if victory in this field hung in equality of choice or chance, but resistance is vain against both eyes and voice, since she has the advantage both of wind and sun in voice and eyes. Thus in this war with created pleasure "all his Forces needs must be undone."

Mourning is another poem on eyes and tears conceived in a contrary mood; here their relations as suggested by the title are trifled with or sophisticated. They are given a macrocosmic dimension in order to magnify possible disparities or paradoxical identities between them, which make it difficult to determine cause and effect. Tears as infants of the eyes should have both likenesses and differences, and these may interpret their astrological meaning. The ambiguity of "Off-springs" relates these waters of love to their cosmological framework, and poses the question of their fate:

> *You, that decipher out the Fate*
> *Of humane Off-springs from the Skies,*
> *What means these Infants which of late*
> *Spring from the Stars of Chlora's Eyes?*

They present the appearance of grief, and the next two stanzas describe it: Her eyes diffused and refracted, by tears suspended before they fall, seem to be bending upwards, in order to restore to Heaven, its source, their woe. When, forming out of the watery spheres of her eyes, drops slowly detach (untie away) themselves; as if she would cover, with these precious tears, the ground where Strephon lay. / Yet some assert, professing art in these matters, that her eyes have so drowned her bosom, only to soften her heart for another wound. And while a vain show of mourning keeps her within her solitary chamber, she courts herself in amorous tears (of self-love), making her both Danaë and the shower (of Jupiter). / But others, who are bolder, therefore think that joy now has grown so much her master, that whatever even seems like grief is thrown from her windows (eyes). Not that she pays, while she lives, this tribute due to her dead Love; but

casts abroad these donations at the installing of a new love. /
But how wrong are they (and also her slaves)?

> *How wide they dream! The Indian Slaves*
> *That sink for Pearl through Seas profound,*
> *Would find her Tears yet deeper Waves*
> *And not of one the bottom sound.*

This is a macrocosmic triumph of poetic innuendo, compar-
ing the seas of pearl divers with her "precious tears" and find-
ing hers more unfathomable. And his conclusion makes the
innuendo more obtrusive:

> *I yet my silent Judgment keep,*
> *Disputing not what they believe:*
> *But sure as oft as Women weep,*
> *It is to be suppos'd they grieve.*

The conclusion is either sardonic or cynical of all, not only
because it bases itself upon the sign of grief that has set the
question, but because its simplicity denies the complexity of
the whole poem, and itself remains a supposition.

The Definition of Love is achieved by Marvell's most brilliant
use of geometry as the metaphor of fate, and also of the qua-
train of *Mourning*. Its triumph over fate is at the expense of
every finite limitation by which geometry can frustrate hope.
His Love is of a birth as rare as it is strange and high in object;
it was born of Despair out of Impossibility. / Only high-
souled Despair could show him so divine a thing, where feeble
hope could never have flown, but flapped in vain its showy
wing. / And yet he quickly might arrive where his extended
soul is fixed (extension belongs only to body); except that
Fate drives iron wedges, and always forces itself between
them. / For Fate sees with jealous eyes two perfect loves, nor
lets them come together; their union would be her ruin, and
depose her tyrannic power. / And therefore her decrees of

steel have placed them as distant as the poles, (though Love's whole world doth turn on them), not by themselves to be embraced; / Unless the giddy heaven fall, and some new convulsion tear the earth, and to join them, the world (or its geometry) should all be cramped into a planisphere (projected or flattened into a plane). / As lines so love's obliquity may well greet themselves in every angle: but theirs, so truly parallel, though infinite in extent, can never meet. / Therefore the love which doth bind them, but Fate debars so enviously, is (in astronomical terms) the conjunction (apparent union) of the mind, and opposition (diametrical position) of the stars; or spiritual union and physical separation.

In the geometry of their world, Fate makes perfect love impossible of realization, and thus Despair in love becomes more high-minded than Hope, and its object divine. It is a product of idealism, and its values are measured by impossibility or opposition to reality, which is also natural necessity.

The Picture of little T.C. in a Prospect of Flowers uses a more complex stanza, intertwined in rhyme, and closed by a shorter and longer line, which draws back before it runs out. Again what promises to be a song of innocence reaches into the song of experience. Perhaps no poem is a better example of the complex vision of Marvell: little T.C. in a view of flowers soon deepens into her future. A young girl begins her golden days in nature, and her career of conquest:

> *And there with her fair Aspect tames*
> *The Wilder flow'rs, and gives them names:*

and to this effect the poet opposes another,

> *But only with the Roses playes;*
> *And them does tell*
> *What Colour best becomes them, and what Smell.*

Thus beauty may learn sophistication, and arouse speculation about her future: for what high cause was she born?

> *Yet this is She whose chaster Laws*
> *The wanton Love shall one day fear,*
> *And, under her command severe,*
> *See his Bow broke and Ensigns torn.*

Happy will be anyone who can appease this Diana, whom Cupid must fear; such militant virtue is the enemy of man. / His own effort to appease this beauty conveys a feeling of apprehension:

> *O then let me in time compound,*
> *And parly with those conquering Eyes;*
> *Ere they have try'd their force to wound,*
> *Ere, with their glancing wheels, they drive*
> *In Triumph over Hearts that strive,*
> *And them that yield but more despise.*
>   *Let me be laid,*
> *Where I may see thy Glories from some shade.*

Before her chariot wheels drive over her victims, while every green thing charms itself at her beauty, let her correct the errors of the spring, by adding sweetness to the beauty of tulips, by disarming the roses of their thorns, but most of all, by making violets endure a longer time. These reforms seem to glance beyond the flower kingdom, toward her future. / But in her floriculture she must spare the buds, lest Flora become angry and make an example of her, and so "Nip in the blossome all our hopes and Thee." Thus we discover with what discordant feelings Marvell can see and praise a nymph in her simplicity.

The Mower to the Glo-Worms suggests one of those exhibits of fancy for which Marvell used to be esteemed. The mower addresses himself, in quatrains, to the possible uses of glow-worms: as living lamps in the summer night for the nightingale composing her matchless songs; as country comets portending only the grass's fall (his work); as glow-worms whose office is to direct mowers who lose their way and stray after foolish fires. But their courteous lights are wasted since Juliana has arrived:

> For She my Mind hath so displac'd,
> That I shall never find my home.

Thus the apparently casual associations of glow-worms order themselves into a dramatic pastoral for the mower: from the nightingale's song, through portents of danger and lost ways, to the infatuated mower forever beyond the help of glow-worms.

The Mower against Gardens opposes the fields to gardens, in limping elegiac couplets, but more generally shows how man "Did after him the World seduce." How fallen man seduced Nature from its native innocence by cultivation, hybridizing, and grafting, vexing Nature in the cherry "To procreate without a Sex." Gardens are the sophistication of nature,

> While the sweet Fields do lye forgot:
> Where willing Nature does to all dispence
> A wild and fragrant Innocence:
> And Fauns and Faryes do the Meadows till,
> More by their presence than their skill.
> Their Statues polish'd by some ancient hand,
> May to adorn the Gardens stand:
> But howso'ere the Figures do excel,
> The Gods themselves with us do dwell.

Again the gardens have artifice in their statues, and the fields the real thing. This poem is Marvell's way of describing the fall of man in the world of nature.

On a Drop of Dew, which is expressed in a complex mixture of measures and rhyme patterns, is an elaborate example of the comparison or conceit in which Hoskins said "there are to be searched out all the several points of a consorted equality." But the form is likely to pass unnoticed in the meaning: "The eastern dew, shed into the rose, is careless of its new mansion because of the clear sky where it was born; incloses round in itself, and in its little globe's extent frames, as best it can, its native element. It slights the purple flower, scarcely touching it where it lies, but gazing back upon the skies, shines with a sorrowful light, like its own tear, because it has been divided so long from the heavenly sphere. Restless it rolls, and insecure, trembling for fear it grow impure; until the warm sun pity its pain, and evaporate it back again to the skies.

"So the soul, that drop, that ray (moving from moisture to light by way of fountain) of eternal day, if it could be seen within the human flower, still remembering its former height, shuns the sweet leaves and green blossoms, and gathering again its own light does, in its pure and circling thoughts, express the greater heaven in a lesser heaven. Wound in so modest a figure, it turns away in every direction; so excluding the world around, yet receiving in the day; dark beneath, but bright above, here disdaining, there in love. How loose and easy to go hence, how taut and ready to ascend; moving only on a point below, it bends upwards all about. Such was the Manna's sacred dew [Exodus xvi]; like hoar frost on earth, but when dissolved, it runs into the glories of the Almighty Sun."

Although the reader may search out all the points of consorted equality, he is more impressed by their expression of a Platonic aspiration like that of Vaughan carried out with the greatest emblematic skill.

The Garden has proved to be the most controversial poem that Marvell wrote, its only rivals being *An Horatian Ode* and *The Nymph*. It is Marvell's conception of the life described by Cowley in *The Wish*. Marvell's *Hortus*, often regarded as a Latin version of *The Garden,* is not the same poem. Although the beginning and end are similar, the middle is radically different. Comparison of the two poems helps to distinguish the nature of each, and the basic difference is exposed in the middle section. It will be enough to regard *Hortus* from this point of view.

In *Hortus* the opposition of society and solitude is basic: all flee from the love of woman which dominates society to the love of nature which prefers solitude, from the beauty of white and red to the beauty of green. Women are disdained for trees: Neaera, Chloë, Faustina, Corynna, for the Elm, Poplar, Cypress, Plane. Even Cupid himself is conquered by nature, and the gods rejoice "to see his lessening rage" as they turn from Juno, Venus, Daphne, and Syrinx to Oak, Beech, Laurel, and Reed. Only the last two examples remain in *The Garden* to show how the gods ran "Passion's heat." In *Hortus* the poet seeks and finds Quiet and Simplicity "concealed in green plants and like-colored shade," where the sun is *candidior,* milder, than in the society of women.

The Garden turns the opposition into one of the active and the contemplative life, where the contemplative life is found in his image of the original Eden, and the active life is outside, in the Fallen world of Eve and work. Here the wit about woman takes a new turn. Marvell's time would have read this poem as a version of the retirement theme, which Marvell had first considered in the retirement of Fairfax to Appleton House.

The poem begins with the rewards of these two modes of life: "How vainly men perplex themselves to win the symbols of victory, civil, or poetic achievement; and see their unceasing labors crowned from some single herb or tree, whose short and ever closing [narrowing] shade does prudently reproach their toils; while all flowers and all trees converge [come together] to weave the garlands of repose. / Fair Quiet, have I found you here, and your dear sister Innocence!

For long mistaken, I sought you then in busy companies of men. Your sacred seeds will grow, if anywhere below, only among the plants. Society is almost [everything short of] rude compared to this delicious Solitude.

"No white or red was ever seen so lovable [amorous] as this lovely green. Foolish lovers, as cruel as their flame, cut the name of their mistress in these trees. Little, alas, do they know or heed how far these beauties exceed hers! Fair trees! wheresoever I wound your barks, no name shall be found except your own. / When we have run our passion's race [and heat], love makes its best retreat here. The gods that chased mortal beauty, always ended their race in a tree. Apollo hunted Daphne only so that she might become a laurel; and Pan ran after Syrinx, not as a nymph, but for a reed [for his pipe].

"What a wonderful life I lead here! Ripe apples drop about my head; the luscious clusters of the vine crush their wine upon my mouth; the nectarine, and rare peach, do reach themselves into my hands; stumbling over melons as I pass, insnared by flowers, I fall on grass. [And all this sensuous but innocent indulgence without work! Neither here nor in *Bermudas* is Providence austere.] / Meanwhile the mind, from this lesser pleasure, withdraws into its own happiness: the mind, that ocean where each land species immediately finds its counterpart [by popular belief]; yet it creates [not merely reproduces] far different worlds and seas, transcending these; destroying by transforming all that is made [Creation] into a green Thought in a green Shade [the abstract or ideal]. / Here at the foot of the fountain's stream, or at some fruit-tree's mossy root, my soul, casting aside the physical garment, does glide [aspire] into the boughs: there it sits and sings like a bird, then trims and combs its silvery wings; and, until prepared for longer flight, wafts in its feathers the changeable light.

"Such was that happy Garden-state, while man walked

there without a mate [original Eden]: after a place so pure and sweet, what other help could yet be meet [proper]! But it was beyond a mortal's share to wander solitary there: it would have been two paradises in one to live in Paradise alone. [Here Marvell reverses the words of Genesis: 'It is not good that the man should be alone; I will make him an help meet for him.' But Eve broke the solitude of Eden and destroyed its quiet and innocence, or the image of Marvell's earthly paradise.]

"How well the skillful Gardener drew this new Dial of flowers and herbs; where from above the milder sun [of the Garden] runs through a fragrant zodiac [or yearly circuit of bloom]; and, as it works, the industrious bee computes its time as well as we. How could such sweet and wholesome hours be reckoned except with herbs and flowers!" Here the bee computes its time by pleasant work, man by contemplation. *Hortus* gives the bee ambiguous "thyme." Thus man learns how to compute his time in "sweet and wholesome hours" until he is prepared for longer flight. As he tries to recapture Adam's original life in the Garden, he ascends the scale of being, and leaves the curse of labor to the bee and disciples of ambition. Yet the bee has an advantage over the recipients of crowns from "some single herb or tree."

We should not, however, lose sight of that side of Marvell which made him a public servant and finally an admirer of the greatest man of action in his time. For his *Poem upon the Death of Cromwell* also conveys a sense of triumph in one man's struggle with the "several families of the necessities":

> *I saw him dead, a leaden slumber lyes,*
> *And mortal sleep over those wakefull eyes:*
> *Those gentle rays under the lids were fled,*
> *Which through his looks that piercing sweetnesse shed;*
> *That port which so majestique was and strong,*
> *Loose and depriv'd of vigour, stretch'd along:*

All wither'd, all discolour'd, pale and wan,
How much another thing, no more that man?
Oh! humane glory, vaine, oh! death, oh! wings,
Oh! worthlesse world! oh transitory things!
Yet dwelt that greatnesse in his shape decay'd,
That still though dead, greater than death he lay'd;
And in his alter'd face you something faigne
That threatens death, he yet will live again.

Thus Marvell introduces into the strong verse of his lament the proud note of Donne's Holy Sonnet:

Death be not proud, though some have called thee
Mighty and dreadful, for thou art not so;
For those, whom thou think'st, thou dost overthrow,
Die not, poor Death, nor yet canst thou kill me.

Even Marvell's *Definition of Love* found its dimension of greatness in the conquest of necessity.

X

Other Dimensions of Wit

When Dryden criticized the wit of Cleveland in *An Essay of Dramatic Poesy* (1668), he was attacking one of the major reputations of his day. Moreover, he himself had once been vulnerable to similar charges in his elegy on Lord Hastings, when Marvell had been less extravagant. But neither had reached the extravagance of Cleveland's elegy for Milton's Lycidas, nor the excellence of Henry King's *Exequy*, whose poems were not published until 1657. What Dr. Johnson called *discordia concors*, Dryden called "Clevelandism," and Addison called "mixt wit" because it depended partly on the ambiguity of words. Dryden judged Cleveland difficult not in thought but in the abuse of metaphor. John Evelyn distinguished a vocabulary peculiar to universities, "as may be observed in Cleveland's Poems for Cambridge."

In 1655 Henry Vaughan had begun his Preface to *Silex*

Scintillans with these words: "That this kingdom hath abounded with those ingenious persons, which in the late notion are termed Wits, is too well known." Not so well known, he felt, were the vicious lengths to which they were prepared to go in their "desire to be reputed poets." Nevertheless, Cleveland was read as Vaughan was not. And so we may conclude our survey by observing some other dimensions of wit in this and later time.

In retrospect we may recall that in simile or metaphor two dissimilar things are united by a likeness or resemblance, which is the point or meaning of their union. When Dr. Johnson called the wit of the Metaphysical Poets *discordia concors*, he was distinguishing a union that emphasized the dissimilarity. In Metaphysical unions the difference is sharp enough to add surprise to the likeness as learning adds subtlety or complexity to the union. *Discordia concors* may involve not only discordant ideas or things, but also dissonant tones such as levity and seriousness or other contrary feelings. Just as levity is not in keeping with the decorum of seriousness, so other violations of established decorum may be a mark of the modern in any time. Although Hobbes observed that the pun conflicts with decorum in the sermon, or elephants with decorum in the sea, wit was not so easily frustrated. It could emerge not only from various kinds of incongruity, but from mixed feelings, or the desire to mask or disguise feeling, or from mixed modes like the mock-heroic.

The older style of this wit produced one of the great triumphs of seventeenth-century elegy in King's lament for his wife. In *The Exequy*, or burial rite, he masks his grief under the disguise of a complaint:

> *Accept thou Shrine of my dead Saint,*
> *Instead of Dirges this complaint . . .*

Rather than the usual funeral song, we are to hear a complaint "from thy griev'd friend," who feels grief and pretends grievance. The latent ambiguity of "griev'd" fixes the complexity of tone that both masks and intensifies his feeling by understating his grief, as the line "Quite melted into tears for thee" does by "quite."

His tears are disguised in tender metaphors of separation that avoid any suggestion of the mawkish. They are expressed in terms of the studious routine which her death upsets, and begin with the understated "Dear loss," which he subsequently computes:

> *Dear loss! since thy untimely fate*
> *My task hath been to meditate*
> *On thee, on thee: thou art the book,*
> *The library whereon I look*
> *Though almost blind. For thee (lov'd clay)*
> *I languish out, not live the day,*
> *Using no other exercise*
> *But what I practise with mine eyes:*
> *By which wet glasses I find out*
> *How lazily time creeps about*
> *To one that mourns: this, onely this*
> *My exercise and bus'ness is:*
> *So I compute the weary houres*
> *With sighs dissolved into showres.*

Thus the wit of complaint translates his weeping into various kinds of difficulty as he tries to read or to measure time with wet (hour) glasses, and all by metaphors that bring reticence through ambiguity.

There is both wit and pathos in the following lines:

> *Nor wonder if my time go thus*
> *Backward and most preposterous . . .*

The last word not only Latinizes "backward" and adds the meaning of "absurd," but epitomizes his sorrow: literally it makes that first which ought to be last, and this reversal makes his time absurd and her fate untimely, for she "scarce

had seen so many years / As Day tells houres." Continuing
the metaphor of time, the measure of mortality, she has "be-
nighted" him because she is his sun:

> But thou wilt never more appear
> Folded within my Hemisphear,
> Since both thy light and motion
> Like a fled Star is fall'n and gon,
> And twixt me and my soules dear wish
> The earth now interposed is,
> Which such a strange eclipse doth make
> As ne're was read in Almanake.

While her fate mocks his time, his feeling expands into
grander images of separation as the macrocosmic figure
magnifies her grave into the earth that eclipses his sun.

His tender bill of complaint allows him to translate his grief
into a grievance against her:

> I could allow thee for a time
> To darken me and my sad Clime,

and all that space (even ten years) he would postpone his
mirth, if she would promise to return. To mention merriment
would be a discordant note in the usual burial song. But such
hopes are empty now that the earth is interposed,

> And a fierce Feaver must calcine
> The body of this world like thine,

before reunion with his "Little World" will be possible.

Then he turns his complaint against the earth and demands
a strict accounting of its trust, that

> Thou write into thy Dooms-day book
> Each parcell of this Rarity
> Which in thy Casket shrin'd doth ly.

And crowns his surrender with the pathetic ambiguity of a separate couplet:

> *So close the ground, and 'bout her shade*
> *Black curtains draw, my Bride is laid.*

But for the poet the exequy, following its literal meaning, never ends, even after the burial; the procession continues until the eventual rendezvous suggested by the ambiguity of bridal bed:

> *Sleep on my Love in thy cold bed*
> *Never to be disquieted!*
> *My last good night! Thou wilt not wake*
> *Till I thy fate shall overtake:*
> *Till age, or grief, or sickness must*
> *Marry my body to that dust*
> *It so much loves; and fill the room*
> *My heart keeps empty in thy Tomb.*
> *Stay for me there; I will not faile*
> *To meet thee in that hollow Vale.*
> *And think not much of my delay;*
> *I am already on the way,*
> *And follow thee with all the speed*
> *Desire can make, or sorrows breed.*
> *Each minute is a short degree,*
> *And ev'ry houre a step towards thee.*
> *At night when I betake to rest,*
> *Next morn I rise neerer my West*
> *Of life, almost by eight houres saile,*
> *Than when sleep breath'd his drowsie gale.*

Thus he journeys toward death and remarriage, and computes his feeling in the measure of mortality and separation.

But his emotions are more impetuous than his journey towards death, though not more so than her conquest of death:

> *'Tis true, with shame and grief I yield,*
> *Thou like the Vann first took'st the field,*

> *And gotten hast the victory*
> *In thus adventuring to dy*
> *Before me, whose more years might crave*
> *A just precedence in the grave.*

This, his ground of complaint, is what made his time "preposterous," but which now gives way to shame and grief at his lesser courage, and thus requires not fanfare, but a muffled drum:

> *But heark! My Pulse like a soft Drum*
> *Beats my approach, tells Thee I come;*
> *And slow howere my marches be,*
> *I shall at last sit down by Thee.*

The thought of this reunion bids him go on, and wait his dissolution "with hope and comfort." Of course his resolve is a crime towards her, but an act of Christian resignation on his part, for which he must be content to live with half a heart. Thus wit has given another dimension to elegy, and to one of the best of its time.

Cleveland was the most prominent of the Wits excoriated by Vaughan. For him "the State of Love," as given by one of his titles, was "the Senses Festival," and religion served to give it wit. His attitude is defined in *The Hecatomb to his Mistress* by his scorn for "Beggars of the rhyming Trade":

> *Charge not the Parish with your bastard Phrase*
> *Of Balm, Elixir, both the India's,*
> *Of Shrine, Saint, Sacrifice, and such as these,*
> *Expressions common as your Mistresses.*

Instead of such Metaphysical vocabularies, he employs in *To the State of Love, or the Senses Festival* the idiom of newer Sects, including the nudist Adamites (with a pun on adamant), to help regale the sense of sight:

I saw a Vision yesternight
Enough to sate a Seeker's sight,
I wish'd my self a Shaker there,
And her quick Pants my trembling Sphere.
It was a She so glittering bright,
You'd think her Soul an Adamite,
A Person of so rare a frame,
Her Body might be lin'd with th'same.
Beautie's chiefest Maid of Honour,
You may break Lent with looking on her.
  Not the fair Abbess of the Skies,
  With all her Nunnery of Eyes,
  Can show me such a glorious Prize.

Macrocosmic imagery is paradoxical for the sense of touch, but now it is without spiritual overtones:

My Sight took pay, but (thank my Charms)
I now impale her in mine Arms
(Love's Compasses, confining you
Good Angels, to a Circle too.)
Is not the Universe strait lac'd,
When I can clasp it in the Waste?
My amorous Fold about thee hurl'd,
With Drake I girdle in the World;
I hoop the Firmament, and make
This my Embrace the Zodiack.
  How could thy Center take my Sense,
  When Admiration doth commence
  At the extreme Circumference?

With Cleveland there is occasional doubt not about his senses, but whether a subject is being caricatured or a fashion in imagery.

In *The Hecatomb to his Mistress*, where he condemns fantastic glossers of poetry, he does ridicule fashions in metaphor; for example,

Call her the Metaphysicks of her Sex,
And say she tortures Wits, as Quartans vex

> *Physicians; call her the squar'd Circle; say*
> *She is the very Rule of Algebra.*

Some of his ridicule, however, could touch both himself and Marvell. Yet he can set the *carpe diem* theme *To Julia to expedite her Promise* in a surprising ecclesiastical context that renews its life by wit:

> *The Candidates of Peter's Chair*
>   *Must plead gray hair,*
> *And use the Simony of a Cough*
>   *To help them off;*
> *But when I wooe thus old and spent,*
> *I'le wed by Will and Testament.*
> *No; let us Love while crisp'd and curl'd;*
> *The greatest Honors on the aged hurl'd*
> *Are but gay Furlows for another World.*

Cleveland's natural impulse seems to be satirical, and difficult to control. In *The Antiplatonick*, which is plainly satiric of Platonic love, his wit opens and closes its attack brilliantly:

> *For shame, thou everlasting Wooer,*
> *Still saying Grace, and never falling to her!*
> . . . .
> *Like an Embassadour that beds a Queen*
> *With the nice Caution of a sword between.*

If this has a Neo-Classical inflection, it can be said that Cleveland exposed, whether consciously or not, the virtuosity of learning encouraged by the pursuit of novelty in wit; but that he also extended the capacity of the Metaphysical idiom for satire.

We should not, however, ignore one triumph, despite some doubt as to his authorship; for it is on a subject that did move him. Although Hobbes condemned the "significant darkness" of "strong lines" as riddles, Cleveland produced his great *Epitaph on the Earl of Strafford* in the riddling mode:

> *Here lies wise and valiant dust*
> *Huddled up 'twixt fit and just:*
> *Strafford, who was hurried hence*
> *'Twixt treason and convenience.*
> *He spent his time here in a mist,*
> *A Papist, yet a Calvinist;*
> *His Princes nearest joy, and grief;*
> *He had, yet wanted all relief:*
> *The Prop and Ruine of the State,*
> *The peoples violent love and hate:*
> *One in extremes lov'd and abhor'd.*
> *Riddles lie here; or in a word,*
> *Here lies blood; and let it lie*
> *Speechlesse still, and never crie.*

This series of contradictions summarizes the paradoxical fate of Strafford, another victim of the Civil War. Its power derives both from the extremes of feeling involved and from the riddling quality of its expression, finally condensing it to one unequivocal word, blood. In his prose Cleveland expressed the same complex attitude towards Strafford in defending an apology for him: "Because it shows wherein the same Man may both condemn and acquit the same Man. Why is that such a Riddle?" The same question has been raised about Marvell on Cromwell.

Among the Restoration Wits, John Wilmot, Earl of Rochester, was the most metaphysical. His *Satyr against Mankind* is in the line of philosophical satire, like Donne's satire *Of Religion*. It attacks both the pride of man and the clerics of "formal Band and Beard"; its tactics involve the scale of being and the monkey of Rochester's most striking portrait. Thomas Rymer, the first editor of Rochester, remarked: "You wou'd take his Monkey for a Man of Metaphysicks." For the *Satyr against Mankind* opens by opposing the Monkey to the Man of Metaphysics:

> *Were I, who to my Cost already am,*
> *One of those strange, prodigious Creatures Man,*
> *A Spirit free, to chuse for my own Share,*
> *What sort of Flesh and Blood I pleas'd to wear,*
> *I'd be a Dog, a Monkey, or a Bear,*
> *Or any thing, but that vain Animal,*
> *Who is so proud of being Rational.*

Therefore he ridicules reason in favor of sense, or the distinctive faculty of the rational versus the animal level, and so produces an inversion of the scale of being. Man's advantage seems to be largely a capacity for dissimulation, to cover the hypocrisy of human motives. Thus fear concealed behind bravado is exposed by his famous paradox: "For all Men, wou'd be Cowards if they durst." The lust for power is associated with cowardice. In his letters Rochester scorns "the mean policy of Court-Prudence, which makes us lie to one another all Day, for fear of being Betray'd by each other at Night."

But if reason helps man to deceive others, it also deceives man himself. Thus the Monkey confounds the Man of Metaphysics.

> *The senses are too gross; and he'll contrive*
> *A Sixth, to contradict the other Five:*
> *And before certain Instinct, will preferr*
> *Reason, which Fifty times for one does err;*
> *Reason, an* Ignis fatuus *of the Mind,*
> *Which leaves the Light of Nature, Sense, behind.*

The sixth sense is "common sense," which judged the other five; reason was not a false light, but the orthodox "light of nature." But its deception is then imaged with a power that may be compared with that of Donne's search for Truth in *Satire III:*

> *Pathless, and dangerous, wand'ring ways it takes,*
> *Through Errour's fenny Bogs, and thorny Brakes:*

Whilst the misguided Follower climbs with Pain,
Mountains of Whimsies, heapt in his own Brain,
Stumbling from Thought to Thought, falls headlong down
Into Doubt's boundless Sea, where like to drown
Books bear him up a while, and make him try
To swim with Bladders of Philosophy,
In hopes still to o'ertake the skipping Light:
The Vapour dances, in his dazzled sight,
Till spent, it leaves him to Eternal Night.
Then old Age, and Experience, hand in hand,
Lead him to Death, and make him understand,
After a Search so painful, and so long,
That all his life he has been in the wrong.

Thus a satire that can echo Lucretius finds another depth in metaphysics, which is presented as strikingly as Donne's way to truth, but with the imagery of skepticism.

Rochester's paradox *Upon Nothing* is reminiscent of the idiom of Cowley's *Against Hope*, but it begins and ends more like Cowley's *Hymn to Light*. Where Cowley refers to "thy Sire the word Divine," which said, "Let there be light," Rochester has Creation come "from the great united— What," and says, Let there be Nothing. But Cowley's poem is more imagistic and his moralizing redounds to the greater appreciation of nature. For perspective we may recall Crashaw's epigram on Christ's refusal to defend himself:

O Mighty Nothing! unto thee,
Nothing, we owe all things that be;
God spake once when He all things made,
He saved all when He Nothing said.
The world was made of Nothing then;
'Tis made by Nothing now again.

Cowley's hymn is to the "First born of Chaos" according to Genesis; Rochester's hymn is to the Original of everything according to scholasticism. Yet his agnostic view of Creation seems baffled by an unknown Something.

He begins by personifying the Nothing out of which the world was made:

> Nothing! *thou Elder Brother ev'n to Shade,*
> *Thou hadst a being e're the World was made,*
> *And (well fixt) art alone, of ending not afraid.*

Shade needs something to cast it, which does not yet exist; all things that have a beginning must have an end. This poem shares basic ideas with Donne's *Nocturnall*. Rochester proceeds to argue that before time and place existed, when the First Nothing directly begot something, then everything proceeded from the great united Unknown. But when Something, which is the General Attribute of everything, is separated from its Original, it falls back into undifferentiated nothingness.

> *Yet something did thy mighty Pow'r command,*
> *And from thy fruitful Emptiness's hand,*
> *Snatch'd Men, Beasts, Birds, Fire, Air, and Land.*

Matter, the most wicked offspring of its posterity, helped by Form flew from Nothing, and Rebel Light (Lucifer) obscured its reverend shadowy Face.

> *With Form and Matter, Time and Place did join,*
> *Body, thy Foe, with thee did Leagues combine,*
> *To spoil thy peaceful Realm, and ruin all thy Line.*

When time and place joined with form and matter to produce body, then Body, the enemy, made an alliance with Nothing, so as to spoil its peaceful realm and ruin all its lineage. Yet Time's defection does not help the enemy, but rather Nothing's short spell of activity, and drives its slaves back to its hungry womb. Although Mysteries are barred from the eyes of laymen, and only the Divine is authorized to pry into Nothing's bosom, where truth lies in private,

> *Yet this of thee the wise may freely say,*
> *Thou from the Vertuous nothing tak'st away,*
> *And to be part with thee the Wicked wisely pray.*

Otherwise, how vainly the Wise would pursue their philosophical inquiries, if the Great Negative were not there to point their dullness!

> *Is, or is not, the two great ends of Fate,*
> *And true or false, the subject of debate,*
> *That perfect, or destroy, the vast Designs of Fate:*

when they have tortured the politician's breast, most securely rest in the Bosom of Nothing, "and, when reduc'd to thee, are least unsafe and best."

Now Rochester begins to elaborate the satiric consequences of Creation. He asks Nothing why its creation, Something, still permits sacred Monarchs to sit at council with persons fit for nothing, while weighty Something modestly keeps away from Princes' coffers and Statesmen's brains, and nothing reigns there like stately Nothing.

> *Nothing, who dwell'st with Fools in grave disguise,*
> *For whom they reverend Shapes, and Forms devise,*
> *Lawn Sleeves, and Furs, and Gowns, when they like thee look*
> *wise.*

To these examples of the ruined lineage of Nothing, he adds French Truth, Dutch Prowess, British Policy, Irish Learning, Scotch Civility, Spanish Dispatch, and Danish Wit. But the most debased forms provide the conclusion:

> *The great Man's Gratitude to his best Friend,*
> *King's Promises, Whores Vows, tow'rds thee they bend,*
> *Flow swiftly into thee, and in thee ever end.*

From Nothing to nothing may be said to mark the mock-heroic decline of *nihil* (*nihilum*) in the story of Creation, and again not the least of its shapes (or perhaps more properly, among the least of its shapes) is the "formal Band and Beard." Thus in Dryden's time could satire affect the metaphysics.

The hard word, odd similitude, and learned wit of Metaphysical poetry came to rest in the satire first of Cleveland and then of Samuel Butler. In *The Rehearsal Transprosed* Marvell's admiration of Butler is not only expressed in words but exhibited in the kinds of wit turned upon Parker. Marvell could not be a Sectarian in wit. Lest the objects of his attack might be mistaken, he says (ed. Thompson, II, 33): "I will assure the reader that I intend not Hudibras: for he is a man of the other robe, and his excellent wit hath taken a flight far above these whiflers: that whoever dislikes the choice of his subject, cannot but commend his performance, and calculate if on so barren a theme he were so copious, what admirable sport he would have made with an ecclesiastical politician." When Parker tried to turn this remark against him, Marvell objected (ibid., p. 492): "I had chanced in my book to speak of Hudibras, with that esteem which an excellent piece of wit upon whatsoever subject will always merit. But you hereupon fall into such a fit and rupture of railing at me, that you have exceeded not only all the oyster-women and butter-whores, but even yourself, pretending that I have done him some dishonour." No doubt Marvell relished Butler's character of the metaphysical Sectarian more than that of the religious Sectarian:

> *In School Divinity as able*
> *As he that hight Irrefragable;*
> *A second Thomas, or at once*
> *To name them all, another Duns;*
> *Profound in all the Nominal*
> *And Real ways beyond them all,*
> *And with as delicate a Hand*
> *Could twist as tough a Rope of Sand,*

And weave fine Cobwebs, fit for skull
That's empty when the Moon is full;
Such as take Lodgings in a Head
That's to be lett unfurnished.
He could raise Scruples dark and nice,
And after solve 'em in a trice . . .

Marvell's political feeling turned him into a Restoration satirist; his lyric voice was lost in a rhetorical voice, his wit degenerated. There was a decline both in the earlier cheap punning of *The Character of Holland* and in the later coarse prolixity of *The Last Instructions to a Painter*. Although his name became prominent in the collections known as *Poems on Affairs of State*, his best satires were in prose, where he was not easily excelled. There he showed his appreciation of Donne, but he referred explicitly to Donne the satirist, and unexpectedly to his most unusual satire. Of course Donne the satirist was relevant to Marvell's purpose, but we may recall that Dryden first mentioned Donne as a satirist and in connection with Cleveland.

When Marvell blames all the answers to his *Rehearsal Transprosed* on Parker (ed. Thompson, II, 274), he finds a ready means of satire in Donne: "I find plainly that 'tis but the same ghost that hath haunted me in those differing dresses and vehicles. Insomuch, that upon consideration of so various an identity, methinks, after so many years, I begin to understand Doctor Donne's Progress of the Soul, which passed through no fewer revolutions, and had hitherto puzzled all its readers." His perception seizes on the stanza pointed by the line: "And liv'd when every great change did come." This use of Donne may testify to Marvell's experience as well as to the reputation of Donne's *Metempsychosis*. Then he follows this progress of the soul or of original sin from the innocent apple through stages appropriate to his ridicule of Parker. For example, when the soul betakes itself into a mandrake, he makes this application:

To show that in love's business he should still
A dealer be, and be us'd well or ill,
His apples kindle, his leaves force of conception kill.

And adds this remark: " 'Tis pity that his Curate of Ickham was not acquainted with its virtues."

He rounds off the conclusion of this progress with these words: "After this soul had passed thorow so many brutes, and been hunted from post to pillar, its last receptacle was in the human nature, and it housed itself in a female conception; which, after it came to years of consent, was married to Cain by the name of Themech." He seems to recognize that Donne's satire involves the scale of being. Then he concludes: "This was the sum of that witty fable of Doctor Donne's, which, if it do not perfectly suit with all the transmigrations of mine answerer, the author of the Ecclesiastical Politie, nor equal the progress of so great a prince; yet whoever will be so curious as himself to read that poem, may follow the parallel much farther than I have done, lest I should be tedious to the reader by too long and exact a similitude." Thus Marvell shows understanding of Donne's most unusual satire, and becomes the only one in his time to approach an exegesis of that poem. In doing so he also illustrates the characteristic method of satire which he employed: a form of caricature that provides a context or outline for his ridicule, exemplified by *The Rehearsal Transprosed* itself.

Indeed, Marvell went so far as to explain his method (ibid., p. 314): "I had a mind to show them by this example, that there was not so much need of prophaneness to be ridiculous, or to take the Sacred Writings in vain; but that if they did but take up at adventure any book that was commonly read, known or approved of, they had the same and better opportunity than out of the Bible, to gather thence variety, allusion, and matter sufficient to make the people merry: and I hope I have attained my end in some measure." John Eachard's

Grounds and Occasions of the Contempt of the Clergy also supported the thesis that one should not, "for want either of reading, wit, or piety," make bold with Scripture in order to be facetious. Although this method applies to his later verse satire, it is in his prose satire that one is reminded most effectively of the wit and learning that distinguished the earlier Marvell. This is how Marvell fits into the course of Metaphysical Poetry which the Grierson anthology outlines from Donne to Butler, who best exposed the dwindling precincts of wit.

Some Bibliographic Aids

EDITIONS

(Note: Syllabic versification must be related to contemporary syllabication. On metrics see Pierre Legouis, *Donne the Craftsman*.)

Cowley, Abraham. *Poems*, ed. A. R. Waller (Cambridge, 1905)

Crashaw, Richard. *Poems*, ed. L. C. Martin (Oxford, 1927); 2nd. edition, 1957

Donne, John. *Poems*, ed. H. J. C. Grierson (2 vols., Oxford, 1912; 1 vol., Oxford, 1933)

——. *Complete Poems*, ed. Roger E. Bennett (Chicago, 1942)

——. *Complete Poetry and Selected Prose*, ed. Charles M. Coffin (New York, 1952), Modern Library

——. *The Divine Poems*, ed. Helen Gardner (Oxford, 1952)

——.*The Elegies and the Songs and Sonnets*, ed. Helen Gardner (Oxford, 1965)

Herbert, George. *Works*, ed. F. E. Hutchinson (Oxford, 1941)

Marvell, Andrew. *Poems and Letters,* ed. H. M. Margoliouth (2 vols., Oxford, 1927); 2nd. edition, 1952

Vaughan, Henry. *Works,* ed. L. C. Martin (2 vols., Oxford, 1914); 2nd. edition, 1957

Gardner, Helen, ed. *The Metaphysical Poets* (Penguin Books, 1957)

Grierson, H. J. C., ed. *Metaphysical Lyrics and Poems* (Oxford, 1921); Galaxy Books

Grierson, H. J. C., and Bullough, G., eds. *The Oxford Book of Seventeenth Century Verse* (Oxford, 1934)

CRITICISM

Alvarez, Alfred. *The School of Donne* (New York, 1961), Pantheon Books

Bennett, Joan. *Four Metaphysical Poets* (Cambridge, 1934); *Five Metaphysical Poets* (Cambridge, 1964)

Brooks, Cleanth. *Modern Poetry and the Tradition* (Chapel Hill, 1939); Galaxy Books

Cruttwell, P. H. *The Shakespearean Moment* (London, 1954)

Eliot, T. S. *Selected Essays* (London, 1932)

Empson, William. *Seven Types of Ambiguity* (London, 1930); New Directions

Ford, Boris, ed. Pelican Guide to English Literature: *From Donne to Marvell* (Penguin Books, 1956)

Keast, W. R., ed. *Seventeenth Century English Poetry* (New York, 1962), Galaxy Books

Kermode, Frank, ed. *Discussions of John Donne* (Boston, 1962)

Leishman, J. B. *The Metaphysical Poets* (1934; New York, 1963)

Nicolson, Marjorie. *The Breaking of the Circle* (Evanston, 1950); Columbia Paperbacks

Praz, Mario. *Studies in Seventeenth Century Imagery* (London, 1939)

Sharp, R. L. *From Donne to Dryden: The Revolt against Metaphysical Poetry* (Chapel Hill, 1940)

Tuve, Rosemond. *Elizabethan and Metaphysical Imagery* (Chicago, 1947); Phoenix Books

Walton, Geoffrey. *Metaphysical to Augustan* (Cambridge, 1955)

White, Helen C. *The Metaphysical Poets* (New York, 1936); Collier Books

Williamson, George. *The Donne Tradition* (1930; New York, 1958), Noonday Press. *The Proper Wit of Poetry* (London & Chicago, 1961)

REFERENCES

Berry, L. E. *A Bibliography of Studies in Metaphysical Poetry, 1939-1960* (Madison, 1964)

The Bible, Authorized or King James Version

Burton, Robert. *The Anatomy of Melancholy*, ed. H. Jackson (Everyman's Library, 1932)

Lewis, C. S. *The Discarded Image* (Cambridge, 1964)

A New English Dictionary on Historical Principles (Clarendon Press); later known as *The Oxford English Dictionary*.

Spencer, Theodore, and Van Doren, Mark. *Studies in Metaphysical Poetry: Two Essays and a Bibliography* (New York, 1939 & 1964)

Tillyard, E. M. W. *The Elizabethan World Picture* (Modern Library Paperbacks, New York)

Index of Authors and
Poems

A NOTE ABOUT THE AUTHOR

GEORGE WILLIAMSON, professor of English literature at the
University of Chicago, was born in Galesburg, Illinois, in 1898.
A graduate of Stanford University, he received graduate degrees
from both Stanford and Harvard. He was selected for the Martin
A. Ryerson Distinguished Service Professor award while teaching
at the University of Chicago. Professor Williamson's first book
was *The Talent of T. S. Eliot*, in 1929, and his books have in-
cluded *The Donne Tradition, A Reader's Guide to T. S. Eliot,
Seventeenth Century Contexts,* and *Milton and Others.*